SATHER CLASSICAL LECTURES
VOLUME SIXTEEN
1942

THE ECLOGUES OF VERGIL

THE ECLOGUES OF VERGIL

BY

H. J. ROSE

UNIVERSITY OF CALIFORNIA PRESS
BERKELEY AND LOS ANGELES
1942

UNIVERSITY OF CALIFORNIA PRESS
BERKELEY, CALIFORNIA

―――――

CAMBRIDGE UNIVERSITY PRESS
LONDON, ENGLAND

COPYRIGHT, 1942, BY
THE REGENTS OF THE UNIVERSITY OF CALIFORNIA

FILIAE MEAE
QVAE MATREM SVAM CVM NOMINE TVM INDOLE REFERT
HVNC LIBRVM DEDICO

PREFACE

ANY VALUE this book may have in the eyes of scholars or of lovers of literature must be accredited chiefly to three great institutions. The first of these, of course, is the University of California, which, when it did me the honour of inviting me to become Sather Professor during the session of 1939–1940, provided me not only with leisure and rest, but also with a place of peace wherein to think sanely while much of the world was going mad. The latter boon neither hosts nor guest knew of when the invitation was accepted; the former is given year by year to those upon whom the choice of this most hospitable University falls.

Next must be named another famous American place of learning, Harvard University. Its vast library and the generosity with which it opens its treasures to every visiting student are well known; it was my good fortune, before journeying to California, to pass a few weeks teaching at a summer school in the surroundings, familiar to me, of the Yard, and within a stone's throw of the entrance to the Widener. I trust my opportunities were not wholly neglected there, nor those which were given me later and with equal munificence in that glorious building which houses California's abundant stores of books.

But no small share of my thanks must go to my own University, whose Court ungrudgingly granted me the necessary leave of absence to take advantage of the offer made by our American colleagues and fellow lovers of learning.

An obvious criticism which will no doubt be made of the following pages is that they do not include a bibliography either of works on Vergil in general or of writings on the *Eclogues* in particular. The omission is deliberate, and my reasons, be they good or bad, are the following. The older scholars, indeed all but the very latest, are named, and particulars are given of what they have written, in the monumental work of Schanz-Hosius. Later additions have from time to time been listed and discussed in such periodicals as Bursian's *Jahresberichte*, the *Year's Work in Classical Studies*, and others.[1] I have read widely in such literature as seemed relevant to the purpose in view; but it has appeared to me neither profitable nor courteous to set down the authors and titles of a number of articles and some few books in which I could discover nothing helpful. Those to which I felt myself in any way indebted I have mentioned in full in the notes at the end of each chapter, together with a few which struck me as lending a touch of comic relief to a serious subject owing to the sheer absurdity of the views they put forward.

My own effort has been neither to write a full commentary on the *Eclogues* nor to discuss every problem which arises for a careful and interested reader of them; for example, practically nothing is said of the more technical matters of their style and metre. The lectures were not intended for specialists, and even if they had been, I had nothing new to say on those points. What I have tried to do is to treat at fairly adequate length such matters as seemed to me of most interest in connection with the genesis of the poems and their worth as literature and as documents throwing light on the mind of a lovable man and on the currents of opinion, hope, and fear which set this way and that in an age as troubled as our own and no less anxious for a happy issue out of its afflictions. It is perhaps even more appropriate than when I originally planned the book that it ends with a consideration of Vergil's vision of a world which shall emerge from wars into peace and find again its lost righteousness and innocence.   H.J.R.

---

[1] I have to thank my friend Dr. Otto Skutsch, son of the lamented scholar whose opinions are often mentioned in these pages, and now an exile in Great Britain, for collecting and placing at my disposal a most useful list of titles not in Schanz-Hosius. It has been my constant companion during many happy and studious hours at Harvard and at the University of California.

CONTENTS

CHAPTER	PAGE
I. THE PASTORAL BEFORE VERGIL	1
II. *Molle atque facetum*	25
III. THE POET AND HIS HOME	45
IV. THE POET AND HIS FRIENDS	69
V. GALLUS, SILENUS, AND ARKADY	94
VI. VERGIL AND ALLEGORY	117
VII. SOME THEOKRITEAN IMITATIONS	139
VIII. A CHILD IS BORN	162
NOTES	221
INDEX	269

CHAPTER I

THE PASTORAL BEFORE VERGIL

It is one of the interesting facts of literary history that a famous author's influence may outlive not only his own death but that of his books. Sophron of Syracuse is represented for us by a few fragments,[1] the longest filling but eighteen short lines on the papyrus scrap which preserves it. Yet we may say, and not without justice, that but for him neither the poems which form the chief subject of these lectures nor the vast, if second-rate, literature which descends from them would ever have been written. So it is reasonable to begin our course by a brief consideration of who he was and what he wrote.

The only mention of his date is vague; he was "contemporary with Xerxes and Euripides," which leaves us practically the whole of the fifth century B.C. to play with. He was a Syracusan, and he wrote in his native dialect, a form of Doric. His works were "mimes," that is to say, imitative or dramatic pieces, probably all of them short, divided by him or his editors into those dealing with women and those treating of men. It is highly likely that these men and women were Syracusans, like their creator, and that their rank was not exalted. Titles such as "The Women watching the Isthmian Games," "The Mother-in-Law," "The Bridesmaid" give some notion of the manner of his portraiture; he supposed a scene of everyday life, a public or private festival for instance, and let us hear the talk of those concerned. In one feature his style departed from realism, for his characters seem to have spoken rhythmically, though not actually in verse. Each of the short lines of our chief fragment comes near to scanning, but never quite arrives; thus, the first is nearly a short trochaic line, the second hovers around

---
[1] Notes to chapter i will be found on pages 221–223.

iambic metre, the third, if it were a syllable shorter, would be two bacchii, and the fourth is again pretty distinctly trochaic. Why this should be so, in an age when Asianic prose, with its elaborate rhythms, almost passing into metre, was still far in the future, we cannot tell; it is a reminder the more of our crass ignorance concerning vast fields of Greek literature. Nor can we say how it happens that a realistic author of this type existed in Sicily, long enough before realism made its appearance in Athens. Doric was not a particularly fashionable dialect with the scholars of a later age, to whose taste we chiefly owe the preservation of what has not perished; and so the literary activities of the Sicilians are even less known than their history, for of all the historians which their island bred, only the late compiler Diodoros has come down to modern times, and he has lost a great part of his bulky compendium.

But let us hear Sophron himself speak, before considering what later ages made of him. I think you will agree with me that he "fades out" much too soon, just as he is getting interesting.[2] The title of the little piece which chance has partly restored to us was clumsy; it is "The Women who say they will drive out the Goddess." It was always a reasonable guess, and is now certain, that the goddess in question was Hekate. She or her emissaries have possessed certain women, or girls, and a professional exorcist has been called in by their friends to rid them of their obsession. The scene is indoors, probably in a house in a mean street of Syracuse; when our fragment begins, the exorcist is speaking. We may assume that she is a woman, for a man would hardly be in the women's quarters and would very unlikely be an expert in matters regarding Hekate.

THE EXORCIST. Set the table down, just as it is, and take a lump of salt into your hand and stick a sprig of laurel behind your ear. Now come here all of you [the gender of the participle shows that not all those present are women; probably the males in question are young boys] and sit down at the hearth. Here, you, give me that two-edged knife. Bring that puppy, will you? And what's become of the bitumen?

AN ATTENDANT. Here it is.

THE EXORCIST. Hold the torch, too, and the incense. Look here, I want the doors open, all of them. You sit there and watch, and put the brand out, just as it is. So; keep silence, please, while I drive off the Sendings from these women. [*Having killed the puppy, burned incense, and performed other rites, she addresses a prayer to the goddess.*] Lady, now that thou hast received a banquet and guest-gifts all perfect . . .

The rest of the prayer doubtless ran "go, take your plagues with you, and come no more to trouble this house," or something to that effect. The powers of the underworld were now supposed to leave through the open doors, as uncanny things commonly do when the place is made too uncomfortable for them. Not all the details are clear to us, for how much do we know of Greek magic earlier than the Alexandrian period, or indeed till the Christian era? But the general sense is perfectly plain, and the vigour and liveliness of these few lines, even in a rough translation into our tongue, seem to me sufficient cause for regretting the loss of the rest, and of the many other similar compositions of this author.

Let us now pass over something like a century and a quarter, and come down to the days when Hieron II sat not too comfortably on the Syracusan throne. In his days the city boasted once more of a literary man of no small merit; his name was Theokritos, and his people were undistinguished citizens. It is in no way impossible that they lived habitually and for choice on some small estate in the country, for certainly their son knew and loved rustic scenes and people. He had for his chief capital a good literary education and his native genius, assets which brought him in something, but not much, in a state on whose northern horizon Rome was beginning to rise, vast and portentous, while to the west the less strange but not less terrible menace of Carthage, strong and unbroken, loomed ever present.[3] He had apparently no taste for other occupations than literary; perhaps his father's estate had passed out of the hands of his family, or some other financial trouble drove him to earn his living by his pen. A poetical address to his own ruler survives, but the absence of any more poems to that or a like patron suggests that Hieron could or would give nothing—to poets, at any rate; perhaps if Theokritos had been a mathematician he would have won more favour.[4] At all events, he quitted Sicily and went, like so many able men of his day who wanted money and were willing to write, paint, carve, or fight to get it, to Alexandria. Here there was a demand at court for flattery well expressed, and Theokritos had no more objection than Kallimachos, whom he admired and supported in the literary controversies of the day, to telling the royal family, in neat verse, what superhumanly admirable people they were. Presumably some kind of return other than graciously expressed thanks came his way; certainly he found himself able to go on writing, and in doing so to follow his own bent.

Being an Alexandrian poet of the most approved school, he was versatile, and tried his hand in several metres and more than one dialect; but the work for which later antiquity and the moderns remember him was all his own, and of high quality. Fundamentally, however, it was as typically Alexandrian as his encomium on Ptolemy or his epyllia, that is to say miniature epics, on sundry mythological themes. For one of the characteristic ways in which that painstaking age strove after originality was by combining techniques which had hitherto been separate. For instance: the lyric ode, intended to be sung by a chorus, had since the days of Terpandros been the recognised way of complimenting a winner at any of the Great Games, or even at minor events, if he was inclined to be sufficiently generous to a poet. The more important the winner's social status, the more likely he was to have a really fine poem written for the occasion; some of the grandest things Pindar ever produced are paid compositions whose ostensible *raison d'être* is the not very thrilling fact, to us, that a Sicilian king's horses had run better than anyone else's at Olympia or Delphoi. Now the Games continued to be held, and one of the great men of Alexandria, Sosibios,[5] won horse- or chariot-races at the Isthmian and Nemean festivals. Kallimachos duly celebrated these exploits, in a poem packed with reminiscences of Pindar, to judge by the fragments we have left of it; but the metre was the elegiac couplet, which in older times was used for personal poems of love or hate, open letters of advice on politics or morals, statements of the writer's views on public or private affairs, in fact almost anything not too exalted except the celebration of anybody's athletic victories. Theokritos was, if he may be labelled in such a way, a Kallimachean; it is therefore not surprising that he tried his hand at a new blend.

The hexameter had served for various kinds of poems since the days of Homer. It was the recognised metre for serious and exalted narrative, for instance; it was the correct metre for didactic poetry; it was freely used, alongside of lyric metres, for hymns to gods; it might be employed, as the elegiac couplet was, as a vehicle for inscriptions of a sort which lent themselves to literary treatment, such as epitaphs. But it does not seem to have been used till Theokritos' time for sketches of common life. He now produced his new blend, the themes and, so far as can be judged, something of the maner of Sophron, handled in a dialect fundamentally the same though more literary, but in hexameters instead of prose. The metre was flexible enough, owing to its long history and the variety of uses to which it had already been put, for a skilful man to employ without being too grandiose in his effects; English blank verse has something of the same quality, for despite their formal similarity nothing could be more unlike in the effect on any sensitive ear than, say, Milton's address to light in *Paradise Lost* and Tennyson's *Dora*. It gave the poet license to use, if he liked, some turns of phrase which did not belong to the speech of any country-side, but to the familiar vocabulary of epic; it did not oblige him to use such phraseology, nor to keep his syntax faithful to Homeric or any other models.

Still keeping to Sophron's precedent (he may, for anything we know, have had other models as well), he wrote his sketches of men and of women, and in them he showed his characters attending shows, chatting of their private affairs, practicing magic,[6] and so forth. But in one respect, whether he took hints from Sophron or not, he became for the future literature of Europe the father of a new kind of composition, the pastoral. Here he was still a realist, for his shepherds are not townsfolk masquerading, but actual inhabitants of the workaday country, such as Theokritos, no doubt, had often seen and chatted with in Sicily, though he sometimes preferred to lay the scene, when it can be identified, rather in Kos than in his native island. Kos was a place he had come to know well since moving east to make his fortune, for he had made the acquaintance of some country gentlemen there and he knew the landscape thoroughly. How long he stayed there and whether or not it was his new home rather than Alexandria, there is not evidence to determine. But to return to his shepherds; without deviating from the truth in the least, he could give them two romantic and interesting characteristics, leisure to discourse with each other and a love of and skill in music. To take a small flock of sheep or goats to a pasture and watch them while they graze is a long day's work, but not an exacting one; the beasts are individually known to their keeper, who may be no more than a child, and they are led, not driven, back and forth. For purely practical reasons, the pasturing is done in pleasant surroundings, for the beasts must have grass, as fresh and green as is to be got, and in a Greek summer that means that they are in a hilly district, comparatively well watered and with some shade. The pine-tree which whispers sweetly by the fountains, the hill-slope with its tamarisks, which provide the setting for the poem generally numbered I in our collection, are not imported into the picture from outside, but are simply there. The only kind of realist who could omit them would be that curious being who has persuaded himself that the real and the ugly are one and the same. As to music, it is to this day the recreation of a Greek or Italian herdsman and part of his method of handling his charges; for instance, on the slope of Monte Rosa each man has his own tune, which his flock or herd knows, coming after him when he plays it. It is a quick way of getting them together, much less tiring than shouting at them or running after them. Since every shepherd is thus perforce something of a performer on a simple wind-instrument, it naturally follows that some of them are skilful, and like to play for their own amusement or that of their fellows. What their songs were really like in the days of Theokritos we cannot now say, for no one thought it worth while to write any of them down, or, if he did, his collection has perished. But it surely is no great assumption that the themes included personal poems, of satire or good wishes, love-songs (such as modern Greece has in plenty), retellings of old stories, and so forth. The poet's contribution was not to create an art for his characters, but to heighten the art which their originals in real life possessed. Probably the songs which the veritable shepherds sang were rude and monotonous, though it should not be assumed that they had no merit as poetry. Theokritos, being a poet, put into the mouths of his goatherds and shepherds some exquisite little poems, but was far too good an artist to make them talk poetry all the time; they sing it, but generally chat with each other in very human style, albeit thrown into verse. Take away the metre, as one does in translating fairly literally, and this is surely not far removed from the actual chaffing of two country boys:[7]

KOMATAS. You she-goats of mine, keep away from that shepherd from Sybaris, Lakon I mean; he stole my sheepskin only yesterday.

LAKON. Shoo, you lambs, get away from the spring; can't you see that Komatas, the fellow who stole my pan-pipe only two days ago?

KOMATAS. "Pan-pipe" indeed! You, Sibyrtas' slave-boy, did you ever get hold of a pan-pipe? Isn't it good enough for you to take a wheatstalk and squawk on that, as Korydon does?

LAKON. It was one Lykon gave me, please, Master Freeman. But what sheepskin was it that poor Lakon ran away with from you? Just you tell me, Komatas; why, even your master Eumaras never had one to sleep in.

When his character is not a simple shepherd, bond or free, but a figure of country-side legend, he has of course a wider scope for his fancy. It is as natural for a Cyclops to talk in verse as it is for Shakespere's fairies. It is pretty clear from the exquisite eleventh Idyll (the word "idyll" has originally no suggestion of idealisation about it, but means simply a little picture or sketch) that the peasantry of Sicily believed in a much less horrific giant than Homer had heard of and placed in his Odyssean wonderland. He is a huge figure of fun, with nothing Homeric about him but his name Polyphemos. His trouble was that he was deeply in love with a mermaid, one Galateia, and she seemed to think him an unsuitable *parti*, being very hairy and also one-eyed. Being a shepherd, he had one resource, his music, in which, Theokritos remarks for the information of the physician to whom the piece is dedicated, he found more relief than he would have got by paying good money to one of the profession. He rather overdid the cure, for he sat and sang all day long, leaving his sheep to tend themselves; fortunately they had rather more sense than he, and went home of their own accord when evening came. The song was such as might have been expected from a bewildered monster in trouble, unintentionally funny where it was not unexpectedly moving. The five lines which describe the first meeting are immortal; we shall see presently that Vergil was among their warm admirers. I am no Theokritos, but the sense is something like this:[8]

> I fell a-loving you, my lass, the day
> You came for flag-flowers and I showed the way.
> Over the hills you came, my mother's guest,
> And still I look and look and have no rest
> From looking; but, God knows, you little care.

And a little later, he is sorry that his mother bore him without fins, for if only he had them, he could dive down to where Galateia lives, and bring her flowers; he lists them, lilies and poppies, but he is a truthful giant, so he adds,

> But these they grow in summer, those in fall,
> So at one dive I could not bring them all.

So, having no fins, he must wait till some ship comes along and he can find one of the crew to teach him swimming, for he is very curious to learn what it is that makes the sea-folk like to live down there at the bottom, when it is much pleasanter on land, tending sheep and making cheese from their milk. But he is a much misunderstood giant, who has no real sympathisers, unless it be the girls on shore, who sometimes ask him to come and play with them in the evenings. And so, with the consoling thought that he amounts to something on land at any rate, he rises and goes, perhaps to make cheese-baskets or get fodder for the lambs, which he reproaches himself for not doing.

Some few pieces, not more than one or two, go a little further still from realism, for they do not deal with the inhabitants of the country-side as they were or the local bogeys as they believed them to be, but with Theokritos' own literary circle. The seventh Idyll tells of a happy summer afternoon spent with his friends in Kos at a harvest festival, and the setting is as real as could be wished, with the hot, dusty road, the arrival at the estate in the country, and the picnic in the orchard, where pears and apples lay on the ground beside the guests, the sloes weighed down the bushes, and the bees hummed about the spring in which the wine was cooling; "everything smelt of summer at its richest, and of harvest-time."[9] The songs, too, which the wayfarers exchange with each other are in character; why should a Greek "hiker" not sing as well as a modern one, if so inclined? But here allegory begins to raise her head; almost no one is called by his proper name, unless it be the good folk who had invited them to their harvest-home, but everyone has a fanciful name which conceals his real one, and a fanciful occupation as well—or at least some of them do. Thus, Lykidas meets Simichidas; that is to say, Theokritos himself is met by another man of letters, perhaps Dosiadas, one of the minor poets of the day, and they talk, under pretence of discussing various people's skill on the pipes and in singing, of the merits of Sikelidas, probably Asklepiades, a man from whose pen we have some little poems in the *Anthology*, and of Philitas of Kos, who is the only literary man called by his name. So "shepherd" can on occasion mean "poet"; to sing or play in shepherd fashion is to write and publish poetry. Also, a not unimportant fact, to be taught by the Nymphs as one pastures cattle among the hills, so that Rumour carries the report of one's singing up to the throne of Zeus, is to win the royal favour and patronage as a writer of verse.[10] This last allegory is also a literary allusion, for it was while he tended his beasts that Hesiod met the Muses and was commissioned by them.[11] The Nymphs are lesser deities than the sacred Nine, so it is a modest claim; Theokritos, who makes it on his own behalf, means that he is not one of the great names of literature, but still has his place among writers who are to be taken seriously and are worth reading.

So we see that, as early as the days of the pioneer of this kind of poetry, realism was being left a little way behind, and to compose pastorals was not merely to sketch the life of the country as it was, or even as it seemed to be through the eyes of one perhaps too long pent up in Alexandria or some other great city. The first step had been taken towards the days when, if anyone was called a shepherd in poetry, it would have been a startling discovery to find that he really was a country fellow who got his living by looking after actual sheep and had never published or tried to publish anything in his life.

The process went on, not perhaps very quickly, but fast enough for it to be complete by Vergil's time. Theokritos, like the other prominent Alexandrians, became a classic, was edited and commented upon and studied by those who would be either learned or literary. We know something of the editions which were produced in antiquity; one consisted of Theokritos only, with exclusion of all pieces which the editor, Theon, thought spurious. Another was a corpus of the bucolic poets; it had been got out by Theon's father, Artemidoros, in the time of Sulla. Someone, we cannot be certain who, but traces of his arrangement survive in our mediaeval manuscripts of the poet and Servius mentions it in his commentary on Vergil,[12] classed ten poems which he and most readers considered "purely rustic" together; nine of them are genuine Theokritos, one a very pretty imitation by an anonymous writer. So imitators knew exactly what they were to imitate; the subject was to be the life of the country-side, the metre was to be the hexameter, and the dialect was to be Doric. If it so happened that the imitator was entirely of the town and had never heard Doric speech, what are difficulties for save to be overcome? The wisdom of antiquity had spoken; country-folk were of literary interest, and information concerning them was to be had in Theokritos, to whom the best of the earlier imitators might be added, if so desired. Hence two worthies called Bion and Moschos gained a place as minor classics. The latter was about a hundred years later than his model, the former somewhat junior to him, though probably not by much. What we have left of their work does not give the impression that the loss of the rest is one of the major disasters of literature, but they were capable of pretty verses. The most noteworthy literary fact about them is that when Bion died, poisoned, as his mourner tells us, someone composed a lament for him which not only is good in itself but was destined to high honours unforeseen by its poet; it furnished the model for Milton's *Lycidas*, although Milton, as usual, dealt freely with his copy, taking hints and improving upon them rather than imitating. But besides being a poem to read and remember, at least for those who know the original tongue, for it loses much of its aroma in translation, it is a literary document from which we can learn a good deal. It tells us very clearly what conventions governed this kind of composition somewhere about the beginning of the first century B.C.; in other words, it teaches us something of the grammar of the poetical language which Vergil learned and wrote in his earliest self-published work.[13]

In general, it keeps close to the equation shepherd = poet, especially pastoral poet. Bion is throughout a tuneful herdsman who has died, and Doric song has died with him. Furthermore, he "drank the waters of Arethusa," the famous Syracusan spring,[14] which means that he was of the school of Theokritos. The nearest it comes to abandoning the stock pretence is in a daring passage which parallels

Bion with no less a poet than Homer, without trying to prove that Homer was a shepherd, or anything but a composer of epic. Since Bion must be a shepherd, his poems of course are shepherds' songs, and the list of them which is given must be interpreted in that light. He chanted, says our author, no tearful tales of war, but "he sang of Pan; clear rang his voice, this herdsman, and singing he tended the kine. Pan-pipes he made and milked a sweet heifer, and he taught the kisses of boys, nursed Eros in his bosom, and provoked the Love-goddess." And, a little earlier, "Herdsman, all the Muses' gifts have died with thee, the winsome kisses of maids, the lips of lads; the Loves are downcast and mourn about thy corpse, while our Lady of Cyprus grieves far more for thy death than for the kiss which but now she gave Adonis as he died."[15] Now the mention of the grief of Aphrodite for Adonis gives, in this context, a pretty broad hint; it was Bion who wrote the *Lament for Adonis* which has come down to us with no name attached. By way of underlining the allusion, our poet imitates quite patently a turn or two of the phraseology of that little work.[16] So the other subjects are themes, perhaps even paraphrased titles, of poems. The pan-pipe is of course a stock feature of pastoral, the more so because it really was an instrument in common use in the country-side, being cheap and not hard to make. One herd-boy gives such a pipe to another in Theokritos,[17] and there is a clever little poem by the same author the lines of which trace the outline of a pan-pipe. Perhaps Bion, however, told the story of Pan's ill-starred love and how he made the first pipe from the reeds which grew over the place where his beloved had disappeared, or into which her body had turned. Exactly how the milking of the heifer came in, it is perhaps rather idle to speculate; part of the reward for a song in the first Idyll of Theokritos is the milk of a particularly fine she-goat, and Bion may have introduced some such detail in imitation of the older poet.[18] The various "kisses" may have been poems describing love-scenes, or short anticipations of Ovid's *Art of Love*, or of Tibullus' curious little treatise on how to win the affections of a boy.[19] A fragment still exists in which Bion, if he does not exactly nurture Eros in his bosom, at least dreams that he is trying to teach him to sing;[20] and to provoke Aphrodite probably means to write a poem about someone or something which vexed her. We shall have occasion later to consider whether Vergil did not use this same poetical method of cataloguing.

The lament is of course written in Doric—book Doric, dropping into the common literary forms pretty often and not succeeding in keeping very close to the true speech of Syracuse in Theokritos' day, if indeed it tries to, which is hardly likely. After all, if a writer of our own times should choose to imitate Burns, it does not follow that he would make an intensive study of the Ayrshire dialect as it was spoken in the eighteenth century, and the ancients were certainly not more scrupulous than we are in such matters. At all events, the poet feels at liberty to vary his speech a trifle to suit the theme; when he says that "lovely Lesbos did not mourn for Alkaios" as much as it does for Bion,[21] the word for "lovely" belonged to the Aiolic speech of Lesbos to begin with, though it had early travelled into other forms of Greek. The next line drops for a few words into pure Ionic to tell us that Paros grieves more for Bion than for her own poet Archilochos. The author tells us that his own home was in the south of Italy,[22] so it is not even certain, though it is highly likely, that he was by race and speech a Greek. If he was, Doric by that time was giving way to the all-pervading "common dialect" of the language almost as fast as our local dialects are being submerged under the muddy flood of so-called "standard" English, as understood by broadcasters and elementary-school teachers, a flat and pointless jargon hardly better than the barbarous noises of Hollywood at its worst.

In a kind of Doric, then, the poet procedes to weave into his own web thread after thread of the tapestries older men had wrought. I give only a couple of instances. The poem is divided, like several other pastoral poems, into groups of lines, not all of the same length in this case, marked off from one another by a refrain, "Begin the lament, ye Muses of Sicily." This refrain, in language and in rhythm, is borrowed from the first Idyll of Theokritos, in which a singer recounts the lamentable death of Daphnis, the hero of a country-side legend imperfectly known to us, but familiar to those for whom the idyll was first written. The anonymous poet's line is

ἄρχετε Σικελικαί, τῶ πένθεος ἄρχετε Μοῖσαι

whereas Theokritos had written

ἄρχετε βουκολικᾶς, Μοῖσαι φίλαι, ἄρχετ' ἀοιδᾶς.[23]

The other instance is not so much a matter of language as of allusion to a subject without which, it would seem, no collection of pastoral poems was complete. One of the mourners for Bion is Galateia, who

laments thy song, for once thou didst delight her while she sat with thee on the seashore. For thy singing was not like the Cyclops'; from him fair Galateia fled away, but on thee she looked more gladly than on the brine; and now she forgets the waves and sits on the lonely sands, and still herds thy cattle.

The allusions are of course to what has already been dealt with, the eleventh Idyll of Theokritos. In that, Polyphemos would have Galateia leave the sea and come and share his country life, but she will not; Bion had had better success with her. But the allusion is twofold; a quotation enables us to say that Bion also had written on the same subject. The surviving lines run thus:[24]

But I will go my own way down yonder slope to the sand of the seashore, still piping, to beseech cruel Galateia; for I will not abandon my sweet hopes till uttermost old age.

When Artemidoros collected the Greek pastoral poets, he was registering for the benefit of posterity the products of an art almost if not quite dead, for little or nothing of the kind was written in the tongue of Theokritos thereafter. Pastoral compositions, some of them delightful, some merely silly, are to be met with in the later history of Greek literature; the best-known of them is the charming romance of Longus, generally called *Daphnis and Chloe*. But these are prose works, by-products of the flood of rhetoric which submerged most of the literary activity of the Greek-speaking peoples in the next few centuries. It would seem that by the time of Nero one of the stock rhetorical exercises, a thing of which every passman was supposed to be capable, was to describe a country feast or to praise the life of the countryman.[25] Those whose interest is in real literature need not spend much time over such phenomena; they belong to the pathology of the subject, not to its normal anatomy and physiology. In Rome, for a little while (part of the activity of one man, to be exact), the pastoral got a new lease of life, and once more proved worth reading.

One of the outstanding features of the last generation of the Roman Republic was the zeal with which a group of clever young men (at least one of them, Catullus, had genius) studied the technique of the Alexandrian poets. For the most part they clearly belonged to the school of Kallimachos, and what survives of their work shows that they were by no means unworthy pupils. They tried their hand at the epyllion; Catullus' *Peleus and Thetis* is one of the best surviving examples of that sort of composition. They tried hard to write elegiacs, which proved unexpectedly troublesome to fit to Latin words and were not perfected till a later generation. They experimented with the not over-wide range of lyric metres which the Alexandrians had used, and found among these some that suited their native tongue very well. Some of them developed a portentous amount of obscure learning, mostly mythological. Between them, they all but perfected the hexameter, which Ennius and Lucilius had left a very lumbering vehicle for poetic thought. They also went far towards providing Latin with a poetical vocabulary; that is to say, they brought into use a number of conventions in phraseology and grammar which proved suitable to verse composition, as another set of conventions had for writers in prose. They wrote a good deal of amatory poetry, some of it instinct with genuine feeling; Catullus again seems to have been head and shoulders above the rest of them in this. But they were one and all of the town. Their interests were either personal or political; if personal, they centered around a good deal of lovemaking and quarrelling, together with endless debate, mostly friendly enough, concerning literary matters. If political, they were generally violent, partly no doubt because to be violent in such matters gives admirable scope for lampoons, and Latin is a beautiful language for abuse. It does not appear that any of them had what we call the social conscience much developed, or possessed any understanding for the vital facts concerning the ordinary, workaday life of their own country, which nevertheless must somehow contrive to go on, however many revolutions there may be. This of course meant that, however promising the start which they had made, they would not continue to produce first-rate literature; for if there is anything certain about art, and especially the art of the writer, it is that it cannot healthily continue to be the property of any clique, however cultured or intelligent, but must keep in touch with the feelings of the mass of the people, adding, however, a contribution of the writer's own, which is essentially a bringing to light of what in the mind of the common man was but dim and vague till, given a genius to express it, there are set forth in unforgettable words fears, hopes, aspirations, and thoughts which the average person of the day never knew he had till they were written down for him to read. In that sense, the great writer is the creation of his age; in another, one might almost say that the age may be the creation of the great writer.

Now into the Roman literary world of those troublous years which followed the assassination of Julius Caesar there came a new figure. It was that of a man no longer in his first youth, but approaching his thirtieth year.[26] He was about seventeen years junior to Catullus (now dead some thirteen years), and had had an education not unlike his, at least on its formal side. Like him again, he came from the north, the chief town of his district being Mantua. His father had owned an estate, probably of no great size, in the Mantuan territory, and his shy, rustic-looking son had learned, as Theokritos had done before him, to know the country at first hand. He had no great liking for towns, then or later, and Rome frightened him; oratory he did not much care for, his one appearance as a speaker being a failure, but he loved poetry and philosophy. Learning of all sorts, especially mythological and historical, he took to very kindly, though he never let it sit too heavily upon him. His share in public business had not been conspicuous or brilliant; the latest revolution, that of which Octavian was the head, had brought confiscation and ruin, or something very like it, to himself and his family. For all that, he had a keen insight into what was going on, and Octavian won his honest admiration and support. At this date, such an attitude did not mean detestation of the other great figure of the day, Mark Antony; that came later, during and after the campaign of Actium.

The form which any great writer's message to his age will take must of course depend on the kind of literature which is then possible. Had Vergil lived in our day and had such a mixture of grievances and hopes to voice, there would have been two principal methods of expression available to him;

he might have written a first-rate propagandist novel, supposing that such a thing is now possible (it was in the days of Dickens, but recent experiments in that line do not seem to get beyond respectable mediocrity), or he might have used the daily or weekly press, if he could have got the needed editorial support, for the part of the great patrons of Octavian's day may be said to have passed, to some extent, to those who, in our times, own and produce influential papers. Had he lived in the reign of Queen Anne, there would have been an opening for him as a pamphleteer, or possibly a contributor to one of the periodicals of that age. There have been times when, with an eye on a censor or the police, he might have made himself heard on the stage. But in the last century B.C., for one who was not prominent as an orator and had not the temperament to sway either mobs or deliberative assemblies (which in any case were fast losing their old powers) the natural vehicle, strange as it may appear to us, was poetry. The reading public was small, but it included most if not all of those whose influence was worth having on one's side. Poetry of the more artistic kinds was a fairly new phenomenon, and several very prominent men were deeply interested in it; one of the most remarkable of the rising statesmen of the day, Gallus, was himself a poet of merit, while another, Pollio, wrote both prose and verse, liked to be told that both were excellent, and showed very fair talent for public affairs, though not the supreme genius he would have had it thought that he possessed. Octavian himself scribbled a little, had enough good sense to know that he was no great poet, and gladly made friends with men of letters, of whom he hardly required more than that they should not actively oppose him, though if they could be got to support him in their writings, he was generous in rewarding them. Of his chief helpers in the business of conquering and then reorganising the world, one, Agrippa, had at least no objection to poetical tributes, while Maecenas appears to have posed as a man of fashion and taste (which, by the way, he was) who dabbled in politics when he had nothing better to do.

Under these favourable circumstances, a poet could be something of a political force, in something like the way that an eloquent and well-informed writer for the better sort of papers may be now, with the difference that his much smaller audience was also much better educated (it was as if the journalist might confine himself to persuading perhaps the best-informed and most intelligent one per cent of his public) and much more powerful than the average readers of anything today. The poet had also a surprising amount of freedom, not only in the technical details of the style of poetry he adopted and the kind of metre he thought fit to use, but in matter also; if he kept clear of the law of libel and did not inform the world that the policy of the government was wrong from beginning to end, he might say almost anything he liked. Octavian's power rested largely on his army; Vergil might say "soldier" and "barbarian" in a breath, contrasting the veteran most unfavourably with the peasant. The new regime was trying, with an increasing measure of success, to remedy the horrible situation created by two generations of strife; Vergil, and Horace too, might declare that things were going from bad to worse, the latter of them not even hinting that there was any prospect of a remedy. Livy, at a later date, might still declare that the times were very bad indeed, unable to bear either their evils or the cure of those evils.[27] It was indeed one of the most remarkable merits of the early Empire that, compared with most strong governments known to the ancients, it set little store by flattery; it was powerful enough to let even a hostile critic go unpunished, so long as he did not add deeds to his words, and wise enough to exact but a moderate amount of panegyric from its supporters. It is remarkable how large a proportion of what the poets say in praise of Augustus, after he had accepted that title, is simply plain fact put into lofty phrasing.

Moreover, it was never necessary for a writer, in verse or in prose, to produce nothing but comments on public affairs. No one whose opinion mattered seems to have been too busy, even in the crises which came almost as thickly as they do now, to read pure literature for his own enjoyment. Vergil, throughout his career, even when he was most active as a government propagandist, wrote for the most part work which would probably have been little different though no such persons as the Caesars and no such thing as civil war had existed. Generally, the propaganda was decorously concealed rather than emphasised; those who knew where to look for it could find it easily enough, but those who did not (and a great number of the later readers of Vergil were in that category) often missed it or found it in the wrong places.

We shall see that of the ten *Poems of the Pastures* or *Select Pieces* with which Vergil appeared before his public, more than half are free of all but purely literary interest; when they mention or allude to public men, it is because they are also men of letters. Of the rest, one does indeed preach a message of hope to the world, but the tone is as much religious as political, and we are still debating who, if anyone, is meant by Vergil to be the bringer of this hope and of its fulfilment. One deals very largely with the poet's own private affairs and his personal reactions to the state of economics and politics in Italy; we are left with one or perhaps two, one-fifth at most of the total collection, which have a good deal to say in praise of Octavian and his adopted father. So if anyone thinks the public affairs of the generation which saw the last flicker of the old Republic die out and the new Empire arise uninteresting, he need not on that account be deterred from studying the *Eclogues*; he will find what he prefers in eight of them, perhaps nine.

One last explanation. Why is it that a man of great poetical genius, with plenty of feelings of his own to express and something to say of the way his fellow countrymen, especially his fellow townsmen, were affected by what went on around them, chose to adopt as his medium an adaptation of the sort of poetry a foreigner, dead some two hundred years, had written in another tongue for a different public and a different environment? Why is Vergil's country-side not all Vergil, nor all Italian, but to a very appreciable extent Theokritos, and Sicilian, or Koan, or some other kind of Greek? I think we are past the stage in which we merely abused the Latin writers for depending on foreign models in this way; it is more profitable to try to understand their methods. Vergil, when he chose to write pastorals, was being original, and original because, not in spite, of the fact that he was imitative. That is the paradox of a classical tradition. Some centuries earlier it was a commonplace that all the techniques were discovered and known; Choirilos of Samos,[28] himself a very tolerable poet and fond of originality, had complained that it was so and looked back with longing on the old days when poets could be also discoverers, pasturing, to use his simile, on an untouched meadow. But the Latins seem to have accepted the fact rather joyously than otherwise; it meant that by study of the accepted methods they could hope to learn to use them as well as their Greek masters in the arts, if not better. Vergil was, so far as we know, the first Latin to write pastorals, certainly the first to write them effectively, as indeed he was nearly the last, for his imitators, Calpurnius and still more Nemesianus and the anonymous poet of the Einsiedeln Manuscript, are but shadows of him. To be the first to attempt a Greek genre in Latin was itself no small thing to be proud of. But he did more than this. Where the Greeks had allegorised a little, he found means to convey in his bucolic poems more than one serious message. Apart from this, he made several technical experiments, which we shall discuss later, combining after the Alexandrian fashion things which had hitherto been separate, and combining them in a way which justified part of Horace's criticism, that the Muses had granted him flexibility.[19]

CHAPTER II

MOLLE ATQVE FACETVM

IN TRYING to appreciate an ancient work, or any work not of our own age and country, it is often useful to discover what the critics said about it when it was new. It is our good fortune to have a contemporary mention of the *Eclogues* by no less a connoisseur than Horace, who says, in a passage mentioned at the end of the last chapter, that the Muses who delight in the country-side have granted to Vergil *molle atque facetum*. Since, in the comparatively small Latin vocabulary, a word is apt to have a confusing variety of meanings, or at least shades of meaning, we may begin by asking exactly what Horace meant by the epithets he applied to his friend's compositions. Certainly he did not mean that they were, or that their style was, soft and comical. *Mollis* can indeed mean "soft," that is to say, it can be used of sundry things which are so described in English, with reference to that quality to which our adjective refers. Vergil himself uses the word of grass, for instance;[1] it is commonly enough used of a man who is what we call a "softy," generally with the further implication that he is rather nastily immoral.[2] But this is certainly not the only appropriate translation of the word. The legs of a thoroughbred colt are not soft, but rather hard and firm; yet Vergil again calls them *mollia*,[3] and the context makes it perfectly clear that he means "springy," "not stiff." If, then, a style is called *mollis*, it means, not that it is lacking in vigour, but that it is flexible, subtle, delicate. What *facetus* means we shall perhaps see most clearly if we look at its opposite, *inficetus*. This can mean "lacking in wittiness," for a good saying is *haud inficete dictum*, a thing uttered not without wit; *irridicule* can be used in much the same sense. But three good authors testify that this is far from exhausting

---

[1] Notes to chapter ii will be found on pages 224–227.

the meaning. Cicero tells a story of a man who was neither *inficetus* nor uneducated, but nevertheless was outwitted by a subtle Syracusan.⁴ He is manifestly emphasising the victim's shrewdness, not his power of making or seeing a joke. Catullus has a grievance against the taste of his age, which commonly compares a certain damsel, according to the poet afflicted with too big a nose, ill-shaped feet, eyes of rather indeterminate colour and coarse speech, with Lesbia (that is to say, Clodia), one of the most beautiful and fascinating women of the time.⁵ His words are, *o saeclum insipiens et inficetum*, "O age devoid of taste and of perception." And, to go back from these moderns (for such they are) to the most ancient surviving well of Latin pure and undefiled, when Diniarchus, in Plautus,⁶ sees that wily courtesan Phronesium for the first time after an absence of some length, she asks him why he is so *inficetus* as not to offer to kiss her; why, in modern phrase, he is such a boob. If therefore Vergil's poetry, in the *Bucolics*, has point and elegance, if it shows quick perception of what it would describe, it may be called *facetum* without our casting about to find jokes in it. Perhaps it may be said that the word comes fairly near meaning "humorous."

So much for what Horace thought of Vergil. Can a modern reader, supposing him to be tolerably well seen in the Latin tongue, that is to say, fairly well educated, and of passable abilities, *nec inficetus et satis litteratus*, like the man in Cicero's anecdote, honestly say that he finds in the pastoral poetry of our author the qualities of a flexible, delicate style and quick, rather humorous perception of a situation? If we would make trial, it happens that there are two of the poems which are peculiarly handy material for such research, in that they offer none but purely literary difficulties. To appreciate them, perhaps almost as fully as Vergil's contemporaries did, we do not need to solve the numerous really thorny problems which we shall have to face later on, but only to know something of the literature which he knew and to get rid of some monstrously bad criticism, too bad to be worth repeating or refuting if it did not clog the pages of a very popular edition of Vergil, that of John Conington.[7] This editor, in his preface to and notes on the second Eclogue, expresses himself in part as follows:

A shepherd gives utterance to his love for a beautiful youth. ... Parts of this Eclogue are closely modelled after the eleventh Idyl of Theocritus. ... We should be glad [with Ribbeck] to believe it to be purely imaginary, though even then it is sufficiently degrading to Virgil [he then quotes some ancient scandal from the scholia, not worth mentioning even to rebut]. ... The beeches (v. 3) and mountains (v. 5) ... point to Sicily, not to Mantua, and Sicily is expressly mentioned in v. 21. ... The strains of Corydon ... are unpremeditated. ... If Corydon is a slave, we must suppose with Keightley that, in falling into the Cyclops' language [i.e., in 19 sqq.] he is really thinking of the advantage he gets from having so much under his charge.

Of this precious critique it may be said that the first sentence, the statement that Sicily is mentioned, and the remark about the eleventh Idyll of Theokritos are true in fact. The rest well illustrates an important principle of criticism, that people who cannot appreciate poetry ought not to talk about it. This "degrading" effort happens to be one of the most exquisite and delicate offerings ever made to the Muses of the country-side; it is to the manners of the age, which the poet had no sufficient ground for ignoring, that we must attribute the choice of subject, a passion involving sexual inversion, then probably commoner than now and certainly more freely talked about. The object of Corydon's fancy is in any case a mere lay figure, who never appears on the scene at all; what matters is Corydon's feeling and the way he expresses it. The poet sets the scene for us in two lines:

> Corin the shepherd for Alexis burned,
> His master's minion; hopeless was his love.

The rest of the poem consists of the complaints which he uttered amid thick-growing beeches (line 3), which cast a deep shade; there was none to hear him except the woods and hills. Since, as we shall see later, there is little or no hilly country near Mantua and few or no beeches, which do not much love hot plains, it is pretty clear that Corydon's haunt is where one would expect a shepherd's to be, on one of the hill-pastures—of which more must be said in a later chapter, when we discuss, not so much where Vergil's father had his estate as what parts of the country the poet in his boyhood had opportunity to become acquainted with. For the present, all that is required is to suppose some region with hills and a certain amount of woodland in it. We may add, if the mention of the singer looking at his reflection in calm sea-water is to be taken literally, that it must not be far from the sea; but it will presently appear that this is a false clue.

The poem falls into a number of irregular stanzas, not marked off by any refrain nor keeping to a fixed number of lines. After the introduction of five verses, in which Vergil speaks in his own person to explain what it is all about, there are eight which describe the lover at noonday, five which contrast old loves with new, nine dealing with the Cyclops, six about the homely country-side, leading up to six more about Corydon's pipe and five concerning some wild kids which he has caught, then eleven which treat of the joys of the country. Now comes the awakening of the singer to his own folly; this is expressed in four lines, which are followed by a last appeal, in nine; and finally, five verses which tell of Corydon's resolve to mend his ways balance the five which brought him and his troubles before us at the beginning of the poem. Except that the Cyclops-song is roughly in the middle of the work, there is no very elaborate arrangement, in fact Vergil himself tells us that there is none. Corydon, he says (line 4), used to sing *haec incondita*, the disordered matter which follows. Dramatically, this is good, for who expects a sorely troubled rustic to produce, offhand, a masterpiece of balanced self-expression? Yet, for the dramatic monologue is a piece of art, the author must not plunge so far into ultra-realism as to make his work totally incoherent, and therefore uncouth and uninteresting. There are clearly defined limits to the imitation of human speech in art, whether the medium be play, poem, novel, or song. One can hear grunts and groans, half-finished sentences and phrases disconnected from what goes before and after, periods which start and never end, and all the vices of ill-trained or emotionally disordered speakers, to say nothing of singers, without either learning Latin or opening a book of verse. It needs but to walk abroad in any country and listen to the speech of its inhabitants. It is for the artist, whether in verse or prose, to make us catch what his more sensitive ears have already perceived, the music which sings behind and through the broken sounds of "real" life. And so Vergil subtly hints at a regular arrangement, blending the fits and starts of his shepherd's singing with the geometrically correct pattern which would lie at the back of a professional poet's or rhetorician's mind if he sat down to compose, on his own behalf, a plea to a hard-hearted love. At the back of his mind, and not on his page, unless he were a very uninspired hack; for as geometry, though an admirable basis for any visible scheme, whether it be the conventional designs of embroidery or the outlines of a great building, yet will not of itself give an artistically satisfactory shape unless the imagination of the artist supplements it, so such rhetorical devices as symmetry, indispensable to the artist in words, must rather lie concealed than appear, if he is to give us anything better than a cold and artificial utterance, uninstinct with the breath of life.

But let us look again at the opening verses. They are worth it, if only for a kind of sentimental value; for although it is probable that we still have a little of the poetry Vergil composed before he wrote the *Bucolics*, yet these are the very first which we are sure came from his pen.

> Formonsum pastor Corydon ardebat Alexim,
> delicias domini, nec quid speraret habebat.

The very sound of them, as of all good hexameters written in the two languages capable of them, is delightful to the ear. Long practice on Vergil's part must have gone to acquiring the power to fit together the words of his native speech into such perfect and smooth melody. And yet longer practice, several generations of it, had gone, before his first beginnings or even his birth, to the same task, from the days when Ennius set out to prove that this difficult Greek metre could be adapted to Latin and incidentally showed that he, small blame to him, did not yet quite know how. By the time of Catullus the Latins had learned, with many experiments and failures, how to write a good hexameter. Vergil was taking the further step of learning, and teaching, how to write a good group of hexameters, all of the same general pattern and yet no two exactly alike. But I must not stray too far into the intricacies of ancient metre, if only because I am myself no expert on the subject.[8] Let us rather consider the words our poet uses, and how he fits them together.

He is writing verse, and so his word-order is freer than that of prose, which in turn is freer than the order in English, for Latin has no grammatical meanings to express by the arrangement of its words; being inflected, it can entrust all that to the case-endings and verbal terminations, leaving the question which word should come first and what ones next to be settled by the more subtle rules of rhetoric. So Vergil begins with two words which serve as a kind of title to the whole poem, *formonsum pastor*, almost "Beauty and the Shepherd." He thus has said already that his shepherd did something which somehow affected or had relation to one more than commonly good to look upon. While giving the names of his two characters (he puts the shepherd's first, by the figure known as chiasmus), he tells us what the something was; Corydon was made in love with the beauty, *ardebat*. That, and not the prose *amabat*. Vergil has no desire to be elaborate here, but to tell us quite simply what subject he has chosen. As in the opening verses of the *Aeneid*, he is perfectly easy to understand. Here his perfect taste contrasts sharply with that of his imitator Statius, for example, who begins his *Thebaid* with two and a half clever lines which say no more than "I tell the story of the Theban Brothers," and then writes fifteen more to add "beginning with a mention of Oidipus."[9] But neither here nor there is Vergil prosaic in his plainness. To write poetry it is necessary to know how to handle verse, as to compose music it is needful to have mastered harmony and other technicalities; and part of the lesson is the difference in phraseology and vocabulary between good verse and good prose. If prose happens to scan, that does not make it verse, but simply bad or at least inferior prose. There was once a mathematician who, to his own great annoyance when the error was pointed out to him, began a chapter of his treatise thus:

> No finite force, however great,
> Can stretch a string, however fine,
> Into a horizontal line
> Which shall be absolutely straight.

This, since it had the scansion and rime-system of a stanza of *In Memoriam*, obviously was not good prose, such as a scientific treatise deserves. But certainly it was not poetry, which does not deal in that kind of truth. I should hesitate also to say that it was verse, for it was not in English poetical diction. "Horizontal line" is a term of art, appropriate to a technical essay, and for that very reason inappropriate to verse. Vergil, by the time he wrote the *Eclogues*, knew when and how to leave the language of Latin prose for that kind of Latin poetical speech which suited his style and subject; *ardebat* was one bit of it, and another came in the next verse, *quid speraret* where prose would have said *quod*; "had not how to hope" for "had nothing to hope."

It is a pity that so many moderns, trying to run before they can walk, seem to despise such necessary learning when they set about composing poetry in their own tongues. I could give, but that the task would be somewhat tedious and invidious, examples, not from those pretenders to art who appear to prefer the promptings of their own untutored senses to the whole experience of the centuries of English poetry, but from writers of real merit who err unbecomingly from ignorance of just such elementary things as Vergil knows and observes in these two lines. But aesthetic criticism, unless very good, is very wearisome and it is more germane to the present subject to consider what manner of songs they were which Corydon sang love-lorn under his shady beeches.

He begins with a straightforward appeal to Alexis' pity and asks if his love would have him die: *mori me denique coges?* The source here, as so often in the poem, is Theokritos, who makes a disconsolate lover[10] ask a hard-hearted mistress if she would have him hang himself. Vergil, in adapting the phrase, shows that he knows how to do it, and makes the necessary alteration to fit a close rendering to the conventions of his own tongue. Greek can without offence use in verse the plain word for "hang," ἀπάγξασθαι. Latin cannot; it belongs to prose to say *suspendio necare, laqueo uitam finire*, or the like. When it is absolutely necessary to speak of that way of putting an end to one's own or another's life, Vergil knows how to do it, or did by the time he composed the *Aeneid;* Queen Amata there[11]

> nodum informis leti trabe nectit ab alta.
> Bound to a beam the knot of hideous death.

But here it is not necessary, so he contents himself with the plain *mori*, which is as good in verse as in prose. Corydon goes on to borrow from another passage in Theokritos and combine it with a third. The language of the next two lines smacks, as it is meant to do, of a totally different noonday scene in the seventh Idyll, the Harvest Festival. There, Theokritos and some of his friends are gathering, on a hot day in late summer, at the estate of certain of their acquaintance in Kos. As he trudges along the dusty road under the noonday sun, Simichidas (that is, Theokritos) is asked by another wayfarer what he is doing out at such a time,"when even the lizard sleeps in the dyke." This is manifestly a country proverb for intense heat and, like many such sayings, contains a jocular exaggeration; my own experience of Greek and Italian weather does not include any day when the lizards found it too hot to sun themselves.[12] Vergil, then, gives us the Theokritean lizard.

> Now even cattle seek the cooling shade,
> Now even lizards hide beneath the thorn,
> While Thestylis, for reapers tired with heat,
> Pounds thyme and garlic in an odorous mess.

Corydon being away from roads and farmsteads in his lonely pasture, there are no dykes for the lizards to run into, so the poet makes them shelter under thorn-bushes. As to Thestylis, while I would not go so far as to measure a poet's excellence by the strength of the scents arising from his verses, I do think that the best artists in words know how to appear to all the senses through the devious channel of the ear. In the hot Italian noon, smells carry far, and the national fondness for strong and pungent herbs is not a thing of yesterday, nor the day before. But to return to Theokritos, whom we have left for a moment, since Thestylis and her salad-making are none of his invention, he puts into the mouth of a girl using love-magic by night a pretty piece of inverted "pathetic fallacy."

> Now sleep the waters and the storm-winds sleep,
> But not the cares that ravage my poor heart.[13]

Vergil takes the hint, and takes it after the manner of a great and a Mediterranean poet. The other period of calm and stillness is noonday, the hour of the siesta, which is no modern innovation, but part of classical usage.[14] In this heavy-scented time of sleep Corydon has no peace, as Theokritos' Simaitha has none:

> But in the glare, while still I track thy steps,
> With me cicalas make the bushes ring.

A few lines follow of contrast between this new love and the older ones, a sunburned country lad called Menalcas and a cross-grained girl named Amaryllis,[15] with a word of warning to Alexis not to put too much trust in his lovely white complexion, carefully sheltered of course from the sun, as was the manner of city beauties of both sexes. Alexis had, it would seem,
>   a skin
> As clean and white as privet when it flowers,[16]

but Corydon reminds him that no one gathers privet-flowers, but prefers the dark *uaccinium*, whatever that may be:[17]

> alba ligustra cadunt, uaccinia nigra leguntur.

This bit of botanising morality over, we come to the most misunderstood thing in the poem. I cannot get the sweetness of it into English, but perhaps a translation will carry with it some slight remnant of the humour.

> Thou scorn'st me, askest not what man I be,
> How rich in herds, how wealthy in milk as white
> As snow; mine are the thousand lambs that roam
> Sicily's hills, and still my pails are full,

> In summer's heat and winter's cold the same.
> My songs are those that once Amphion sang,
> The Theban herdsman, for his cattle-call,
> On Attic Aracynthus. For my face,
> 'Tis none so ugly, for I saw it late
> Reflected off-shore in a windless sea.
> Judge thou; if mirrors lie not, I dare cope
> Even with Daphnis' self, that comely wight.

This passage contains a designed absurdity, which Vergil's learned readers (he did not write for the unlearned) were meant to notice, though the later commentators, Servius and the rest, did not and missed the joke entirely. Corydon has been at some pains to remember the name of Amphion and his upbringing among shepherds, and even to get him on the right hill with his herd;[18] Arakynthos is the name of some high ground in Boiotia, also of a mountain in Aitolia, which does not now concern us,[19] and its suffix shows that it is a very ancient name, older than the coming of the Greeks to the country. But the singer is led by association of sounds to think of and distort another famous Theban name, that of Aktaion, and so proudly brings out the fine-sounding Greek line

> Amphion Dircaeus in Actaeo Aracyntho,

thus putting the hill on the wrong side of the frontier, for *Actaeus* can only mean "Attic." For the rest, he ministers to his own self-respect by bringing himself and his doings into association partly with the sons of Zeus and Antiope, but still more with Polyphemos. He is for the moment not poor Corin the slave-herdsman, but the amorous giant, scorned, not by a brat from the city, but by Galateia the mermaid. The Sicilian hills are of course part of the setting and throw no light whatever on the scene of the poem, the thousand lambs are an improvement on the Theokritean Cyclops' flock, which had a thousand head altogether,[20] and the milk seems to be a poeticising of the original's cheese; for some reason, it does not seem to have been elegant to call cheese by its name in Augustan verse,[21] but no one minds in a Greek pastoral. The singer continues with another Cyclops-passage, this time from a less-known Idyll, the sixth, where the giant says,

> For truly even in looks I am not so bad as they make me out; indeed it was but t'other day that I peered into the sea, when it was calm, and to my judgement my beard showed handsome and also my one eye, while from my teeth there came a glitter whiter than from Parian marble; but lest the evil eye should hurt me, I spat thrice into my bosom, as old Kotyttaris had taught me.

All this borrowing is but pastoral convention; Theokritos is a shepherd, so is Corydon, and one shepherd may be assumed to know another's verses, supposed to have been heard, not read.

But modern commentators have introduced new merriment into the lines, at least for those readers who have any feeling for literature and any power to see the fun lurking behind bad criticism, by their ridiculous assumption that Corydon is singing here in his own person and the consequent solemnity with which they inform us that a man of ordinary stature could hardly use the sea for a mirror and that Corydon is not in a position to own property on a large scale and is not, or should not be, in Sicily. Some day perhaps there will arise a critic who will take Victorian literature for his subject and interpret it through the eyes of A.D. 3000 or so. He will find, it may be, a passage in which one of the characters, in a drawing-room of the 'nineties, sings "I am the Bandalero," and will gravely take the novelist to task, pointing out that on page 63 he mentioned that the singer was a very honest tradesman and no bandit, while pages 123 and 258 make it clear that he had never been in Spain and was quite ignorant of Spanish. And the criticism will be quite as good as that on Vergil, or on Corydon, for choosing to sing here the song of the love-lorn Cyclops instead of describing naturalistically the feelings of an Italian herdsman. Instead of blaming an ancient author for doing, without elaborate explanations, what a modern perhaps would not do in like case, it is better to examine ancient literature a little more closely, including a poem which we know served Vergil as a model, the sixth Theokritean idyll, already mentioned. In that, two shepherd-boys have a friendly singing-match while their flocks rest at noon by a spring. Both of them sing of the Cyclops, one addressing him and teasing him about Galateia, the other assuming his part and singing his song for him. Whether or not real Sicilian shepherds were fond of ballads about their local monster, it is pastoral convention to suppose they were, and for my own part I am very ready to take Theokritos' word for a fact which he must have known if it was a fact, since I can see no sufficient reason why he should invent it if it was not. But be that as it may, once he had become a classic, anyone else writing about shepherds and their songs had his paramount authority for such a theme to put into their mouths, just as he had for expressing their songs and their conversation alike by hexameters. To quarrel with Vergil for following authority in this respect, still more to imagine that he is not following it but making his *pastor* speak of himself in this Gargantuan manner, is to show oneself incapable of understanding what a pastoral poet would be at, or at least to condemn him for writing in this vein at all; in which case, why be at the trouble of reading him?

Corydon goes on to praise the unkempt country-side, *sordida rura,* and here I think we have less of the learned Vergil than of Vergil the country-bred boy. It is hardly the scholar so much as the rustic who knows the exact kind of plant from which to pluck a tough switch for driving a flock of kids. It was the *uiridis hibiscus,* which our botanists say is marsh mallow.[23] But it is worth looking at this passage a little closely to see how convention mingles with realism. This Greek-derived genre ought to have a Greek flavour; therefore the shepherds of Corydon's acquaintance do not worship any Italian deity such as Faunus or Inuus, but are devout followers of Pan. It is true that to the theologians of Vergil's day the Greek and the Italian gods were identical.

> Here in the woods we'll mimic in our song
> Pan, him who first conjoined with wax the reeds,
> Who cares for sheep and for the shepherd cares.

There follows a section, pretty but not very remarkable, for Vergil, on the joys of the country, especially its flowers and fruits. Now comes the awakening. Corydon reminds himself that he is of the country and could offer Alexis nothing that would really please him, or if he could, would be outbid by his master (who for the purposes of the poem has a Greek name, Iollas, like the rest). But, as he rouses himself to a sense of his own folly and consequent neglect of his work, there comes a half-humorous consolation in the shape of a last appeal.

> Whom do you fly, poor fool? the gods themselves
> And Dardan Paris in the woods have dwelt.
> Let Pallas have her towns, she founded them,
> The woods be all our joy. The raging lioness
> Follows the wolf, the wolf the playful kid,
> The kid the clover, each his own desire;
> So Corin for Alexis. Look, the ploughs
> Are lifted and the oxen drag them home,
> The sun descends, the shadows double long,
> Yet love consumes me; love no measure knows.
> Poor Corin, why so moonstruck? See, your vines
> Hang on their elms half-pruned. There's work to do;
> At least take withies, take a pliant reed,
> Weave thee a basket. This Alexis lost,
> Thou'lt find another will not be so coy.

Vergil is an Alexandrian on one side of his literary ancestry, and Alexandrians, when they quote or half-quote, do their reader the compliment of supposing that he knows the context of the quotation and can apply it if necessary. It is easy to do so here, for Corydon is simply giving us more of Polyphemos:[24]

Eh, Cyclops, Cyclops, whither have thy wits wandered? If thou'ldst go and weave cheese-baskets and gather fodder to take to thy lambs, it were better sense in thee. Milk the cow that's at hand; why run after the one that flees? Thou'lt find another Galateia, belike, fairer than this one.

Having just said that gods and princes lived in the woods, that is to say, the untilled land used for pasture and forestry, Corydon once more adds his favourite giant, also of the "woods," being a herdsman like himself. Well, then; if the matter is looked at aright, is there not something fine in being a lovesick herdsman, like the great ones of fable, Apollo when he longed for Admetos' society, Paris while yet unrecognised of his royal kin, Polyphemos while he wooed Galateia? Come, come; things are not going so badly for a poor rustic if he is matched with gods, heroes, and giants in his very woes. Corydon goes away with something of a swagger, thanks to his music and his fancies, thinking of himself as somehow great and desirable, in the same class as the uncouth but mighty monster who, as some say, did after all win his Galateia and become by her the father of the whole race of Gauls.[25]

Compared with the second Eclogue, the third is slight and has less originality, yet it is not without a contribution of Vergil's own to this branch of poetry. Essentially, it is an adaptation of Theokritos' fifth Idyll, whereof a little, part of the opening quarrel between the herd-boys, was quoted in the last chapter. Menalcas and Damoetas meet, pass from rude jests to downright abuse of each other, and in the course of their dispute mention music, which makes one challenge the other to a contest then and there. There is a preliminary wrangle as to what the stake shall be; one wants to wager a heifer, the other dare not for fear of his parents, who always count the beasts at night. Finally they agree to stake a pair of carved wooden bowls. Palaemon, another herdsman, appears on the scene just as they need an umpire, and they begin to cap couplets very prettily, until Palaemon finally decides he cannot prefer either and the match is a draw. A later chapter will have more to say about the fashion of the contest; for the present we may note that, being the kind of imitator he is, Vergil is not content to follow one Theokritean model. He commences with the opening line of the third Idyll and ends with the drawn match of the sixth. He is not at his best in the more colloquial parts of the work, for Latin hexameters, pastoral or other, pay a price for their stateliness in that they cannot be quite natural, as the more flexible Greek can, without ceasing to be pleasing in sound and rhythm. Four men of great talent tried the hexameter for writing about everyday matters of life and conduct, and of these, Lucilius produced some of the worst specimens of Latin metre ever read or heard, but kept the naturalism of language to a greater degree than most of his imitators; Persius combined a designed ruggedness of metre with the most extraordinarily contorted style that has come down to us under the name of a respectable author; while Juvenal produced rather machine-made lines embodying rhetoric of the most effective, bitter, and completely artificial. Only Horace ever managed to be both natural and elegant, and his secret was born and died with him. Vergil had not that kind of genius. He could not write like Terence in a non-Terentian metre, nor, probably, would he have succeeded in those measures which Terence himself used. He gets away therefore from the slanging-match as soon as he decently can, to imitate yet another passage of Theokritos, the description of the cup in the first Idyll. He does not here translate the Greek passage nor imitate it closely, but uses it as a starting-point for giving us his own idea of a piece of artistry in wood by an imaginary craftsman. Soon after, when the umpire arrives to decide the match between the shepherd-boys, Vergil again slips away from his immediate subject into three lines (not undramatic nor without significance, as shall presently be shown) of pure poetry. Palaemon speaks:

> Say on, for now soft grass provides our seat,
> The birthtime's coming for each field and tree,
> The woods in leaf, the year at its most fair.

To anyone who knows Italy, the picture is complete; the grass is fit to sit upon, as it is only in the cooler parts of the year or the country.[26] It is springtime.

The two lads now begin to sing against each other, one starting with two lines and the other answering with two of like style and subject. The matter of the forty-four verses which they sing varies from love to literature, and so to the troubles of countrymen (snakes, treacherous streams, burning heat), then back to love again, ending with a pair of riddles which are distinguished by the fact that no one hitherto has succeeded in solving them to the general satisfaction.[27] The literary references include one to Pollio, which we shall have occasion to deal with in a later chapter, and one to that famous couple Bavius and Mevius, poetasters so obscure that we should not know they ever existed but for their having annoyed Vergil and Horace, of whom the latter devoted a little poem to calling Mevius a "stinker" and genially wishing him ill luck on a voyage,[28] while the former here pairs them (it would indeed appear that they were close friends)[29] and remarks that he who does not hate the one is at liberty to love the other, but only a fool big enough to use foxes for draught-cattle or try to milk he-goats would do either.[30]

But the end of the poem contains a wholly original touch. Generally the umpire in these contests is a mere lay figure, at most giving the author's opinion on the songs of the competitors. Vergil's Palaemon suddenly comes to life—indeed he had given signs of it in his charming little description of the spring weather—and in a few lines (the best of the ancients liked their psychology and character-drawing brief and good) is sketched for us as a romantic and amatory poet, probably young, not much older than the singing shepherds themselves. His judgement is no more than a modest refusal to judge, and makes it clear that his mind has been busy at least as much with his own thoughts and desires as with what they have been singing.

> Non nostrum inter uos tantas componere lites;
> et uitula tu dignus et hic, et quisquis amores
> aut metuet dulcis aut experietur amaros.[31]

> So great a quarrel is not mine to end;
> Ye both deserve the heifer; so do all
> Who fear love's honey or who taste its gall.

The umpire's absence of mind is betrayed by two little points. In the first place, the fears and woes of lovers have hardly been mentioned, and love has by no means been the only theme. In the second, the heifer has not been wagered. Before Palaemon came up, the stake had been decided, and the offer to make it a heifer declined; he does not know what they are singing for, but merely assumes that so earnest a contest must be for a considerable prize. Then who is the third, indeterminate claimant, the person, "whoever he is," to render Vergil's perfect verse into very plain prose, "that either shall fear love in its sweetness or taste it in its bitterness"? The two competitors, after a pious couplet apiece, to Iuppiter and Apollo respectively, have started with the names of loves—Galatea, Amyntas, Delia. It is obvious enough that they are bragging of affairs which have no existence but in their own imaginations, for they are still very young, and no great credence can be placed in the sincerity of a passion which calls a mistress first Galatea and then Phyllis. Of love's bitterness neither has said or hinted anything. But Palaemon is of a different cast of mind, a kind of shepherd whose existence has been assumed at least since Theokritos wrote his third Idyll, the passionate lover. The convention, like many others, may well go back ultimately to truth and nature, but in any case it exists. As the serenader in Theokritos (if we may call that a serenade which is not sung in the evening) addresses a hard-hearted and unresponsive Amaryllis, so we may suppose Palaemon to have spent much thought and song over his love, whoever she may be, and it needs but a few notes of music to set his mind on that familiar theme once more. I much doubt if he has heard more than the amatory lines which came early in the contest, unless it be a passing *Phyllida amo ante alias*, "Phyllis is my chief love," from Menalcas. Therefore, when the singers pause, as they do unbidden, it dawns on the poor umpire that he has not really been listening, and is in no position to decide which has done better. So he hastily declares a draw, and assures them that they have sung enough:

> claudite iam riuos, pueri; sat prata biberunt.
> Shut off the waters, for the fields are moist.

No one, at this time of day, can be sure that he sees in Vergil all, or nearly all, that Horace saw and admired. On the contrary, it is probable that we miss many delicate points of language and allusion that were perfectly clear to him and to other educated contemporaries of the poet. But I think we may fairly claim to see those qualities which he mentions and which I have tried to point out. There is in these two poems, perhaps the simplest and least interesting of the ten, a power of passing easily from theme to theme and from mood to mood, from the desperate earnestness of Corydon's passion to the slightly ridiculous figure of Corydon himself; from the rough chaff of Damoetas and Menalcas to their dainty singing and from that again to the slight but vivid sketch of their umpire, with his love of poetry and beauty and his preoccupation with his own affairs. This may serve to show why Horace styled his friend's work *molle*, flexible. And as to the humour, surely that is present in works which handle with so light a touch matter over which it would be quite easy to grow sentimental and rhetorical, letting us see at once that Corydon's woes are a trifle absurd and that, for the moment, they are the most important things in the universe to Corydon. For it is the destiny of the little man that his affairs, however intensely he may feel them, still remain little in comparison with the scheme of things and that to make them out important must always be just a shade absurd to the impartial observer. It is not snobbishness but sound judgement which lies behind the old precept of critics, that the proper subjects for tragedy are kings and princes, not common folk.

Now this sense of humour, a rare thing among Latins, which Vergil shows that he had, is nothing but a particular form of the sense of proportion, which is none too common in any people or age. That sense is put to an acid test in the next group of Eclogues we have now to examine. Vergil could see that his imaginary shepherds were not space-filling figures and became less, not more impressive when they tried to make themselves out to be such. Could he continue to see troubles and misfortunes in so sane a light when they were his own? Was he capable of realising that although he or his household might suffer, the world at large could not be expected to join in their complaints; in fact, that Publius Vergilius Maro, his father and his friends, might weigh little heavier in the scales of the world than a slave-herdsman, who might be very wretched, or very angry, and yet leave the district of Mantua generally content and prosperous? Such detachment needs, not merely native humour or sense of proportion, but more than a slight tinge of philosophy, inborn or acquired. Now Vergil had had a philosophic training, and, if the little poem which generally stands fifth in the *Catalepton* is really his, as many think, he had been an enthusiastic pupil. He was, or had been, an Epicurean, and Epicurus, like most of the later teachers and their followers, made it his chief task to liberate the mind from the disturbances which it would otherwise suffer in this mortal life. So Vergil, if indeed it was he, had thought when he looked for the reward of "a life set free from every care"[32] as a result of his studies under his teacher Siron. If we are to judge how he faced his share of earthly miseries, we must first make up our minds what exactly these were and then ask concerning his reaction to them. We of today, used as we became to two or three fresh crises every month till the last of them once more plunged Europe into open and declared hostilities, do not need much imagination to realise how easy it was for a man of Vergil's generation to fall a prey to what we inelegantly term "jitters," while Latin more plainly styled it *formido*, fear. Economic distress, again, is nothing new, although Vergil's word for it is *egestas*, and it was extremely common when Octavian, afterwards the Emperor Augustus, was fighting for his position and his supremacy. Both these evils seem to have come the poet's way, and he spoke his mind about them after his fashion. We must therefore proceed in the next chapter to consider the situation in which he found himself during the composition of at least some of the *Eclogues* and the way in which his emotions found voice.

CHAPTER III

THE POET AND HIS HOME

THERE ARE two of the ten poems which by common consent have something to do (though what, is still undecided) with the personal and bitter experiences of Vergil, his family, and his fellow Mantuans during the disturbed conditions which resulted from the long-continued civil wars. To read them through, they are simple enough in contents; but there is hardly a line in either which has not been the subject of sharp controversy and of criticism ranging from really penetrating and tasteful interpretation to the utterance of some of the absurdest views ever heard outside, perhaps, of the commentaries on Homer and Shakespere. These poems are the first and the ninth of our collection, and the chief difficulty is to decide, not so much if they are figurative or allegorical, for that is pretty generally admitted, but where and how, and what exactly is the prose which their poetry conceals from us and probably revealed to those for whom it was first written.

Since so much is doubtful, it is perhaps best to begin by setting down briefly what exactly the two poems say. In No. I, a poor herdsman, or rather a small farmer who keeps a few goats, by name Meliboeus, meets his friend Tityrus, an older man of like occupation, under distressing conditions. Meliboeus has been forced to leave his farm and betake himself and such of his possessions as he can transport away from Mantua and its neighbourhood, to seek a new home, he does not know where, but gloomily fears it will not be in Italy at all, but at the ends of the earth. Tityrus, somewhat to his friend's surprise, is not at all affected personally by the conditions which have ruined Meliboeus; he is resting in the heat of the afternoon under a beech (the two friends, then, cannot well be on low ground; indeed

Tityrus mentions that they are near hills and can see farmhouses a long way off),[1] playing his pipe and singing a love-song in honour of his wife, or quasi-wife, one Amaryllis. Meliboeus, enquiring how it is that he is not dispossessed, gets a curious reply; he has been to Rome. In answer to further questions, he tells his story a little confusedly, omitting what he would ordinarily have dwelt upon, that he went there to see his master, evidently a man of some importance who lives in the capital, and to buy his freedom with money he had saved from his quasi-property or *peculium*, the little croft which he farms, the pasture of which he has the use, and the produce of both, especially of his flock. This he has at last managed to do, under Amaryllis' wise direction, for his former mate, Galatea, had been a spendthrift and had made him one. He hastens on to the surprising part of the story; at Rome he had seen (besides his master, whom he must obviously have met and satisfied) a wonderful *iuuenis*, whom he regards as a god and means to sacrifice to every month. This *iuuenis*, who can be no one but Octavian, has told him to go on quietly with his usual work, implying that he will not be turned out from what is now his patrimony to make room, like Meliboeus,[2] for a time-expired soldier. Meliboeus congratulates him and sadly contrasts his own hard lot, the horrible result of civil war. He probably will never see his bit of land again, and will have no heart to sing the songs he once used to sing. Tityrus has but one small comfort to offer him; at least he may pass the night with his old friend and have a good supper of familiar rustic fare—fruit, chestnuts, and cream cheese.[3]

That this is a sketch of the sort of thing which might happen after Philippi, when Octavian's men were being given land (a modern government would have given them some kind of pensions) and the existing owners were being

[1] Notes to chapter iii will be found on pages 228–233.

dispossessed on every excuse and none to supply it, is obvious enough. That Octavian might, out of good nature or for some special reason, exempt a smallholder here and there is also pretty clear. But the question arises, Why Tityrus in particular, and who is Tityrus? Before we consider the answers, ancient and modern, to this natural enquiry, let us look at the companion piece, the ninth, which also treats of dispossession.

Its framework, but only that, belongs to the seventh Idyll of Theokritos; two friends encounter each other during a noonday walk, and go on together, singing and chatting. But their conversation deals with other matters than those which engage the care-free young men of the Greek poet's *Harvest Festival*. Moeris, the slave, freedman, or even partner[4] of a certain Menalcas, is on his way to the town, carrying, it would seem, a pair of young kids on his shoulders.[5] It is a sad mission, for the beasts are, or their price is,[6] for the benefit of a new owner of Menalcas' estate. He is met by a younger man, Lycidas, who is surprised at the bad news; it had been gossipped that Menalcas' estate had been preserved to him for the sake of his poetry. That, says Moeris, was the current report, but so far from its being true in these terrible days, Menalcas and I owe it to a celestial warning, an omen sent through a raven, that we are alive at all. Lycidas expresses his horror at the danger to so sweet a singer, and they begin to quote tags of the poems of Menalcas, till at last Moeris will sing no more, declaring that his voice and memory are failing as he grows older, and the pair walk towards the town in silence.

Here the interpretation is pretty generally accepted by ancients and moderns alike. Menalcas is Vergil, and the misfortune which has overtaken him is the confiscation of the property on which he had lived in boyhood, the land which belonged to his father and which he might naturally look to inherit, and so to live modestly but comfortably on its revenues, if not actually reside there.[7] This is stated at length by Servius, who gives the following sketch of the opening situation: "Vergil, after having been nearly killed by Arrius the centurion, returning to Rome, gave directions to his agents to look after his estate and in the meanwhile to take their orders from Arrius. Moeris therefore, an agent of his, according to his patron's instructions, is now taking kids to Mantua to present to Arrius."[8] For the present, we will set aside the question of the historicity of this Arrius and of his murderous assault on Vergil-Menalcas and stick to the main fact of the identification. That it is correct is made sufficiently clear by the nature of the scraps of song which are quoted in the poem; they include two excellent imitations of Theokritos,[9] one appeal to (Alfenus) Varus[10] to save Mantua, and what appears to be the beginning of a little hymn of praise to the memory of Julius Caesar, with the implication that under his successor all shall yet be well.[11] In other words, they are thoroughly Vergilian in style and content, admirably fitted to give an idea of his poetical methods and his interests. But there is a further indication. In the fifth Eclogue a Menalcas is one of the singers in a friendly display; at the end, he presents his pan-pipe to the other poet, Mopsus, and says that on it he composed the second and third Eclogues. Menalcas therefore is Vergil in that poem, and there is no reason why the same name should not have the same significance here.[12]

Now in the first poem Servius is equally certain that Tityrus is Vergil,[13] but he makes a curious qualification to his statement; "we must understand Vergil under the mask of Tityrus, but not everywhere, only where reason so bids." This may mean that Tityrus is not necessarily Vergil when the name occurs casually in other poems, or even that he is not always and everywhere Vergil in the first Eclogue itself. It is true that in *Ecl.*, VI, 4 Vergil is addressed by Apollo himself as *Tityre;* but it is by no means unlikely that this simply means "my poor rustic."[14] Be that as it may, the objections to taking Tityrus as Vergil anywhere in Eclogue I are formidable, and have been well emphasised by Leo in the best short commentary that has ever been written on that charming but difficult poem.[15] Vergil was free-born and wrote the first Eclogue somewhere about the age of thirty; Tityrus is a slave just freed and is getting old and grey.[16] Tityrus had never been to Rome before, we may add, and Vergil probably had lived in the capital for some time, to say nothing of his sojourn in Naples or its neighbourhood.[17] It is allowable of course for a poet to introduce a little fiction if he bring himself into one of his own works under a feigned name; any imaginative writer has that privilege. But what possible point is there in such a travesty as this would be? Who would readily recognise a young man in an old one, a freeman in a slave-born peasant just set free, a town-dweller who was born in or near the country[18] in one to whom the capital is a strange place, so strange that he is not quite sure if his friend knows the name of it[19] and is lost in wonder at its vastness, of which he had had no sort of conception before? Certainly Theokritos, Vergil's presumable model in his allegories, or masquerades, put on no such heavy disguise; he merely calls himself by a fictitious name and puts himself in country surroundings which apparently were not fictitious at all. I think therefore that we must refuse to recognise Vergil in Tityrus, although the identification is still quite popular[20] and was common in antiquity. Who he is must be considered when we have striven to see some daylight through the mist which surrounds much of the ninth poem as completely as that which Venus provided hid Vergil's later hero from inquisitive Carthaginians.[21]

Menalcas has been turned out of some kind of property at the risk of his life and that of Moeris, his friend or servant. The property is described, briefly, but in a way which suggests a real place and characteristics recognisable to anyone who had been there, in the speech of Lycidas:

> Certe equidem audieram, qua se subducere colles
> incipiunt, mollique iugum demittere cliuo,
> usque ad aquam et ueteres, iam fracta cacumina, fagos,
> omnia carminibus uestrum seruasse Menalcan.[22]

Surely I had heard that your Menalcas had saved by his songs everything at the place where the hills begin to run down and lower their crest in a gentle slope, as far as the water and the old beeches whose tops now are broken.

It is of course obvious that there must be many places in Italy where hills tail off into a plain and there is water somewhere near the foot of them; it is obvious also that there may have been old beech-trees growing in hundreds or thousands of spots in Vergil's day, and old trees, of whatever sort, if fairly big, form natural landmarks and boundaries. Vergil does not tell us what kind of water he means, but a stream or river of some sort is a sufficiently unforced explanation, unless some lucky topographer finds a suitable pond or lagoon in the right neighbourhood, or proof that there once was one. It would therefore seem that Vergil's estate, or that of his father, was on sloping ground, but not a very sharp slope, part of it perhaps being quite flat, and had at least two boundaries which it ought to be possible to find today, a line of hills, big or little, forming a recognisable ridge, and either a body of (probably flowing) water or at least the indication that such a thing once existed, at a not impossible distance from the higher ground. There is nothing in tradition or in our general knowledge of Mantua and its inhabitants, or of the two *gentes*, the somewhat obscure Vergilii and the rather better-known Magii, from whose happy union the poet sprung, to suggest either that his parents were very rich or that they were very poor. Very poor people cannot send their son far from home to expensive places of education, and the very rich are not so concerned over the loss of one country home as Vergil and his family appear to have been. Therefore we ought, if we can identify the estate at all, to find something considerably more than a poor peasant's holding, yet less than a *latifundium*.

But evidently we must have some idea where to look, for the topography of Italy is not so poor or monotonous as to have but one ridge of hills and one body of water at places where it is conceivable that an inhabitant of Mantua might have owned some land and brought up his son. To make matters worse for the modern, the face of the country near Mantua itself was somewhat profoundly changed during the Middle Ages. The river Mincio, Vergil's *uiridis Mincius*,[23] probably flowed in classical times, not in one bed, as now, but in two, before it reached Mantua. Of these, it seems likely to one of the best and most loving explorers of the region, Professore Bruno Nardi,[24] that one ran into what is now the Larione, joining the Osone on the way, while the other formed, as it still does, a loop running past the town from north-west to south-east and widening out into the swampy valley mentioned by Livy.[25] It may be, but it cannot be proved, that part of the stream also ran south-east and south of Mantua. In those days the Po kept its distance from the neighbourhood of Mantua, which stood "well above" the formidable marshes on its banks, since removed by modern engineering,[26] and indeed was a good deal farther from the city than it now is. Hence, if Vergil talks of marshes, as he does, though not in the ninth Eclogue, and means any considerable swamp in the territory of his own city, it is the Mincian and not the Paduan marshes that he means. And when anyone speaks of water and rivers, it is but natural, unless he specifies the contrary, to suppose that he is thinking of the principal river of the district, itself no very huge stream, not of some insignificant rivulet.

Hence the banks of the Mincio have the first claim to be examined for the estate of Vergil's parents.

Here tradition points a guiding finger which most ages since the death of the poet have been willing to follow. While the majority of our authorities[26] content themselves with saying that Vergil was born near Mantua, or simply that he was a Mantuan, one, the so-called Probus,[27] who, let his real name be what it may, was clearly a well-informed man, tells or tries to tell us just how far away the birthplace was from the town. It was, he says, in a country village (*uicus*) known as Andes (here several of the rest agree and no one contradicts him), and its distance from Mantua was ... how far? The existing manuscripts of his commentary on the *Bucolics*, all late (fifteenth century) and therefore of an age when learned humanistic interference with the text is perfectly possible and scribal error conceivable as it always is, agree that it was thirty (Roman) miles: *rustico uico Andico, qui abest a Mantua milia passuum XXX*. But the scarcely later *editio princeps*, printed in Venice in 1507 and edited by Egnatius, reads clearly *milia passuum III*, which certainly, if correct, agrees better with the assertion that it was "near" Mantua, since "near" is a relative term, and a distance which certainly would take us to the very bounds of the city's territory would rather be "far." But this very agreement makes the reading somewhat suspicious. Neither Egnatius nor any editor of his day had heard of an apparatus criticus, and all were much too fond of altering, without notice, what they did not understand or thought obviously wrong. Hence the fact that Egnatius prints III is no proof that he found it in whatever manuscript he used for his edition. Without going so far as Sabbadini in supposing that wherever he differs from the surviving copies of the work he is printing his own conjectures and nothing else, we may query this departure, for it is the very change which a man of learning might well make to bring Probus into line with the local tradition.

For it is well known that Andes is traditionally identified with Pietole—Old, not New Pietole,—which is veritably three miles (Roman) from the town, to the east, near the Mincio. Not only was this identification known to Dante,[28] but it is preserved in more than one local name, such as the *fossatum Virgilii*, at a large farm called Fornicata or Fornicatula near Pietole, and the *mons Virgilii*, a small hill not a great way off. Moreover, the whole region is and was abundantly provided with pottery-kilns, and the assertion, be it true or false, that Vergil the elder started life as a potter fits this very well.[29] All this so hangs together that any document which contradicted it would stand an excellent chance of being altered to bring it into line, much as, by an easier emendation than that from XXX to III, St. Jerome proposed to alter the text of Mark 15:25 from "third hour" to "sixth hour," to fit the concurrent evidence of Matt. 27:45 and John 19:14.[30]

Pietole then is the traditional site, and can appeal, a little doubtfully, for the inscription is now lost and has been declared spurious, to archaeological evidence of a sort. There was once an epigraphic record of a certain P. Vergilius, and we are assured that it was found at Pietole.[31] This man cannot have been the poet, but if the record was geniune, it at least shows that some members of the family did live in classical times, although later than his, at about the place where his monument now stands.

But there is a serious reason for not at once assuming tradition to be right, however likely it may be that the inhabitants of a place not otherwise very famous would remember just where their best-known fellow citizen had been born and brought up. Pietole has nothing that could fairly be called a ridge of hills. The country is all flat, with a few gentle rises at most, the famous Mons Virgilii being the best-known of them. Now Vergil implies that Menalcas' estate was next to a district anything but flat; the hills "begin" to slope down there, hence they presumably have not been sloping down a little farther on, but forming something of the nature of a small range, ridge, or table-land. One would at least expect a river flowing at the bottom of a fairly deep valley, such as may be seen in scores of places in Wales, for instance, a *dyffren* as the speech of that country calls it. There is no such thing on the Mincio east of Mantova, although the fact that its banks are partly composed of glacial deposit makes them not always dead level with the surrounding country.[32] Why should Vergil, or any poet, add so conspicuous a thing as a hill, or rather a line or ridge of hills, to a place which had no more than a hillock or two? I would not overstress this, for some at least of the ancients seem to have found the very place, presumably at or near Pietole, to their satisfaction; Filargirius, commenting on the lines already quoted, knows of a lake or pool which formed one boundary of the estate, and is quite content to take the "slope" as that of the bank of the Mincio. But that it is a difficulty, no one who reads the Eclogues carefully and notes how vivid their descriptions are can reasonably doubt.

Hence it is that the late Professor Conway[33] abandoned Pietole altogether, as Sir William Ramsay and others had done before him, and looked for a place which should at once fit Vergil's *colles* and Probus' alleged *milia passuum XXX*. With the help of Professor Braunholtz he found it, and defended his discovery in the face of an incredulous Mantova. The theory he put forward teems with ingenious elaborations, but may be briefly stated thus. Vergil arranged his Eclogues, so to speak, geographically, the odd-numbered ones having a local and the even-numbered a foreign setting. No. I we shall come back to later; VII mentions the Mincius, IX as we have seen speaks of what seems to be Vergil's own estate, V consists of two songs concerning Julius Caesar (we have to discuss this later), therefore it is no great assumption that the series is complete and III refers to the Mantuan district also. Now these pieces teem with references to hilly scenery; No. I speaks of the shadows of mountains as visible,[34] III has beeches and irrigation-ditches[35] (incidentally, the latter at least are to be found near Pietole to this day, so prove nothing for the nature of the district; Conway apparently imagined they required a far greater slope than they really do),[36] V has a cave,[37] VII is laid in "these mountains."[38] Ergo, IX has hilly scenery, and its *colles* are no mere small differences of level, but recognisable hills, such as are not to be found near Pietole, but perhaps might be if one went Probus' supposed thirty miles away.

Furthermore, Vergil's farm was lost, or at the very least threatened with loss, when the wholesale seizures of land were made by Octavian's government, after Philippi. Servius explains the circumstances.[39] "Augustus, having won the war, gave the lands of the people of Cremona, who had sided with Antony,[40] to his soldiers. These being insufficient, he added the territories of Mantua, which were taken away for no fault, but because of their nearness to Cremona, whence the poet himself says in the *Bucolics*,[41] 'Mantua, alas, too near hapless Cremona.' " Daniel's Servius is more explicit:[42] "To this spot [i.e., the one described by Vergil above] Octavius Musa had extended his surveying-poles, that is to say, through fifteen miles of the Mantuan territory, since that of Cremona was not enough," and again,[43] "Others say Vergil wished to show that through the unfairness of Alfenus Varus nothing was left the Mantuans except their swamps," and there follows something of great value, a quotation from a speech of Cornelius (Gallus) accusing this Varus of having left the unfortunate town barely eight hundred paces of land, and that waterlogged, when he had been told to leave it three miles (presumably every way) from its walls. Now, if it was the intention of

Octavian to seize fifteen miles of Mantuan territory, or if, whatever his intentions, that was what his commissioners did, the natural thing would be to seize the portion nearest to Cremona. Pietole, being on the side away from Cremona, would be one of the portions least likely to be touched, especially if a three-mile strip was to be left the town, it being pretty exactly three miles away.

Conway therefore searches for a hilly or relatively hilly place on the side towards Cremona and thirty, not three miles from Mantua, and finds it to the north-north-west, approximately, of the latter city. This chosen site is the neighbourhood of the two towns of Calvisano and Carpenedolo. Of these the former is rather unpromising; though on a higher level than Pietole, it is quite as flat. It lies exactly at Probus' limit, supposing the reading XXX to be right. Carpenedolo, which is but twenty-three Roman miles from Mantua, is better, having a ridge which does indeed slope down to the plain, also water, the little river Chiese, though not so near as might be wished; the distance to it from the ridge is about a mile and a quarter. The nearest hills are the Brescian Alps, the shadows of which would hardly be visible, if we try to find Tityrus' land hereabouts, as well as Vergil's.[44] Tradition in favour of Vergil's having lived here there is none, but good inscriptional evidence from the neighbourhood (not very near, the place in question being Casalpoglio, fourteen kilometers off)[45] of the existence there of both a Vergilia and a Magius, sometime in the first century A.D. Unfortunately for a theory urged by its author with eloquence and conviction, the whereabouts of a man's collaterals in a later generation (for it is well known that Vergil, never having married, had no descendants) are no guide whatever to where he himself lived, something like a century earlier.

Thus far, then, we have two sites, whereof one has for it tradition, but against it some features at least of the scenery;

the other, partly right scenery, but not tradition, on its behalf. I say "partly right," for even if the Calvisano-Carpenedolo neighbourhood was backed by every scholiast and every biographer, and were by unanimous consent part of the ancient territory of Mantua (it is nowadays Mantuan neither in province nor in dialect, but Brescian),[46] it fails to satisfy two of Vergil's indications of the site of his land. Moeris and Lycidas are walking from the estate to the city, presumably Mantua. Half-way there, the tomb of one Bianor is just in sight, and to suppose that there was no such tomb and Vergil invented it merely because the tomb of Brasilas, an equally unknown worthy, is a landmark to Theokritos' wayfarers,[47] is so ridiculous that few commentators on any other author would venture it. Unfortunately, we have no idea where it was, nor what was the real name of the man Vergil chooses to call Bianor. If by any chance Servius is right[48] and he is Ocnus, the founder of Mantua (to whom, in that Hellenising age, it is just possible there might have been some sort of monument, or an identification with it of some old shrine), then it would presumably be somewhere at or very near the city itself, and in that case it must have been remarkably conspicuous if it could be seen, even dimly, by men twelve to fifteen miles away. That the distance is not very great, indeed considerably less than even twelve miles, about half-way to Carpenedolo and its ridge, is indicated by the fact that old Moeris is apparently not tired with trudging so far carrying the kids and refuses to sit down and rest.[49] Another point is that about the same place there is an *aequor* in sight.[50] In itself this might be a plain, but it is spoken of in terms which could apply only to *aequor* in the other sense, the surface of a not inconsiderable body of water; *stratum silet*, it lies flattened out and quiet. This of course implies that if the weather were different it might be rough and noisy. Neither the sea nor any existing lake is near enough for the purpose; but if the then course of the Mincio ran through a swamp, as we have seen that it did, there might be enough flood-water about to make a lake of some pretensions, at least in the rainier times of the year, and Lycidas hints that they may perhaps be overtaken by rain before nightfall;[51] the season, then, is probably not summer. That the region is wooded tells nothing for any identification;[52] the ancient and mediaeval Mantuan territory was much more overgrown than the modern.[53]

Since, then, we seem to be dealing with a very will-o'-the-wisp of an estate, which recedes for ever and for ever as we move, it is worth while to glance for a moment at the view (ancient and somewhat inclined to by Professors Tenney Frank and Rand)[54] that no individual's property is really meant and what Menalcas-Vergil tried to save was the territory of Mantua as a whole, or some considerable part of it. But here we meet a fresh difficulty. It is true that along the banks of the Mincio towards Cremona, where Ramsay tried to find the Vergilian patrimony, there are to be seen tolerably high ground, fields running down thence to the river, and of course the stream itself to provide the water of which the poet speaks. But what of the beeches? Considering that there seems not to be a single specimen of them today at either Pietole or Carpenedolo,[55] it appears none too likely that ancient Mantua had so many that a line of them formed the boundary, perhaps stretching for miles, of her territory. This is supposing that Vergil really spoke of a plurality of beeches, which is far from certain, since there is a very well attested variant which reduces the number to one,[56] a single aged tree, such as might continue for many years to mark a corner of a property, but surely would be too small to serve as the boundary of a whole region.

Frankly, then, I have no solution of the mystery. Conway's theory, which captivated me for a while, I have now abandoned as untenable, or rather as supported by so slight evidence that its difficulties are not worth clearing away. Flat Pietole may be a district where the Vergilii or the Magii owned some land, but I can hardly think it is the spot described by Moeris. I would point to one small indication, anything but a proof, that Vergil's father possessed more than one stake in the country, perhaps getting some land with his wife and having already another, not adjacent, property himself. This is the much-quoted poem in the *Catalepton* which most moderns think to be Vergil's own and to refer to his own affairs at the time we are considering.[57] It is an address to a little country house, *uillula*, with a bit of land, *agellus*, attached, which once belonged to Vergil's teacher of philosophy, Siron. The poet "commends" to it his loved ones, and especially his father, that is to say, implies that if expelled from their Mantuan estate they are going to live there. Probably Siron was by that time dead and had left the land to his promising pupil; or it is conceivable that it had been bought from him or his heirs. But the poem concludes:

> tu nunc eris illi
> Mantua quod fuerat quodque Cremona prius.
> Thou now shalt be to him [i.e., the elder Vergilius]
> What Mantua erst and what Cremona were.

Now, as we hear of the family circumstances, they lived in the Mantuan territory on their estate. How, then, can Cremona have been to old Vergil what the *villula* is to be, that is to say, a familiar and beloved dwelling-place? Mantua might be so called, even if they seldom set foot in the town, for it is an easy metonymy for the *ager Mantuanus*. It is of course well known that Vergil went to school in Cremona for a while,[58] but this seems to me little to the point. If I may judge by my own feelings, it does not give a man any great affection for a place that he has had a son at school there, though he may wish it well; and Cremona certainly was by no means the climax of the poet's education, for he had his mind finally developed in Rome and Naples; they were, so to speak, his university, Cremona but his preparatory school. But supposing his father had owned land, little or much, sufficiently near Cremona for that city and its immediate environs to be familiar to him, he might well regard that, as well as Mantua, as being in some sort his home. It would seem therefore possible that the estate at Pietole and the estate, of unknown position, mentioned in the ninth Eclogue are both Vergilian, in the sense that Vergil's father lived in both at one time or another, and both formed part of his own property or his wife's dowry. If this or anything like it is really the truth, I should not think it impossible that Vergil on occasion gives us a composite picture, made up of reminiscences of his boyhood at Pietole, if indeed he lived there, and of the other steading, wherever it may have been.

And now to turn to Tityrus' little estate, big enough for him, says Meliboeus, although it is stony soil and the marshes cover it with reed.[59] It is a healthy neighbourhood, not liable to the diseases which afflict stock; there are rivers and springs, some at least of the fields are hedged, and somewhere about it is a high rock, overgrown with trees or large bushes. Elms grow there and two of the local industries are bee-keeping and apparently the breeding of pigeons. Once more, it is hard to place this holding on Mantuan territory; for the swamp suggests (it does not prove) that the land borders on the Mincio or one of its tributaries, and we shall see in a moment that the part of the river east of the city is the likely one; in other words, that we are once more near Pietole. But the high rock is a difficulty, unless we suppose Vergil to mean some very modest elevation of the soil with stones amid its trees; the trees were there until fairly recently, as many mediaeval documents show,[60] but intensive cultivation in the last few centuries has replaced that beauty by one more to the taste of the husbandman, the *laetae segetes* of the first line of the Georgics.

On the whole, then, Tityrus owned land at a low level. But, and I think this is a point which has not been sufficiently noticed, he is not there when he meets Meliboeus. Look once more at the picture which ends the poem:

> et iam summa procul uillarum culmina fumant,
> maioresque cadunt altis de montibus umbrae.
>
> Now rises smoke from distant farm-house roofs,
> And longer grow the shades of lofty hills.

If this means anything, and I refuse to side with the many critics of Vergil I have dipped into who assure us that in the *Bucolics* the poet often means nothing in particular, or such a mixture of things that there is no pinning him down to one meaning, we are on a hillside, or hilltop, and not a very low one at that. It is the roofs of farm-houses which Tityrus sees, which strongly suggests that he is looking down at them, or that they too are on hill-slopes and standing out clearly in the evening air. Moreover, he sees what is not visible from Mantua or anywhere near it, the shadows of great hills lengthening as the sun sets. I do not think that he can be in Mantuan territory at all, unless that extended farther towards the Alps than we have any reason to suppose it did. Furthermore, the whole scene is one of peace; the country-folk are quietly preparing their suppers after the day's work. But Meliboeus has told him that the whole country-side (of Mantua and of course Cremona too) is in confusion: *undique totis usque adeo turbatur agris*. He himself apparently would go supperless if he had not met Tityrus and been invited to take pot luck with him (on uncooked food, by the way; Tityrus lights no fire and prepares no *puls* or other rustic dish). The season is summer, for there are ripe fruits, *mitia poma*, to be had. There is nothing to show that Tityrus' holding is anywhere near.[61]

I believe the key to this and many passages of the *Bucolics* is to be found in a remark of Varro.[62] He tells us, what our own common sense might tell us if we know anything of stock-raising in warm countries, that flocks and herds used to move about Italy a great deal, up or down hill according to season, and implies that local boundaries did not stop this; the herdsman (no doubt under traditional restrictions, or rules made from time to time to prevent confusion and overcrowding of one pasture while others were neglected) took his beasts more or less where he saw fit, up the hills in summer and down to the plains in winter. How else, indeed, could grass enough be had, even for a very moderate number of beasts, all the year round? As it is, Vergil's rustics supplement the available fodder by gathering leaves of trees to give the animals in times of scarcity[63] when the grass of the plains is exhausted. Hence, in summer, the nearest hills, wherever they might be (possibly, for Mantuans, the Brescian Alps) would be familiar places to the herdsmen. I suggest that they would also be familiar to the young Vergil. We know[64] that he never was robust, and that it was heat (a sunstroke or the like) that killed him in the end. We have no reason at all to suppose his parents harsh or injudicious in their treatment of him, or that they kept him too steadily at books in the hot weather, when, says Martial, keeping well is lessons enough for children.[65] I conjecture that, like the young Walter Scott, he was often packed off to healthy places with the country people whom his father employed or knew; in his case, to the comparatively cool hillsides, where there was always fresh air, shade, and good water, things which he keenly appreciated.[66] His pictures are largely reminiscences of these pleasant holidays, as a glance through the *Bucolics* will show, though naturally he did not forget the lower levels which he also knew well. Let us look for a moment at some of his scenery. We have already seen that Tityrus and Meliboeus are on high ground. Corydon, in Eclogue II, is somewhere in the noonday heat; one would have to go very high, at a point south of the Italian frontier of today, to find a place where it was not hot at noonday in full summer (it is harvest-time,[67] which means about June or July, though there are mountainous districts which get in the crops as late as August). But the beech grove under which he strays suggests that he is not very low down, and his familiarity with both deer and wolves[68] points to one of the more sparsely inhabited districts. We may pretty safely put him on a hill-pasture. Eclogue III gives us little guidance to its scenery; once more there are beeches (Vergil appears to have been fond of this tree), but one of the shepherd-boys is near his own home, whither he returns each evening with his beasts. This is not surprising; it is still spring, and apparently early spring,[69] and there is no reason why both should not be in the lowlands as yet. No. IV, being a dream of the future, is situated nowhere, except that it is vaguely in Europe and the temperate zone, if not actually in Italy, that the wonder-child is to be born; the growth of the balsamic cardomom, *Amomum cardamomum* in the parlance of modern botanists, is a wonder (it seems also to have been a country proverb for something too good to be true, or Vergil's adaptation of one),[70] and the usual occupations which the Golden Age renewed is to end are those of Italians, trading, tilling the soil, and tending vines. No. V has a cave as part of its setting,[71] but caves need not be on high ground; all that can be said is that it is not near the Mincio, which has no formations capable of containing caves. The filbert is cited to witness the piteous death of Daphnis, and as that is also styled the nut of Abella, and supposed to be called after the Campanian town of that name, the passage has nothing very reminiscent of high levels.[72] No. VI takes place in fairyland, or whatever we should call that part of the ancient literary world where casual shepherds might catch a Seilenos asleep, as Midas did in the old days. No. VII is near the Mincio,[73] but Vergil gives fair warning that he is not to be taken too literally, for he says that the singers were both Arkadians.[74] No. VIII is at a level low enough for olives to grow, and early enough in the year for the nights to be cool. That is to say, we are not inland or on high ground in northern Italy,[75] but might perfectly well be somewhere near the mouth of one of the rivers. Of No. IX enough has been said. No. X is in Arkadia, and more will be said of it in another chapter.

It may, however, be asked why, if I abandon the immediate neighbourhood of Mantua, indeed the whole *ager Mantuanus*, for the scenery of a great part of the *Eclogues*, I do not adopt the theory of the most thorough-going deserter of the traditional region, Professor Tenney Frank, and lay at least the majority of the pastoral scenes in the hilly country near Naples, where it is reasonably certain Vergil had been at the date in question and where "along the ridge of Posilipo... in the mountains about Camaldoli, and behind Puteoli all the way to Avernus—a country which the poet had roamed with observant eyes—there could have been nothing but shepherd country. Here, then, are the crags and waterfalls and grottoes that Vergil describes in the *Eclogues*."[76] I have several reasons. One is that I dislike calling a favourite author a gratuitous liar. Whenever Vergil mentions a geographical name not patently out of Theokritos, it is one belonging to his own country. When he speaks of confiscations, they evidently menace himself and those in whom he is interested, and we have no evidence that he owned land likely to be seized by anybody in the Neapolitan area; Siron's villa,[77] if it was near there, is spoken of as a safe retreat, not a threatened spot. No names belonging to Naples and the district occur in the *Eclogues*, and the mere fact that part of the scenery is hilly and part of the land near Naples is likewise hilly is scarcely better evidence, it seems to me, than that with which the slave of Demos, in Aristophanes, supports his assertion that by "serpent" the oracle means "black-pudding," namely, that both are long.[78] Another is that we know Vergil's boyhood, the most impressionable time, was spent at home or largely at home, and the landscape most likely to come to the eyes of his mind when he sat down to compose would probably be that of those early days. And thirdly, if around Mantua we have to look some distance for a sufficiency of caves and rocks, I am not aware that Naples is very well stocked with swampy ground and slow-flowing rivers. A composite picture, especially for the background of a whole group of poems, not a single piece, is understandable, but I do not see sufficient reasons for supposing it. Till I do, I shall continue to think that Vergil is describing adequately and accurately the country in which he was brought up, touching now on one feature of it and now on another, and that where he seems to speak of foreign places (except in passages like the Cyclops-song of poor Corydon) it is a kind of challenge; he is singing the song, not of Askra,[79] but of Syracuse, through the country-side rather than the towns of Rome. There are Arkadians (that is to say, romantic figures) enough, if one looks at them with the understanding eye of the poet, to be found without leaving the ancient land of Saturn.

But we must not lose sight of the question with which the chapter began: Who is Tityrus? We have decided, I think, that he is not Vergil; who is he, then? Rejecting some ingenuities, I hold to the answer of F. Leo, which is in substance that of Servius in another context;[80] he is a poor rustic, and nothing more, neither a literary man nor in any other way distinguished, except that the almost random favour of Octavian has lighted upon him. In other words, he is the population of a part of the Mantuan territory, and specifically, I think, the part that is saved. This, we may conjecture, is why Octavian is represented as addressing him in the plural,[81] though nothing indicates that, so lately a slave himself, he in turn employed slaves. We have seen that Octavian meant to leave the wronged inhabitants of the city at least something of their territory, three miles around their walls, and that a subordinate is said to have stripped them of most of that. Now the injustice found no less a person to protest against it than Cornelius Gallus; what success his speech had we do not know, but putting it together with what Vergil says, or makes Tityrus say, I suggest that Octavian's attention was drawn to the state of affairs, whether by Gallus or another, and that he insisted that his original orders be carried out. This would surely be reason enough for the modified gratitude and laudation which the poem expresses; for modified it is. Tityrus, indeed, declares that Octavian is a very god and to be worshipped as such. This might sound the extreme of flattery to us if we did not know how long such a compliment had been in use, and that to less exalted people. Later on I shall have more to say of the relations between human and divine nature as then conceived; for the present, I content myself with one example. Lucretius can hardly be accused of flattering out of self-interest a man long dead and unable to hurt or help him directly; indeed, by his own philosophy, incapable of knowing whether he was praised or not, because he no longer existed. Yet he emphatically says Epicurus was a god,[82] and compares him favourably with popular figures, such as Herakles, whose right to the same title he does not deny. What he means by Epicurus' deity he himself tells us; he excelled other men in the greatness of his genius. Now Vergil knew his Lucretius and was well versed alike in the philosophy of the day and in the vocabulary of the Alexandrian poets, who used very similar language to that which he employs concerning the new head of his own state. When therefore he makes an honest peasant say that he thinks Octavian a god, he is merely saying that he is a very remarkable man indeed, and especially that he is a benefactor of mankind on a large scale. But, so the entire poem implies, his benefactions are limited; Tityrus is saved from eviction, and so is well content for himself, and can spare a little pity and practical help for Meliboeus, at least to the extent of giving him food and a night's rest in his temporary cabin on the hills. But Meliboeus sings no psalm of thanksgiving; his encounters have not been with gods in human form, but with rough and uncouth soldiers who are not even Italians (perhaps Vergil was thinking of the Gaulish auxiliaries of Julius Caesar's recruiting). The new god is a force for good, but the powers of evil are terribly strong.[83]

This may throw a little light on the vexed question of which of the two poems is the older. I think that the Ninth is a record of Vergil's earlier hopes and their blighting. Mantua had not offended; the poet had, or thought he had, some influence with at least one or two of the officials charged with the acquisition of land for the veterans; he was not very old nor very experienced, and perhaps, like so many contemporaries of violent events, had little realisation of how violent they were. He may seriously have thought for a while that a little urging of the justice of the Mantuan claim to be spared would gain its end, and nothing be left for him to do but praise the equity of Alfenus Varus, or of him and his colleagues. A short trial convinced him that even to appeal to personal friendship for the preservation of his own property was likely to result in nothing but repulse; he could save neither himself nor his fellows. Servius says that he actually was in personal danger; he had been restored to his property, but found a soldier in possession, one Arrius, a centurion, who chased him ignominiously into the Mincio. I should be readier to believe the story if I found any real evidence that Vergil was ever given back a single foot of his patrimony, and also if Daniel's Servius, to quote but one variant, were not equally sure that the intruder's name was Clodius.[84] But be that as it may, Vergil had good enough reason, practical as well as poetical, for putting on record his regret at failure and the fact that it was no fault of his; the good will had been there, but not the power.[85] Now, as I see it, when all was over and the very worst had not happened, since not all the rural free population of the territory was left homeless, he could properly add to his poems, and it was good policy to put in a conspicuous place, a word in praise of Octavian, though modified with implied condemnation of the measures Octavian had found himself obliged to use and the character of his subordinates and helpers.

I have hitherto said almost nothing of the prominent men who are mentioned by name up and down these and other poems. The questions connected with them are so intricate and involve consideration of so many aspects of the *Eclogues* that they deserve a separate treatment; the next chapter will attempt to deal with them.

CHAPTER IV

THE POET AND HIS FRIENDS

THAT VERGIL in the *Eclogues* makes mention of several persons known to him is so obvious that no one has yet tried to dispute it. Nevertheless, their number and relations to him are as far from being decided as the precise position of his property, if not more so; for some have been so fortunate as to prove to the satisfaction of others that the poet did or did not live at Pietole, but scarcely anyone seems yet to have determined to the satisfaction of any but himself what names in the poems, if any, mean more than they say.

It is therefore well to begin by noting what are the undisputed facts. In *Ecl.*, I, we may, I think, assume that Vergil hints at Octavian; in II, Corydon and Alexis are not said to be the actual names of any persons known to him; in III, apart from gods and one or two historical characters by that time long dead, the singers speak of Pollio, Bavius and Mevius, and, on one interpretation of a disputed line, a certain Caelius,[1] apparently no longer living. In IV, Pollio is again mentioned, whoever else may be hinted at; in V there is no reason to suppose that any real person is named by his own name; in VI, Varus is directly addressed, Gallus mentioned. No. VII speaks of no one but imaginary people, so far at least as the names go, but we shall see reason by and by to ask if Codrus was really so obvious a Greek as he sounds. In VIII, Pollio, though not actually named, is once more addressed; in IX, as we have seen, Menalcas is probably Vergil and Varus is named, as are also the living poet Varius and the recently dead Cinna. No. X deals with Gallus and his Lycoris.

So far, then, the list is short, but select enough: Octavian, the three prominent statesmen C. Asinius Pollio, Alfenus

[1] Notes to chapter iv will be found on pages 234-239.

Varus, and Cornelius Gallus, of whom two were also poets; the poets Varius, Cinna, probably Vergil himself, and at least one other; the poetasters Bavius and Mevius, and, if the common assumption is right, the notorious freedwoman Volumnia, better known under her stage name of Cytheris or the metrical equivalent thereof, Lycoris, used in Gallus' poems.

But if we look in Servius, to mention no other ancient, the list begins to lengthen. Tityrus, as we have already seen,[2] is Vergil to him, although the named characters in the first Eclogue are lessened by two; Amaryllis and Galatea are not mortal women, but Rome and Mantua respectively.[3] The fountains and bushes which seemed to regret Tityrus' absence are respectively senators, presumably of Mantua, and *scholastici*;[4] Octavian remains Octavian, though his title of Augustus is anticipated. In No. II, either Alexis or Corydon, for the commentator gives us our choice, is a handsome slave (if Alexis, he was really Alexander, who belonged to Pollio); or, if we prefer, he is no other than Octavian himself.[5] Amaryllis and Menalcas are respectively Leria and Cebes, two slaves belonging to Maecenas whom their master gave to Vergil because he had a fancy for them.[6] In III, he mentions but does not approve an explanation of the words *tu post carecta latebas*, concerning Varus "writer of tragedies," his wife, who was Vergil's mistress, and a tragedy which the lady received from Vergil and handed to her husband, who promptly passed it off as his own.[7] Apparently the Damoetas of the poem is Vergil again, for the Tityrus to whom he gives advice about the management of kids is Mantua,[8] and the promise of Damoetas to wash them in the river is a hint that the poet will make all right with Augustus. The child in the fourth Eclogue is given a variety of identifications: the elder or the younger son of Pollio, or Augustus himself.[9] The dead Daphnis of No. V is Julius Caesar or Quintilius Varus;[10] we shall have more identifications presently. Some say, but Servius is not so sure, that the Stimichon of line 55 is Maecenas.[11] No. VI, still according to Servius, introduces us to philosophical circles, the Silenus being Siron, the two shepherds Vergil himself and (Alfenus) Varus.[12] Many say, he tells us, that in No. VII Daphnis is Caesar (Octavianus), Corydon Vergil, Thyrsis either Bavius or Mevius, or perhaps Anser.[13] Codrus is a contemporary poet, but he does not give his name.[14] No. VIII makes a curious addition; the unnamed person addressed in lines 6 sqq., who is plainly Pollio, is suggested to be Octavian.[15] Nos. IX and X add nothing to the list. The fact is that Servius, although he mentions some quaint interpretations, is not very fond of allegorising, coming as he does rather before the great age of that form of comment. He knows of its existence, but for his own part prefers to decline allegorical explanations, unless they are necessary consequences of the incidents relating to the loss of Vergil's, and the Mantuans', land.[16]

Setting aside the mediaeval interpreters, who were very apt to find hidden meanings everywhere, and their successors of the Renascence or somewhat later times,[17] and coming to our own day, we have still alive and producing ingenious work one upholder of a most thorough-going theory of identifications, Professor Léon Herrmann of Brussels.[18] He is fully convinced that the *Bucolics* are in effect a continuous work, and a *roman à clef* in verse. The characters are all members of literary or other society, but chiefly literary, of the poet's time, and all personally known to him; no names are introduced merely as stopgaps, but each corresponds to a single real name and no more, while the relations between the characters are those which existed between their prototypes. So, if Corydon and Thyrsis, for instance, in the seventh Eclogue, are rivals in song, they stand for two literary men who were rivals in their art; if Amaryllis is mated with Tityrus in one passage, beloved by

Corydon in another, we must look for some woman who was the wife or mistress of a real person, known to Vergil, and for a rival in her affections.[11] By a series of most ingenious but most hazardous arguments, the author finds the face which underlies every mask, or at least, for he is not dogmatic about it, a possible face; that the masks are there, he is certain.[20] Menalcas is Vergil himself; Tityrus is the learned freedman, Q. Caecilius Epirota, and the first Eclogue refers to some trying experiences of his about the year 49 B.C. Corydon is Valgius Rufus, and his beloved Alexis the slave of that name who belonged to Atticus, Cicero's friend,[21] for being a slave he might be called by his real name and needed no disguise. Iollas, Corydon's rich rival, is Maecenas. Daphnis, dead or alive, is Catullus; Mopsus is Domitius Marsus; Damon, Calvus; Aegon, Furius Camillus; Damoetas, Helvius Cinna the poet; Alphesiboeus, Varius Rufus. The Seilenos who sings so eloquently to the two shepherds is Parthenios, and the shepherds themselves, Philodemos of Gadara and Siron.[22] The Varus of No. VI is not Alfenus, but Quintilius, the critic esteemed by Horace and lamented by him.[23] The women, even those most casually mentioned, can often be identified, or at least their social status (Greek freedwomen for the most part) clearly made out. And the little Micon who gets one passing mention in VII, 29–30, is P. Volumnius Eutrapelus the banker, to whom Lycoris-Cytheris-Volumnia formerly belonged.[24]

This work seems to have convinced nobody but its author; certainly it has not convinced me. Quite apart from the general difficulties of accepting the fundamental thesis that anyone in that age would have written poems in which every person (with the odd exception of two of the most important) is called by an assumed name, when the literary conventions as we know them permitted quite free mention of almost any man and referred to women under names which scanned like the real ones, and apart from some improbabilities of detail which confront the reader from time to time, it is hampered by the sheer lack of anything like cogent proof, even plausibility, for practically every identification save the one or two already proposed by others. I am not even very sure of the truth of the late Professor J. S. Phillimore's far more moderate explanation of the poems, that they are "a personal history" of the years 42–39, whereof Vergil and his friends are the subject.[25] Yet the poet does speak of himself and of some persons whom he knew. Can we find a mean between the extremes of identifying everyone and identifying no one, and, what is rather more to the point, can we say who his principal friends and acquaintances were likely to be at the time when he wrote these poems?

It is easy enough to generalise, as Phillimore does in the work already quoted, and say that pastoral poetry is the poetry of a clique[26] (why this rather than any other works in the Alexandrian manner, written for the cultivated few?), and that "Vergil the artist, already a master of his craft... found himself actually in the situation of literary clubmate"[27] to persons such as Varus and Gallus, whom, since they all came from the North of Italy, he would meet "like brother Scots in London."[28] It may have been so; we do not know how clannish these northern Italians were, nor to what extent such a feeling, if they had it, would overcome the not inconsiderable social and probably economic differences which existed between them.[29] It is easy to note, what has again and again been noted, that Vergil's poetry shows the influence of the neoteric school, Cicero's *cantores Euphorionis*,[30] but less safe to conclude that he and the members of that school, or such as survived till he was at all prominent as a literary man, knew one another, apart from merely being aware of one another's existence. Ovid, in a later age, was not so very much younger than Vergil nor so wanting in self-esteem as to shun an introduction to the most celebrated poet of the time, yet he no more than saw Vergil, apparently on one occasion.[31] It is more profitable, though less picturesque, to look for the few facts we have and try to judge from them whom Vergil certainly, or with a high degree of probability, may be said to have known during the years, about 51–41 B.C., between his ceasing to be a schoolboy and becoming prominent as the composer of the *Eclogues*.

The Lives say that he studied at Cremona, Milan, Rome, and Naples,[32] places in themselves likely, even highly likely, for him to have visited, if he or his parents wanted him to receive the best education that was to be had. But the first teacher and the first fellow pupil whose names any tradition, true or false, offers us are Epidius the rhetorician and Octavian, who by the way was seven years younger than the future poet.[33] Epidius we may provisionally accept; he was a celebrated teacher, and we know it was intended that Vergil should try to become an orator.[34] But Octavian, or Octavius as he was then, seems to me most unlikely as a fellow pupil of Vergil in any proper sense. It is of course conceivable that Epidius had them both under his charge at the same time, especially if we suppose, as Professor Tenney Frank plausibly does,[35] that Vergil started rhetoric late, Octavius early. But seven years is an enormous difference at the time of life Vergil had reached; even if he went to Rome very shortly after he took the *toga uirilis*,[36] he would be about sixteen or seventeen, and what sort of friendship would he be likely to form with even the cleverest little boy of nine or ten, especially when we remember that the little boy's family was wealthy and distinguished, the big one's unknown and probably of but moderate means? I am much inclined to think the whole story of their being fellow pupils (did Epidius, by the way, teach in classes or private lessons?) made up long after the event, and part of the same sham tradition that gave us the most glaring of all Vergilian frauds, the *Culex*, in which Vergil, with the prescience which a great poet should have in the imagination of a *grammaticus* and is no more likely than other people to have in real life, already sees that his young schoolfellow is something more than ordinary humanity and so proceeds to read him a poetical lesson on mythology and other things, thrown into the form of a story suitable for youth.[37]

If *Catalepton*, 5, is really Vergil's, as many think, we have a name or two to add to our scanty and slow-growing list. He bids farewell to a number of people (not to Epidius by name, although he is probably implied, for the first line takes leave of the "swollen phrases" [*ampullae*, λήκυθοι] of rhetoricians, and so presumably of the chief purveyor of them whom Vergil knew), whereof several are highly doubtful, for if the guesses of modern scholars concerning their names (corrupted in our very bad textual tradition) are right, they are at least as likely, I should say much more likely, to have been represented for the author by their books as their persons. But one has a separate farewell; he is named Sextus Sabinus, and Vergil, if it is he, professes to have been very fond of him: *o mearum cura curarum*, he calls him. I conjecture that he was a younger school-mate for whom the poet had formed a romantic attachment. Finally, the Muses are bidden *au revoir*, for they are invited to come and see the author now and then, modestly and not too often, *pudenter et raro*. He is going to study philosophy under Siron, and nothing must be allowed to interfere with this, for it will lead him to a blessed life.[38] So we gain two more names, Siron the philosopher and Sex. Sabinus. Unfortunately, we know nothing whatsoever of the latter; the *Catalepton* has another Sabinus,[39] but, again supposing the poem to be genuine, it is evident that he was not of an age for Vergil and him to have gone to school together, and also that Vergil disliked and rather despised him.

But at least we know who Siron was; both Vergil, says Servius, and Varus learned the Epicurean philosophy under his teaching.[40] He lived apparently in or near Naples,[41] was one of the most prominent Epicureans of the day, and was associated with Philodemos, the author of the bulky works found at Herculaneum. The two were something of a power in both philosophy and literature, and there can be no doubt, whatever else we may know or guess about Vergil and his entourage, that here he would find a learned and cultured atmosphere, with as much philosophy as one could expect a young Italian provincial of the day to absorb. It is also possible, indeed probable, that he would at least see, if not become intimate with, several prominent men of the day. Professor Tenney Frank gives a list,[42] which makes no pretence either to being exhaustive or to confining itself to those of about Vergil's age, of well-known Roman Epicureans of that and the previous generation; Julius Caesar himself heads it, with Piso his father-in-law and Cassius the assassin not far behind; others are Hirtius, Pansa and Dolabella, Paetus and Gallus, from among the correspondents of Cicero, and of course Atticus. It is very likely that many who knew and cared nothing about philosophy were yet acquainted with this group, because, as the fragments of Philodemos make abundantly clear, one of the interests of these Neapolitan sages was literary criticism, and Philodemos was himself a very tolerable poet in his own tongue. It is further likely that among the men who knew Philodemos and Siron there would be several with enough literary insight to see the talent of the delicate, shy, and awkward[43] young man from the North who could already turn out capital imitations and parodies of Catullus, if nothing more,[44] and several others whose political ambitions would cause them to keep their eyes open for a poet, in other words a useful indirect propagandist, whom a little encouragement might attach to them for the future. But this is conjecture, not established fact, and the estimate of its probability must vary with different investigators. At best, it does not yield us definite names.

The rest of the *Catalepton* helps us a little, always assuming that we are really dealing with early works of Vergil, and not amusing and clever efforts of later readers, trying to imagine what sort of lines he might have written at that age.[45] No. 7, a trifling epigram, is addressed to Varius, presumably that Varius, the epic poet, whom we find as his travelling companion in the Journey to Brundisium.[46] This gives us little new information. No. 1 b, in Birt's enumeration, addresses Tucca, again presumably Varius' fellow executor and co-editor of the *Aeneid*. No. 4 addresses and No. 11 laments the death of Octavius Musa, apparently a poet, certainly a writer of some kind.[47] But beyond this, they tell us nothing. No. 9, addressed to Messalla, presumably M. Valerius Messalla Corvinus, is certainly not Vergil's; the Sabinus of No. 10 is evidently not a literary acquaintance; 12 and 13, exercises in lampoon-writing, are not addressed to people whom one would expect to find mentioned in a politer style, such as is that of the *Eclogues*. That Vergil somehow and sometime made the acquaintance of Maecenas is certain, but our only chronological indication, apart from biographers and scholiasts, is in the *Georgics*,[48] with nothing to tell us how long the two had known each other. The story in Donatus[49] that Maecenas, though as yet Vergil was but a casual acquaintance, helped him against the soldier who threatened his life, sounds highly improbable, though it is not impossible; certainly there is no mention of the great patron by name in the *Eclogues*, and no "mask" under which he can with any real plausibility be said to lurk. The sober Life of Vergil ascribed to Probus[50] says it was after the writing of the *Eclogues* that Maecenas introduced him to Octavian, but has no information about the date of the first meeting of patron and poet. The impression one gathers is that they can scarcely have known each other earlier than the thirties of the century; after all, Maecenas, much as he loved literature, could not be a wholly disinterested patron of it, for what we should call the Ministry of Propaganda was, unless I am much mistaken, largely in his hands, and it was well to make sure that a poet or other writer was not disaffected and factious before encouraging him. Vergil could pass this test, and the *Eclogues* showed it.

We must therefore pass on to the troublous times which cost the poet his estate, in order to make up the list of his known friends. Here we meet once more the familiar figures of Gallus, Pollio, and Varus and must ask exactly what they were doing and how Vergil came to know them. It is also necessary to be as sure as we can to what degree and in what way he knew them, whether as personal friends whom he liked for their own sakes and of whom he could ask a favour without embarrassment, or simply as well-known men whom he might approach as a member of the general public or as a representative, official or other, of his city or district. To the first of these questions we can give a sort of answer, imperfect but not wholly unsatisfactory, from the scanty historical records of those times; for the second, we are dependent chiefly upon the text of the *Eclogues*.

The victory of Philippi left Octavian in anything but an easy position. The self-appointed triumvirate, driven together by common necessity and by no mutual liking or trust, had agreed, at its first and fateful meeting "on a little island of the river Lavinius" (near Bologna) to "rouse the hopes of the soldiery for the rewards of victory by sundry gifts and especially by awards for settlement of eighteen cities of Italy."[51] In other words, they were to have for their own, on discharge, the territories of these unfortunate towns, for certainly nothing less would be nearly enough to accommodate such large numbers. The soldiers carried out their part of the bargain, Brutus and Cassius were defeated, Octavian returned to Italy, and Antony went off to his share of the world, the East, leaving two formidable agents in the West, his terrible wife Fulvia and his brother Lucius, consul in the year 713/41. Now the discomforts of the whole arrangement began to show themselves acutely for all concerned. "The soldiers," says Appian, "asked for the cities which had been picked out for them as being the best before the war began, and the cities demanded that the assignment should be spread all over Italy, or else that they should cast lots (to decide which cities should thus sacrifice their territory). Also they asked the price of the land from the recipients, and there was no money to pay them."[52] Octavian, thus caught between clamorous veterans and civilians with an unanswerable claim for compensation, vainly tried to arrange some sort of compromise. The veterans were on the verge of mutiny, and riots and murders common,[53] while the relations between soldiers and civilians grew worse and worse, for "the army insolently trespassed on neighbours, helping itself to more than had been granted and picking out the best land."[54] The insolent *haec mea sunt, ueteres migrate coloni*[55] which Moeris heard was no invention of Vergil's. To make matters still worse, L. Antonius, inspired by Fulvia and aided by Antony's agent Manius,[56] began busily to fish in these troubled waters. First he and his supporters posed as the champions of his brother's time-expired men in Italy. The specious proposal that nothing should be done till Antony returned found no favour with the impatient men, and was hastily replaced by another, that Antony's men should have commissioners (οἰκισταί) of their own to assign lands to them.[57] But Octavian, who by wholesale sacrifice of civilians' rights kept his popularity with the soldiery,[58] was not to be thus easily thwarted, and his opponents tried another line of tactics. They came forward as champions of the oppressed, declaring that land enough could be got by confiscation of the property of those who had actually fought against the triumvirate. No attempts at compromise between the two parties being successful,[59] as was natural when only one, apparently, wanted peace, they came to open conflict and the campaign of Perusia began.

All this while Pollio, commander of a considerable force in what was now the North of Italy (for Cisalpine Gaul, Gallia Togata, had recently been made Italian),[60] seems to have tried to keep some kind of balance between the two powers, that of Antony, whose supporter and *legatus* he was, and that of Octavian, in whose sphere of influence he found himself. His part in the campaign consisted of a series of not too energetic attempts to relieve Perusia, and by the time it had fallen, he found himself still in command of an army in being and apparently not out of favour with either party. Indeed, Antony had no quarrel with him, for Pollio remained his supporter as long as it was safe to do so, while Octavian, already so desperately short of money that he was forced to seize on temple-treasures to pay for the advance on Perusia[61] and certainly with no desire to incur new obligations to veterans or the surviving relatives of the fallen,[62] would not, if he could help it, offend mortally a man with so many swords at his command as Pollio. What precisely the latter's legal position was, it would be hard to say, for clearly he was neither *legatus* nor proconsul of Cisalpine Gaul, seeing that no such province now existed, and the express intention of Octavian in joining it to Italy was to prevent anyone from having an army there.[63] But Pollio, so long at least as he took no very drastic steps against Octavian, was left in peace. It seems not at all improbable that, highly as he thought of his own abilities, he cherished some dream of using the masters of the East and

West for his own aggrandisement. At all events, it was he who brought about their meeting at Brundisium in 714/40 and so may be credited with the subsequent treaty which gave Octavian a measure of quiet for eight important years, during which he consolidated his power and popularity in Italy and won the adherence of Vergil, and probably many other honest men, who guessed what his ultimate ends were, and that they were for the general good of the Empire.

But we have to speak of Pollio's relations to Varus and Gallus, for they are commonly grouped together in our authorities[64] almost as if they were in some way colleagues. That they formed an actual board for the division of the lands, *tresuiri agris assignandis*, after the Republican and especially Gracchan model, seems in the last degree unlikely. Yet it is by no means so improbable that they all had, perhaps not simultaneously, some official position in the matter, for legalism was too deeply ingrained in the Roman mind for Octavian to neglect, if he could help it, some show of proper forms even in his enforced injustices. I suggest that Varus and Gallus were Octavian's own land commissioners and Pollio represents an acquiescence in the suggestion of L. Antonius and his backers, that an Antonine commissioner should see to the awarding of land to Antony's veterans. His authority in his own party and the nearness of his command to the former Cisalpine Gaul, and therefore to the neighbourhood of Cremona (another piece of legality; it was alleged that by siding with the rebels they had made themselves *hostes*, or so I would interpret the excuse Octavian made),[65] would make his an appropriate appointment, and that he was never legally and formally out of favour with the provisional government might seem to be indicated by the fact that we never hear that his consulship-designate, if it may be so named, was called in question, and he did in fact take up that office sometime in the year of the Treaty of Brundisium.[66] The difficulty is to know, supposing that he was recognised as an Antonine land commissioner, when he had any duties in respect of Mantua; for the seizure of Mantuan land was consequent upon that of the territory of Cremona, Cremona became forfeit as a result of the war of Perusia, and therefore Mantua was not in danger till after that war; and it is not easy to find a time for Pollio, between his activities, such as they were, in the campaign, immediately after which it would hardly have been politic for him to thrust himself into notice in a territory controlled by Octavian, and his appearance at Brundisium as negotiator between the two great rivals, to do much in the direction of taking away or giving back any Mantuan estate. Let us see if Vergil implies that he did.

The first two Eclogues never mention Pollio; the third has his name three times in as many songs of the two contending shepherds. The first of these says that Pollio likes pastoral poetry, the second that he is a poet himself, the third wishes happiness to any who love him, that is, probably, who esteem his writings as they should.[67] The fourth Eclogue is notoriously dedicated to him and dated 714/40. No. VIII compliments him on his recent foreign campaign.[68] Here is nothing which could not have been said of any man powerful in the state, which Pollio was, and particularly, powerful as a general commanding a region not far away, and interested in literature. The compliments are politic, and they cover much the same ground as those of Horace, who certainly did not fear that anyone would confiscate his Sabine farm nor hope that in that case Pollio would restore it.[69]

It may, however, be objected that in the last passage Vergil declares that his "strains" (*carmina*) are begun at Pollio's bidding. Does not this denote a fairly close acquaintance, for one does not "bid" a sensitive artist like Vergil to write this or that without knowing him well, for fear of a rebuff or a literary failure resulting? But "bid," *iubere*, has a wide range of meanings, and it is not at once evident which of them is to be understood here. A general can *iubere* his men to perform some manoeuvre, when the verb is equivalent to *imperare;* a friend can "bid" his friend good-day with the formula *iubeo te saluere*, which certainly does not mean "I command you to be in good health." Between these extremes of full authority and none at all there are many shades. The "stern commands," *haud mollia iussa*, of Maecenas produced the *Georgics*, according to their author (*Georg.*, III, 41). The great man probably had conveyed a polite but broad hint of what was wanted. But Pliny the Younger tells us how a fellow countryman of Propertius, who, like him, wrote elegiacs, began his effusion, "You bid me, Priscus" (*Prisce, iubes*), whereat the man addressed, whose wishes had not been consulted in the matter, replied from his seat in the audience, "No, I don't" (*ego uero non iubeo*).[70] The merest suggestion from Pollio that he would like to see another specimen of Vergil's poetry, or that Theokritos' second Idyll would make a pretty Latin poem if well imitated,[71] would be enough to set the poet's brains to work, if it happened to suit his mood. We cannot build up a theory of friendship or close acquaintance on so slender a footing as this.

And this is all; Vergil might have said every word of it if no such thing as the land question had ever arisen and there had been no war anywhere in Italy. The implications of the ancient authorities that Pollio had something to do with the distributions may have a basis of fact (he might, for instance, have been a commissioner before the affair of Perusia); true or false, they are of very little importance, and all we need conclude is that Vergil knew Pollio and thought it worth while, out of interest, esteem, or both, to win his good graces.

Let us now ask if he addresses him in any tone which suggests personal attachment. The decision must be in large measure subjective, but I for my part can hear no such tone. Pollio is named as a lover of such Eclogues as had then been published or circulated in any way, that is, the second and perhaps one or two more; that is the utmost that can be got out of the first of the passages mentioned above, and not even that is necessary. Pollio, says the singer, loves my Muse, rustic though she be. Now, the words are put into the mouth of a neatherd, and so far as he may be taken (as I have no doubt he may) to be Vergil's mouthpiece for the moment, anything he—that is, his creator—had composed must be called "rustic," to fit the picture. I do not see how else Vergil could have phrased it if this were his very first attempt at pastoral, as we know it was not, provided only that Pollio had seen something he had written, some of the poems of the *Catalepton*, if we like to say so, or any longer pieces which we may imagine him to have composed. At the very most, Pollio will be sufficiently of the inner circles of the latest literature to have seen a poem or two of Vergil's, say the second Eclogue, which was circulating among his acquaintance; and in the days before printing, when the gap between published and unpublished was so much narrower than it is now, once the work had got out of the author's own desk at all, I do not see that this indicates any close intimacy. In any age, does a powerful man need to know a writer very well to say to him, by word of mouth or by letter, "I hear you have composed a charming little poem recently; So-and-So quoted a bit of it to me. Might I have a copy?" The rest of the reference in the third Eclogue is compliment and nothing else; it might have been penned by anyone who knew that Pollio wrote verse and had no violent dislike of him.

Even the high honour of dedicating the "Messianic" Eclogue to Pollio proves little for the relations between the two men. Let us take a modern parallel. In a disturbed part of the world, Spain, China, or where you will, a soldier of literary tastes, himself something of an author, has had his headquarters near the birthplace of a young writer. He has, at least, done no wanton harm to the district the writer has known and loved all his life; perhaps he has found time to send him a polite message or two and enquire if his work is managing to continue under such unpropitious circumstances. Soon after, the soldier is instrumental in negotiating a settlement from which, at least for a while, much is expected.[72] The writer produces a book or a poem in which he expresses vague hopes for the future of mankind and the restoration of lasting peace, at the same time hinting at political leanings supposed not to be distasteful to the soldier. Should we be much surprised if it were dedicated "to the illustrious General X, leader of the movement to end our differences and holder of such-and-such a post in the enlightened Y government"? Or should we at once conclude that the two must know each other very well for one to be so complimentary in print to the other? I think we know too much of modern human nature to conclude anything of the kind, seeing that there are newspapers and other means of knowing the tastes and habits of persons whom we have never seen; and we should know too much of ancient human nature, which differed from that of today in no perceptible fashion, and too much also of the smallness of the total reading public, to forget the high probability that, of the few score prominent men of Vergil's time who cared for rustic or other Muses, most would be well known by repute to the writers of the day, and certainly those of them who did a little in the way of literature themselves, like Pollio, would be known to all authors, whether they had met the persons in question in the flesh or not. Armies especially are hotbeds of gossip, unless the Roman Tommy was unrecognisably unlike his later comrades, and we may be tolerably sure that if Pollio called for parchment or wax tablets and did not soon after dispatch a courier with a message to some subordinate or a report to either of the Antonies, it would be all over the legions in an hour that the general was writing some more verse: *Pollio et ipse facit noua carmina.* How long would it take for so interesting a scrap of information as that to reach Vergil, whether he was in the neighbourhood of Mantua or in the south? So, knowing of the general, even if he did not personally know him, as a fellow poet (it is politic to assume that the poetry of the great is very good, as Quintilian knew when he quoted Vergil's praise of Pollio to Domitian),[73] having no objection to gaining the good graces of a possible patron (suppose Mark Antony were in the end to win, would not Pollio be a likely candidate for the unofficial "portfolio" of Maecenas?), and perhaps feeling a sort of negative gratitude towards one who had not made the bad state of affairs at Mantua any worse, Vergil did an entirely natural, tactful, and nowise unworthy thing in making his dedication, likewise in inserting a complimentary allusion to Pollio's campaign into the eighth Eclogue. We may of course, if we like, suppose all manner of ways in which real acquaintance and mutual esteem could have sprung up between the two men; but it is entirely unnecessary on the evidence available to do anything of the kind.

Coming to Varus, we are confronted with quite different circumstances. In the first place, he was apparently of lower social standing than Pollio,[74] a man of ability but self-made. Secondly, he was certainly no poet. Finally, whereas Pollio had done Mantua no harm, so far as we know, Varus did it much. It would appear that he grossly exceeded his instructions with regard to appropriating territory and was sharply attacked for his excesses by Gallus.[75] How much of this was his own doing and how much the work of Octavius Musa, who according to the grammarians' tradition[76] measured off fifteen miles of the Mantuan land for assignment to soldiers, to avenge a small private quarrel he had with the local magistrates, we do not know, for, ill-informed as we are of the exact size of the territory, we cannot say definitely how much this would leave, whether the three miles intended by Octavian or the eight hundred paces spared by Varus.[77] It may be that Musa was Varus' subordinate. But there are good grounds for saying that Vergil knew Varus. He was a native of Cremona[78] and it is said that the two had studied together under Siron,[79] from which it is not a wild guess that they may have been schoolfellows in Varus' native place. It is therefore a further not unlikely supposition that Mantua, threatened with wholesale evictions, should turn to her best-known literary man and ask him to use any influence he had with Varus to spare the land. And it seems to me that such a supposition as this will explain not a few things in the part played by Varus in the *Eclogues*.

He is mentioned twice, both times in a laudatory fashion. The first twelve lines of the sixth Eclogue are all about him, though the rest of the poem does not mention him, even to say good-bye. In other words, the little work is dedicated to him, and a dedication may be added later. Furthermore, Vergil asserts[80] that he is writing "by request" (*non iniussa cano*),[81] though he does not say from whom the request came. In the other passage,[82] Menalcas (that is to say, Vergil) has begun but not finished a poem in honour of Varus, assuring him that if he will but spare Mantua, he shall have his name exalted as high as heaven by Apollo's birds, the swans; in other words, if we make allowance for classical literary convention, that he shall be immortalised by mention in a serious work.[83] In all, then, there are fifteen verses which speak of him. Now, we know that Vergil was a slow composer and very fastidious.[84] We know also that the time must have been short, for the confiscation began after Perusia and the *Eclogues* were finished and published perhaps a year or two later. Between the two dates had come, no doubt, a good deal of polishing and revising on the poet's part, and also, as I think, at least one event of importance for Mantua, the intervention of Gallus. A very few months, perhaps but a few weeks, would be available for Mantua to appeal to Vergil (if indeed he did not try to intervene without being bidden, though I think his *non iniussa cano* hints strongly that he is his town's mouthpiece) and for Vergil to accede to the request, compose his message to Varus, and send it to him. This is further shortened by the circumstance that Vergil was but doubtfully in the neighbourhood of his birthplace at the time; he may still have been in the south, perhaps at Tarentum, where Propertius implies some of the *Eclogues* were written.[85] Hence it would not have been possible for him to do himself justice with a whole new poem in honour of Varus; also, as he himself says, he did not feel capable of writing either an ordinary panegyric (*tuas laudes*) or a poem of epic character which might show him, or his party, in heroic action (*tristia condere bella*). But, I would suggest, he had on hand and nearly complete the charming episode of Seilenos and the young shepherds. A little work would preface this with a dedication, and that, I think, was what Vergil did, and sent the completed poem to Varus.[86] It is a most tactful dedication. I cannot, it says in effect, write anything really worthy of your greatness; I am but a pastoral poet, a failure at epic, which I once thought of trying. But there are plenty of epic poets and panegyrists in the world, and no doubt many of them will do you justice. Meantime there are some people who seem to like my trifles, and this one will surely be good, for it is recommended by your name. Varus, we may imagine Vergil thinking, ought to appreciate this and to listen favourably to a request for bare justice coming from the same source. Besides, he knows well enough that it is possible to praise someone in a pastoral, and that the model of all bucolic poetry also wrote honeyed flatteries of King Ptolemy and King Hieron. He shall have his poem of praise if he will be reasonable. Unfortunately, Varus was, as we have seen, anything but reasonable towards Mantua, and we have no proof that he paid any attention to Vergil's modest approach. This, I think, made the poet as nearly angry as he was capable of being.

Let us look once more at the second reference to Varus, that in Eclogue IX. The two speakers are discussing Menalcas' works and quoting from them. Lycidas quotes as his a pretty imitation of Theokritos; in other words, he says, "Vergil can write good adaptations of the Greek pastoral." It is not like our author to praise himself in this way, certainly not without reason. But he surely has a very good reason here; he has been slighted, and he knows his own worth too well not to be aware that it is an unmerited slight. "Our songs," he says, "have no more power amid the weapons of war than the doves of Chaonia have, they say, when the eagle pounces." The epithet *Chaonias* is not idle. It means "of Dodona," and the doves of Dodona were no ordinary birds, but sacred beings, whether literal pigeons or priestesses called by that name.[87] The insult and the wrong have been done to a poet, and a good one, or so say people who know what poetry is and can compose it themselves: *et me fecere poetam Pierides*, says the speaker, "by the grace of the Muses I too am a poet." Now comes the reference:

> Nay, the unfinished strain that Varus heard:
> "Leave us but Mantua, Varus, and thy name
> (Mantua, to poor Cremona all too near),
> The singing swans shall carry to the stars."

It is not underlined, the talk going at once to other subjects; but it is there. If Varus could have been induced to spare Mantua, something really fine could have been written about him, but as it is, the song is "not yet finished," *nondum perfecta*, and is not likely to be finished now. Old

Moeris, after searching his memory, produces another Theokritean reminiscence, a Cyclops-song freely imitated from the eleventh Idyll,[88] as if to show that the second Eclogue had not exhausted that fruitful theme for Vergil any more than for his model. But, says Lycidas, what was that song I heard you singing one clear night? I have the tune in my head. And, with that, he sings the few lines he can remember:

> Daphnis, why gaze you on the ancient stars?
> Lo, now, where Dionaean Caesar's orb
> Blazes in heaven, to make the harvests glad
> And ripen grapes on every sunny hill.
> Daphnis, graft pears your grandsons yet shall pick.

Everyone then alive knew what Caesar's star was; it was the famous comet which appeared while the Dictator's funeral games were being held, and was taken to signify that he was now a god.[89] Vergil as good as says that he was a peaceful god, despite all his warlike exploits, and had the good of the country-side at heart (we shall have to ask presently if he does not say that again in another form).[90] It needs but little reading between the lines to see the appropriateness of it here; Octavian is Caesar's (adopted) son, and it is for him to carry on Caesar's work and show himself in truth of that divine stock. The singing ends here, Moeris declaring that his memory is failing him for very age and refusing to be coaxed into producing any further samples of his master's work. Vergil had said his say, and, I think, come as near spitefulness as was in his gentle and forgiving nature. Caesar's star is in the heavens, and under it a man like Varus, who might have won the praises due to the merciful and the just, turns men out of their holdings, and men of letters at that, who can trumpet his shame to the world. Is that what Octavian expects of his followers?[91]

I think, though all such judgements are subjective and liable to change without notice, that a line in this same passage gives a clue to a question already discussed, namely, which of the two Eclogues relating to the loss of the land is the earlier. In IX, as we have seen, lines are quoted from a supposed poem of Menalcas concerning the star

> quo
> duceret apricis in collibus uua colorem.
> insere, Daphni, piros; carpent tua poma nepotes

which I have inadequately rendered,

> (To) ripen grapes on every sunny hill.
> Daphnis, graft pears your grandsons yet shall pick.

Now it has been pointed out often enough already that these words, especially those of the second line, either echo or are echoed by a verse of Eclogue I:[92]

> insere nunc, Meliboee, piros, pone ordine uitis.
> Graft, Meliboeus, pears, set vines a-row.

But which is echo, which original? The first-quoted passage echoes the second, say those who believe that No. I is earlier than No. IX: "il [Vergil] fait amende honorable," says R. Waltz,[93] who supposes that the "songs" which were thought to have saved everything are simply the first Eclogue. But it seems to me far more likely that it is the other way around. Under the star of Caesar vines are meant to ripen, and therefore the vine-dressers to be rewarded for their labour; but Meliboeus has to leave his fields for a soldier to plough, his crops for a barbarian to gather;[94] a pretty reward, he seems to imply, I have for trusting the promises of the star, in other words, those of the new regime. We have already seen that his part of the poem is very far from consisting of honeyed flattery. It seems to me that this is much more effective as Vergil's last word on the subject, and thus for the poem which he deliberately chose[95] to begin his first published collection.

I have hitherto said little of Gallus, reserving him for the next chapter. Enough has perhaps been said to show that of the three alleged friends Pollio need hardly have been even an acquaintance and Varus was probably an acquaintance but not a congenial one, at least during and after the affair of the confiscations. Gallus therefore remains.

Perhaps also the question has been answered which was asked at the end of the second chapter, namely, whether Vergil showed, in the face of real and personal misfortunes, any fruits of his philosophical studies. Surely we may answer in the affirmative. He never, at least not at that time, affected to be a Stoic or to reject all emotion as unworthy of the wise man; but Epicurus' teachings were in favour of controlling the feelings. This we may honestly say the poet did. His complaints are not unmanly; the tone has more quiet resignation than grief, and there is no whine in the voices of his speakers. Also, there is, if we remember what the conventions of the time were, no base flattery even of the mighty Octavian, of whom Pollio is recorded[96] to have said that he would not reply to some lampoons of his, because it was not well to write (*scribere*) against one who could include the writer's name in the list of the condemned (*proscribere*). The tone is courtly, not base. Over and above this moderation in addressing the great and powerful, there is more than a little honest and frank indignation. The voice of Vergil speaks rather through Meliboeus than through Tityrus[97] in the first Eclogue, and we have seen how pointed are the quotations from supposed poems of Menalcas in the ninth. In some ages and some countries such honesty would not have been safe; indeed there are places where it would be highly dangerous now. But the great poet addressed his rebuke and his modified praise to a man deserving indeed of the former but increasingly meriting the latter. As he felt himself more firmly in power, Octavian was great enough to value this new poet aright, and I have little doubt that Maecenas had unmistakable hints from his chief that here was one to be attached to the Caesarian cause at all reasonable costs, for he was much too good to suppress and too honest to keep his own feelings altogether hidden, whereas his support might be invaluable alike among those who loved poetry and those who could appreciate honesty.

CHAPTER V

GALLUS, SILENUS, AND ARKADY

THE CONSCIENTIOUS student of the Eclogues has no sooner made up his mind, or reconciled himself to not making it up, concerning the position and fate of Vergil's farm and his relations to the alleged land commissioners of the day than he finds himself faced with new problems, which are all the more unwelcome to those of purely literary tastes because they haunt two of the most charming of the poems, the sixth and the tenth. These, like all the even-numbered pieces,[1] are non-dramatic in form. Both are narrative, the former telling how two shepherds caught a Seilenos asleep and he ransomed himself with a song, while the latter describes the poetical agonies of Gallus, who found himself somehow in Arkadia and like to die of unrequited love. Both are unconcerned with the spoliation of Mantua, if we except the dedication to Varus prefixed to the former, which might be dated sometime in 714/40[2] and throws no light on when the rest was written; No. X announces itself as the last of the Eclogues,[3] but again this does not necessarily signify that it was written last, since it would have been easy for the poet to add or modify a line or two at the beginning when he gathered together his "selections" to give to the literary world. Its date, be it late or early, before or after the confiscations, lands us in a mass of difficulties as soon as we try to particularise; these we must discuss later.

Let us take the poems in the order which Vergil gave them. The setting of No. VI need trouble no one, not even the keenest searchers after realism or its absence in the poems. Chromis and Mnasyllus, two shepherd-boys, find the Seilenos asleep in a cave, which presumably means he was not on the banks of the Mincio, but leaves us a great

---
[1] Notes to chapter v will be found on pages 240-244.

part of the rest of the world to choose from, with an inclination towards Greece, since the song that he sings had apparently been overheard from Apollo when the god was practicing on the banks of the Eurotas.[4] The plain geographical fact is that the whole scene is clean outside this workaday world, in the region where wood-spirits and water-nymphs (the boys are helped to play their tricks on the drunken godling by *Aegle Naiadum pulcherrima*) are still commonly to be found and the only serious businesses are love-making and singing, with drinking for an occasional change or as the regular occupation of Seilenos and his kind. Through the fairyland scenery and characters peeps a reminiscence of such a prank as Vergil may very well have seen in his own land when children came across one of their elders sound asleep after a cup or so too much of the local wine. The lads, urged on by their pretty minx of an immortal, tie him hand and foot with his own wreaths, while she bedaubs his face with mulberries. The blessed privilege of the gods enables him to awake with no trace of either headache or ill temper, and he acknowledges himself fairly caught and ready to pay forfeit; to the boys, the fulfilment of a long-standing promise to sing to them sometime, and for the Naiad, as many kisses as she or he likes, later on.

So far, all is as readily intelligible as it is lovely. Poets of many ages, especially those which have built great cities, have had the key to a land which is where you please, only not in Alexandria or Rome, London or Paris or New York. Now begins the core of the poem, and of the difficulties, for Seilenos, says the poet, proceeded to sing, *namque canebat*, and the matter of his song (no one with a shred of taste will quarrel with the manner) has set controversy a-going to the extent of far more pages than it contains lines, or even feet.

He begins very properly with the creation, or rather the

evolution, of the world, and here the ancients at least found him Epicurean.[5] This is his doctrine, whether seriously from that philosopher or merely expressed with literary reminiscences of Lucretius:

> How, forced together in the void of space,
> The seeds of earth, of air and sea and fire
> The ever-moving, met; how these began
> And all beginnings from them,[6] till there grew
> This world's great sphere, but soft and tender still.
> Next, earth grew hard; its shores confined the sea,
> And step by step the formless changed to form,
> The new-born sun lighted amazèd lands,
> The clouds retired and farther fell the rain,
> And the first forests rose, while here and there
> Some living thing roved hill-sides unexplored.

Then comes the re-creation of man, after the deluge, by Deukalion and Pyrrha; next, against ordinary mythological chronology, the Golden Age, and, with another jump from the reign of Kronos to that of Zeus, Prometheus and his theft of fire, with his punishment on Mount Caucasus. The next leap is wider still; we are suddenly in the midst of the Argonautic expedition and they are searching for the lost Hylas. Then the story turns back a generation, and we hear of Pasiphae, with a side-glance at the daughters of Proitos. Pasiphae and her laments are interrupted by the story of Atalanta, that in turn by the woeful tale of Phaethon's sisters, who mourned for their brother's fall until they turned into trees, and immediately after them comes, it would appear, a sketch of the prelude of one of Gallus' poems, an epyllion, probably, after the Alexandrian manner. As he wanders by the banks of the Permessos, a Muse meets him, the rest give him courteous welcome, and Linos gives him Hesiod's pan-pipes and bids him use them to sing of the grove of Apollo of Grynion. Of this we must shortly say more. The song of Seilenos goes on with stories of shape-changing—Skylla, Tereus, and Philomela. The rest of its contents we are not told, but it took all day to sing and contained all that Apollo had sung before while he practiced by the Eurotas.

Human curiosity being what it is, the question has been asked, first, why Seilenos sings of these matters in particular, and secondly, why Gallus suddenly intrudes, and that too in a poem supposed to be addressed to Varus. Few are content to say that they do not know, and fewer still are likely to rest satisfied with the solution of Cartault,[7] that Vergil simply looked through a handbook of mythology and put in those stories which happened to catch his fancy at the moment. Even if this were accepted, Gallus and his Gryneian grove remain puzzling.

It is therefore well to consider the most thorough-going and ingenious explanation which has yet been suggested, that of the late F. Skutsch.[8] He takes the grove and what goes with it, the meeting with the Muses and Linos, for his starting-point. That this does describe a poem by Gallus is not doubtful. The legend was an obscure one and the grove far from being one of the best known of Apollo's many sanctuaries; Servius, both the ordinary and the longer, tell the story, and the former adds that it was to be found in the works of Euphorion, the very place where one expects a *cantor Euphorionis*[9] to go for inspiration, and that Gallus translated it into Latin. Here it is well to stop for a moment and consider what Servius' notions of translation and close imitation are. We cannot compare Gallus with Euphorion, for we have neither poem; but we can compare Vergil with Homer, and thereby check similar statements of the commentator. In his note on the *Aeneid*, XII, 206 sqq., Servius assures us that "this is a passage out of Homer, word for word" (*Homeri locus, uerbum ad uerbum*). It is actually a close imitation of one; but let us see how nearly true Servius' remark is. Here is a literal rendering of Vergil:

As this sceptre (for by chance he bore a sceptre in his right hand) never shall put forth light-leaved twigs nor cast a shade, since once for all in the forest it has been cut close off from the trunk, lacks its mother-tree, and has lost leaves and shoots to the iron, though once it was green wood, while now the craftsman's hand has sheathed it fairly in bronze and given it to Latin elders to bear.

The speaker, King Latinus, is swearing a treaty with Aeneas. The original is from the *Iliad*, where Achilles is swearing that Agamemnon and the other Greeks shall yet feel the need of him:[10]

By this sceptre, which shall never put forth leaves and twigs, since first it hath left the place whence it was cut in the hills, nor shall grow green again; for the bronze hath stripped off its leaves and bark, and now the sons of the Achaians bear it in their hands, the dispensers of justice, who guard the dooms that are from Zeus.

The general resemblance is obvious, and the imitation equally so; but Vergil is full where Homer is brief, brief where he is full. Homer's hills become a forest, the staff is sheathed in bronze in Vergil, where Homer's Achilles gives no such detail and Homer himself later says that it was decorated with gold studs. Homer's barons and their judicial functions are mentioned at some length, against Vergil's two words, *patribus Latinis*. This is certainly not what we mean by translation, for it is hardly even paraphrase. It is imitation of the best kind, the reëxpression in one's own way of what had been well said by another in his. Like Johnson speaking of Addison, Vergil might have said of the great Greek, "Sir, Homer had his style, and I have mine."[11] Other examples might be given, for instance of the resemblances and differences between *Aen.*, XII, 754 and Apollonios, *Argon.*, II, 280 sq., which Servius again declares

Vergil has translated "word for word"; but one is enough. Gallus did not make, so far as Servius' authority goes, what we should think at all a literal rendering of Euphorion, but he may have imitated him pretty closely. The result commended itself to Vergil, as we may see by his alluding to it long after Gallus was disgraced and dead. In the Eclogue he declares that after Gallus has sung of the Gryneian grove, Apollo shall pride himself on that as much as on any other. In the *Aeneid*[12] Vergil has to represent Aeneas as stating his own case to Dido with all the eloquence at his command, for he is telling her that he must leave her. His reason for departure is of course the explicit commands of the gods, and of them he mentions Apollo first. He is an Easterner speaking to an Easterner, therefore he mentions the god by Eastern titles, and the first of these is *Gryneus;* the "Lykian oracle" (*Lyciae sortes*) takes second place. It is a boldly anachronistic compliment to the dead poet; Grynion is one of Apollo's chief shrines, not for any reason which could have affected the real Aeneas, but because Gallus has sung of it.

However, let us return to Skutsch. His statement of his own case is not easily bettered, so let us have it in his own words.

Silenus sings in one place what Cornelius Gallus had sung; he reproduces in brief the proem for us which introduced the song of the Gryneian grove. But before and after he sings of matters which have, so far as their content goes, no connection with this, and yet must have some kind of connection. He does not sing all these things at length, but in more or less epitomised form, sometimes very much epitomised. Therefore the common feature of all these sketches is surely that they are synopses, of course synopses of works by one and the same author, namely Cornelius Gallus.

He goes on to argue, what indeed is fairly obvious, once his main thesis is granted, that the works were little epics, *epyllia*, in the style of the Alexandrians and of Catullus and his fellows. Once the poem on the beginnings of the world is over, if Seilenos is really giving the outline of a poem, all the subjects would do excellently for such works; they might be handled in perhaps three to five hundred hexameters apiece. As to the creation, so to call it, that again is the sort of thing Siron's pupil might write, if he knew his Lucretius, and why should not Gallus know his Lucretius very well?[13] Indeed, it would be rather odd if he did not, for not only was he Vergil's personal friend (see below), but also Lucretius was much in fashion about the beginning of the Augustan period, and even Vergil's supposed teacher of rhetoric, Egnatius,[14] was the author of a *de rerum natura*, a poem Lucretian in title and, to judge from the little that is known of it, in content also.

The whole Eclogue, then, according to Skutsch, is a catalogue-poem of an unusual kind, a poetical synopsis of the work of a poet whom Vergil admired and liked. Though unusual, such a thing would not be unheard of; the unknown author of the *Lament for Bion* paid a similar compliment to the subject of his exquisite lines, and Propertius did as much for Vergil himself.[15] It would not, however, be easy to find so long and continuous a versified account of another's verses, one extending, not to a dozen lines or so, but to a whole poem. And the difficulty remains, why so much should be said of Gallus—why, indeed, the whole body of the work should concern Gallus and no one else—when the dedication is to Varus. It is true that Varus was in some sense Gallus' colleague; it is said[16] that the latter's task was to exact contributions in money from those cities north of the Po which were not deprived of land. It is also true that Gallus was Vergil's friend by Vergil's testimony,[17] of about the same age,[18] and, it would seem, already of some celebrity as a poet. But all this leaves it a very singular manner of approach to one man by praising another at length, even though a compliment or two is paid to the nominal recipient of the address in its opening paragraph. Besides this negative objection to Skutsch's theory there is a positive one, emphasised by Leo[19] and not sufficiently attended to by Skutsch himself. Gallus was, at the date of the sixth Eclogue, something like thirty years old; on this theory he had already written at least some of the elegies for which he was afterwards remembered, and also about eight epyllia. Now an epyllion was not a thing to be dashed off at a sitting; Catullus wrote but one in his whole career and it would be hard to find a Latin poet who had many more than that to his credit. It must be, by the laws of its genre, highly finished, full of learned allusions, as well as poetically good. On Skutsch's theory, this amateur poet, so to call him, for literature never claimed his whole attention at any time, so far as we know, and his political career must have consumed much of his energies, had at this early age done more, at least in bulk of production, than any neoteric of whose output we can form an opinion. This, too, was not the scribbling of a writer with a flux of words and no concern for form; all the evidence we have is to the effect that his work, while not faultless,[20] was serious literature, and we have seen that Vergil, surely no bad judge, thought well of it; just how well and how much use he made of it is a matter of opinion and depends partly on what we think of another doctrine of Skutsch, that Gallus wrote the nameless poem called the *Ciris*,[21] which either imitates Vergil or, as is rather more likely, is imitated by him. Fortunately for our present discussion, it is not necessary to go into that complicated question; be it a work of Gallus or not, some poem about Skylla is one of the epyllia which, on Skutsch's general theory of the Eclogue, must be attributed to him.

Nor is this all; for besides the epyllia, Skutsch supposes that Gallus had by that time written some of his elegies at least, if not all of them.[22] But this is a subordinate point and, as I think, depends on highly doubtful interpretations of a passage of Vergil and another of Propertius.[23] With all that could be urged against it, however, Skutsch's doctrine might yet hold the field because it produces an intelligible reason why Seilenos sings of these themes and no others. If we can find another reason equally intelligible, we may abandon a hypothesis which rests on so slender a foundation of certain fact and so large a superstructure of clever deduction; though whether we keep it or leave it, honesty obliges us to thank a scholar who, always more careful for the discovery of truth than for his own glory, has drawn attention anew to a fascinating and beautiful but puzzling poem.

I must confess that I am ill-satisfied with the accounts I have seen of Vergil's reasons. Leo frankly admits that he does not know what they were,[24] and I have found so far but one writer who, in searching for them, seems to me even to help his readers to the right track, provided always that there is a right one and the agnosticism of one so well seen in Latin poetry as Leo is not the last word.

The guide I mean is a student of Vergil otherwise unknown to me, Severinus Hammer.[25] To him, the lines about Gallus are a hopeless difficulty as they stand (*locus conclamatissimus*). But the themes fall into two groups, if for the moment we neglect Gallus; from the beginning of his song, the passage about the cosmogony, down to line 61, Seilenos sings of matters which have at all events a negative characteristic in common; they are not stories of metamorphoses. Now he changes his theme, and sings of nothing else in 62–63 (the sisters of Phaethon), 74–77 (Skylla), 78–81 (Tereus and Philomela). These two groups would make quite an intelligible poem, still omitting Gallus and his meeting with the Muses. How, then, did Gallus enter? Hammer will have it that the whole passage is an interpolation, but that its author is none other than Vergil himself. Deceived in his hopes of Varus, and hearing that

Gallus had turned from elegies to epyllia, Vergil turned the work into a compliment to his friend by thrusting into the midst of it a mention of what was presumably his first attempt in the new mode.

Adverse criticism of this theory is only too easy; Hammer explains neither why Vergil spoiled his own poem in this clumsy manner nor why he did not suppress or alter the address to Varus; it was easy to substitute Gallus' name for his everywhere, since they scan exactly alike, and the laudatory remarks and excuses addressed to the one would need little change to make them fit the other. It is more profitable to take up the challenge and see whether we cannot find in the mention of Gallus what, from its position, it should be, the climax of the poem, and not a parenthesis, original or of later addition.

Seilenos, after his cosmogonic passage, sings of the doings of Pyrrha, the Golden Age of Kronos, Prometheus' offence and its punishment, the loss of Hylas, the sorrows of Pasiphae, and incidentally of Proitos' daughters, then of Atalanta, Phaethon's sisters, Gallus, Skylla, Tereus and Philomela. Is there, after all, a link between these tales? I think there is, namely that all of them recount how the gods interfered in human affairs for good or ill. Pyrrha (and Deukalion) cast the stones by the direct command of the Earth-Goddess.[26] In Kronos' days the gods dwelt among men, to their great advantage. Hylas was stolen away by water-nymphs. Pasiphae was the victim of the anger of Poseidon, or Aphrodite,[27] the daughters of Proitos of the wrath of Hera. Atalanta was caught by the golden apples because Aphrodite interfered on behalf of Hippomenes; Phaethon's fall and therefore the grief of his sisters were due to the dealings of the unfortunate youth with Helios, less directly with Zeus, and the metamorphosis of the sisters was of course a miracle. Now, says Vergil, listen to another intervention of the gods, this time wholly for good. Gallus was as yet but a beginner in poetry, wandering at the foot of Helikon or on its lower slopes, when the Muses themselves took an interest in him and gave him such inspiration as they have granted to few since the days when they showed mercy to another wanderer, Hesiod himself. I need not go on with the other tales Seilenos told; there were more metamorphoses and much else.

This, it seems to me, gives us the unity we are seeking (a loose unity, enough for a short poem which never tries to rise to great heights) and also could turn into an endeavour to win the interest of Varus. The gods have manifestly interfered in favour of his own colleague, his fellow supporter of Octavian and co-worker for the rewarding of his veterans. It hardly need be said that this is not a serious warning that divine favour or vengeance will pursue Varus according as he treats another follower of Apollo, Vergil himself, well or ill. It was centuries since any educated man had believed in the conventional gods in that way. But I think it does convey a fairly broad hint of a different kind. If Varus wrongs Mantua, he is wronging not an inarticulate and insignificant country town, but the home of a poet; perhaps we may say, if we accept certain of the *Catalepton* as genuine, of a poet who had already shown his skill in lampoons and therefore could on occasion bring Varus before the public in a way he would not like, but certainly a poet whose praise was worth having, however much he might assure Varus that there were plenty of panegyrists already. And I would further suggest that Vergil published his work unaltered, with the frustrated dedication left standing, as a companion piece to the significant lines in the ninth Eclogue[28] about the unfinished song in Varus' honour.

We pass now to another Eclogue, equally beautiful and equally associated with the names of Gallus in antiquity and of Skutsch in modern times. It is the Tenth, which announces itself as the last of the series, whether it was originally composed last or not.[29] Its plot and setting are simple. Gallus, to whom the poem is addressed and at whose request it was written,[30] is in evil plight, dying of love. He is in Arkadia, surrounded by sympathetic auditors, human and divine, of his plaints, and the gist of them is this. Lycoris has deserted him and gone away, through the ice and snow of the Alps to the cold waters of the Rhine, with another. He still loves her, though he heartily wishes that he were a simple Arkadian shepherd with a rustic beauty at his side. Indeed, he has thoughts of becoming one and leaving all his over-sophisticated culture for simple songs and a simple life. But he knows that even this would not cure him, for love knows no cure; therefore the poem ends on a note of gentle despair. Here Gallus' part stops, and Vergil himself continues with the epilogue, not to this poem but to the collection as a whole.

Two facts concerning the composition are quite beyond dispute. One is that the death and dying speech of Daphnis in Theokritos' first Idyll are imitated, not slavishly, but with such closeness as to make Vergil's indebtedness, and his great skill in adapting Greek material to his own language and manner, as evident as he meant them to be. The other is that Servius says a part of the poem is taken from Gallus' own work.[31] Over this statement a controversy raged for some years, again starting from the treatise of Skutsch already quoted.[32] He finds a number of inconsistencies in what Gallus says. In lines 9–43, he is peacefully lying in an idealised Arkadia,[33] surrounded by sympathetic mourners, and wishing Lycoris were there so they might live and die quietly together. But in 44–45 he is at war, *duri Martis in armis*. The very next line, 46, complains that Lycoris is far from her own land, which seems to suggest that Gallus is in his; if he is in Arkadia, he would still be separated from her if she were at home. In 52 sqq., he has apparently left the quiet pastoral region in which we found him for a wilder part of the country, where he means to hunt, until he gives up the idea because he knows it will not cure his mad passion. Moreover, his mood changes from one passage to another; now he would be a shepherd, now a huntsman, now he laments that Lycoris is exposed to hardships in her new adventure, and so forth; I omit some difficulties which seem to be created by nothing more solid than the pleasure of finding them there. For all this Skutsch has a remedy to suggest. The poem, as Vergil wrote it, is a unity in multiplicity, for it contains again a sort of versified catalogue, albeit drawn up with the finest skill, of several other poems, namely the amatory elegies of Gallus. Finally, two lines put into Gallus' mouth acquaint us with an interesting fact about his literary development; he intended, whether or not he carried out his intention, to try his hand, like his friend, at writing pastorals. The lines are 50–51:

> ibo et Chalcidico quae sunt mihi condita uersu
> carmina pastoris Siculi modulabor auena.

> I'll go and turn my high Chalkidian strains
> To lays of the Sicilian shepherd's pipe.

In plain prose, he will give up the style of Euphorion and imitate Theokritos instead.

Again Skutsch found a doughty opponent in Leo, who was supported by lesser but nowise contemptible scholars. Their strongest line of counter-attack was to deny the hopeless discontinuity which Skutsch thought he had discovered in the Eclogue. To begin with, the situation as seen by them is not wholly imaginary, at least not impossible. Gallus is for some reason in (or near) Greece[34] and has taken an opportunity for a furlough, which he spends in Arkadia, amid romantic pastoral surroundings, poetised of course by Vergil. Once the Theokritean motif is disposed of, and it is well-nigh at an end after the thirtieth line or so of the poem, there is no worse instability of subject-matter than may be found in the surviving elegiac poets; the theme after all is, as Vergil himself says,[35] the troubled passion of Gallus, and one does not expect a man in his situation to speak with strict attention to logic and the best arrangement of his thoughts. He is in his quiet country retreat and wishes he could stay there, nay, that he were a native of it and in love with one as simple as he then would be. He addresses the (supposedly poetical) Arkadians:

> And would I were of you, to tend your flock
> Or at the vintage pluck your ripened grapes,
> Some Phyllis or Amyntas at my side,
> Some love (what though Amyntas swarthy be?
> Violets are dark and irises are dark.)
> Some love beside me 'neath the willow shades
> And vines, she plaiting garlands, singing he.

Now the mood changes; instead of a rustic, he will have his own Lycoris there, to enjoy the delectable country-side. Then (44 sqq.) he comes back to reality again; he is a soldier, by his own foolish whim,[36] she is in some bleak district of Gaul or Germany, or half-way over an Alpine pass, where he hopes that the ice and snow will not hurt her little feet. Then, since he is in Arkadia, he will stay there (50 sqq.). He will write no more learned poetry, but learn to sing and play on the pipe like any shepherd; he will cut Lycoris' name on trees (instead of writing her any more clever and artificial elegies); he will go up into the wilder parts of the country and be a huntsman; he will—but he knows that none of these things, if he did try them, will do him the least good. There is nothing left but to despair quietly.

With this general interpretation of the poem, which seems to me to do more justice to Vergil and be far more likely in itself, I am in agreement. Nevertheless, it leaves a number of problems to be solved, and these are by no means uninteresting. When is all this supposed to happen, and how far, if at all, is Vergil serious? And what exactly is the meaning of Servius' statement about the quotation from Gallus?

To determine the first of these points, it is well to start from the assumption that Lycoris really is Cytheris-Volumnia. The evidence for this is tolerably good,[37] the objections to it not over-convincing; indeed, they largely spring from the very difficulty of fixing a date. But this difficulty itself arises from an assumption which we have no right to make, namely that the man with whom Lycoris had gone away to the north was Mark Antony. That he was for a time her lover is notorious; indeed, it was he who was her first protector and launched her on her career as actress and *femme galante*, by getting her ownership transferred to Volumnius Eutrapelus, his own dependent, who set her free, no doubt by Antony's directions. All this happened some years before Vergil began writing any Eclogues of which we have any knowledge, in 705/49 or a little earlier.[38] It is generally assumed, and with reason,[39] that she ceased to be his *maîtresse en titre* when he married Fulvia, that is, in 708/46. Even Antony, marrying a woman of such force of character as his wife showed herself to be, would hardly flout the conventions to the extent of keeping a double establishment, like the misguided heroes of Menander's Ἐπιτρέποντες and Terence's *Hecyra*. If it is really true that she became the mistress of Brutus, it presumably was after Antony left her.[40] So far, there is little room for Gallus; what opportunities would he have had, between the ages of about twenty and twenty-five, to acquire so expensive a luxury as Cytheris in the face of strong competition, amounting to a monopoly for the time being? Consequently, there is no date at which she could have left him to go to Gaul, or anywhere else, with Mark Antony. Yet this is what Servius appears to say, and very likely thought that she did do.[41] There are two ways out of the difficulty, both of which are easy and natural, and we have our choice between them. One is that Servius is merely indulging in a false combination, based on some literary but not much chronological knowledge. Cytheris was celebrated by Gallus in his poems, she was not faithful to him, she was the mistress of Mark Antony; therefore she left him for Antony. Or it is just possible that what he says (*eo spreto Antonium euntem ad Gallias est secuta*) may be literally true, for he gives no *praenomen;* her new attachment may have been for L. Antonius, if it was for any of that family at all.[42] It is to be remembered that these affairs, for a woman like Cytheris, were chiefly matters of business. We have not the slightest reason to suppose that she ever in her life had any moral scruples—indeed, chastity for other than prudential reasons would not be an indulgence permitted to a pretty slave-girl—or that she had in her anything of Propertius' Cynthia, who apparently was capable of a genuine and enduring affection for no selfish ends. By any date at which Gallus was at all likely to be in the neighbourhood of Greece (and if he was not in or near Greece, why put the scene of the Eclogue in Arkadia, instead of the equally conventional Sicily or South Italy?) Cytheris must have been a dozen years or more at her two exacting professions; since there is no year in the forties to be found for the poem which will fit Cytheris and the new lover and account for Vergil's finished art and Gallus' having written both his elegies and his "Chalkidian" pieces, that is to say, his epyllion or epyllia,[43] we must look to the beginning of the thirties. Suppose that Cytheris was about twenty years old when she so captivated Mark Antony, she would be about thirty-one or thirty-two when the year 714/40, a busy one for Vergil, was over and Gallus was no longer in Italy, occupied with the business of exacting contributions from the cities of the Transpadane region." As a reasonably prudent woman, she would certainly know that she had not many years of attractiveness left and that younger beauties were coming to the fore in Rome. Gallus with his elegies had been an excellent advertising agent, whether profitable or not as a lover; she would jump at an offer financially advantageous and having the added attractiveness of getting her away from Rome to a place where competition would not be nearly so keen and perhaps she might even aspire to marry and settle down with some not too exacting provincial. Whether L. Antonius or another made her the offer is a matter of small importance; she took it and left Italy.

Now Gallus, being a man of the world and no longer a boy, must have known that some such end as this would come of his little romance. He may well have been piqued and annoyed, but his heart-break was mostly literary convention, a good subject for a new and moving elegy or series of elegies. His life continued for another decade or so and was full of incident and activity, not in the least that of the despairing and melancholy figure described by Vergil. Vergil, knowing him and probably knowing also that he had been quite able to leave Cytheris and go away to Greece without her, was doubtless aware of all this, but he, like Gallus, saw the excellence of the literary material involuntarily furnished by the latest immorality of a totally immoral woman. Our knowledge of the surviving elegiac poets is enough to enable us to imagine how Gallus would vary and embroider the theme, "I am far away at the wars, and Lycoris, safe at home, will not await me, but has proved fickle." One can even reconstruct the mythological allusions, beginning perhaps with the faithless wife of Diomedes and provided with an effective contrast in the conjugal troth of Penelope, which would decorate the poems. Vergil, his Theokritos in his head, at once saw an admirable situation in the bucolic manner; Daphnis had died for love,

Gallus should be on the point of doing so, and, to add an effect, he should sing some of his own verses, with the necessary changes of metre, to a grieved and admiring auditory. Or, better still, he should speak them, for as he was not a bucolic poet and the setting was to be rustic, it would be better not to make him, with his learned style, be found performing in a manner so out of tune with his surroundings.

And here, I think, is the great difficulty of supposing either, with Skutsch, that the speech of Gallus is a sort of index or catalogue of all his elegies, or a group of them, say the last of his four books,[45] or, with Leo and his followers,[46] that any one elegy is the source. These scholars have perhaps paid too much attention to the natural wish of a *Gelehrter* to have all his material nicely in order and not enough to the actual procedure of a poet who pays another the compliment of borrowing from him. Their own literature might have taught them something of the latter. Schiller[47] is to be found on occasion lifting a verse bodily out of Seneca, giving it a wholly new meaning with its new context, and then going on with lines of his own, as independent of the older author as if no such person had ever existed. Vergil is crammed with most subtle procedures of this kind;[48] to prove that he got this or that line from a given poem tells us absolutely nothing about what the next line of the original was, whether the sense has come over with the wording, or, even if it has, whether the application in the source was that given it by the imitation. Indeed, no author who borrows a phrase or two from another is thereby obliged to borrow more than the bare phrase or phrases. So, when Servius says that "all these lines" are taken from Gallus, apart from his inaccuracy in such matters, of which we have already seen an example, and the fact that we really have no idea what "all" the lines are, we still do not know how Gallus used them, nor what he said before and after. Supposing that Vergil has borrowed the whole of the sentence against which the note stands and the sentence before that; his Gallus then laments,

> But now a madman's lust for savage War
> Holds me in arms, amid the foeman's points,
> While thou (how can I bear it?) far from home,
> Leav'st me, ah cruel, to tread Alpine snows
> Or Rhenish hoar-frost—may they chill thee not,
> Nor sharp-edged ice make those soft feet to bleed.

This hangs together sufficiently well as Vergil writes it; but so do, for instance, lines 32-43 of the third Eclogue, in which Menalcas refuses to stake one of the beasts he tends on the singing-contest but is willing to wager a pair of bowls finely carved; and yet the first part of what he says is from the eighth Idyll, which is not Theokritos at all, the next from the fifth, where there is no mention of a bet, but only of an intended present, and the rest from the first, profoundly modified. If we had not the text of Theokritos, it would be quite impossible for us to reconstruct any one of these three passages from Vergil, who nevertheless might be said with quite as much accuracy as is usual with Servius and his like to have taken "all these verses" from the Greek.[49] I therefore would reject, as utterly alien to Vergil's technique in imitation, any theory which makes him give us the substance either of one or of many elegies of Gallus. If we had the elegies, we should, I have no doubt, see that his friend had a number of quotations and half-quotations in his Eclogue, but I also have no doubt that we should find them adapted in half-a-dozen different ways, and especially, that we should seldom find one passage imitated by itself, without admixture of another, whether or not from the poems of Gallus. There is another consideration which would seem to forbid any looking for very close reproduction of Gallus' poems. This is the necessary difference of tone. Even if we suppose, with Skutsch, that Gallus wrote a "bucolic elegy,"[50] like one or two of those in the Tibullan collection, the fact remains that classical elegy is definitely of the city; it may describe the country, in fact often does so, but it is from the point of view of the town-dweller, perhaps on a visit to some rural scene, his own estate or another's. The tenth is one of the least pastoral in its note of all the collection,[51] but even it is essentially written from the point of view of the country-dweller, though here he is most sympathetically recording the woes of a townsman visiting his region. However much Vergil may have laid Gallus' words under contribution (and I do not know of any considerable or even perceptible difference from the language of the other pieces which would suggest this), the music is transposed into a wholly other mode; the Chalkidian strains are modulated to fit the scale of the Sicilian flute.

We may turn in conclusion to a question which has been more than once raised,[52] to what extent Vergil is serious in his celebration of Gallus' unhappy love. Is the poem one of real sympathy, an address to a friend in sorrow whom the author would like to console, or is it a mildly jocular effort, poking good-natured fun at woes which are, after all, not so very profound? It may help us if we run through the poem once more, to see what the topics are which others than Gallus dwell upon. Vergil first asks, following his Greek model with the necessary changes of scenery,[53] where the Nymphs were who might have been expected to sympathise. The other country deities were present, and some mortals with them; Mount Mainalos, or its daimon (it is seldom easy, in a passage like this, to determine whether the actual earth and stones of a mountain or a vague spirit which haunts them is meant) and the very rocks on its sides; a little group of country-folk (they include Menalcas, who possibly here again is Vergil himself), Apollo (of course Apollo Nomios, the god of herdsmen), Silvanus, and Pan.

Apollo and Pan address Gallus, the former to remind him that Lycoris is gone and he is mad to go on loving her, the latter to tell him that weeping will do no good, for Love can never be glutted with a lover's tears. The framework continues Theokritean, but with endless alterations of detail, many of them due to the fact that Gallus is but rhetorically dying, Daphnis in the original is really near his end.

All this, it seems to me, is a very odd way to console a man for any trouble. Besides his own mournful speech, which we have already discussed, here are two bystanders, both of divine rank, who tell him that the affair is going as badly as it well can and that he is taking the worst possible way to cure it; they do not suggest anything else that he might do, unless we suppose Pan to be urging him indirectly and by hints to forget Lycoris and everything connected with her. Meantime, Vergil is insisting, by the framework and details of the Eclogue, that Gallus' situation is hazardously like that of a famous victim of love, Daphnis himself. Surely it is no great comfort to be told that one's circumstances and behaviour (for the Theokritean Daphnis also makes an elaborate speech) are like those of one who perished miserably. The speech of Gallus comes to its melancholy end, and with his resolution to yield to Love, that is, to die of his unrequited passion, the poem ends too, for the lines which follow are nothing but an epilogue to it and to the series. Vergil imagines himself a countryman, sitting weaving a basket, apparently the regular occupation for industrious folk when they had nothing more pressing to do.[54] As he weaves, he sings, either this Eclogue or all ten, one after another, as we may prefer to understand the passage. But now, with a final protestation of his great and increasing affection for his friend, he rises; it is late, the shadow of a juniper is unwholesome (especially, it would seem, at sundown),[55] and he must get home with his goats. Here is not a word of what one would expect in a poem or speech of consolation, not a hint of any of the stock topics, even Corydon's suggestion that there are other fish in the sea.[56] But Vergil implies that his task is finished and he has done what he set out to do for Gallus, nay, that with the help of the Muses he has done it not so ill and his friend will be well pleased with it.[57] If the consolation has got no further than to say that the case is doleful and there is much need of comfort, how can the poet have done all that he might?

At the same time, I see nothing in the least ridiculous or even the mildest humour in the piece. The other speakers and Gallus himself, be it in his own words or Vergil's, paint his grief and despair strongly and effectively. It is an excellent and, to my mind, a wholly serious picture of love-melancholy, which Vergil knew how to depict better than most.

If, then, it is neither a consolatory poem nor a gentle and friendly joke, what is it? I think we can find an answer, conjectural indeed, but all answers to a question why a poet wrote as he did are apt to be conjectural and subjective, and this one seems to me to fit the known facts and the probabilities alike. Vergil, as we know, admired Gallus' poems; there is no reason to suppose the admiration was all on one side, for Gallus apparently was a good poet and may be credited with enough taste to see that his friend's verses were no ordinary performances. It is clear enough that Vergil had access to Gallus' poetry, and there is little doubt that the two would exchange copies of their latest works. Now Gallus, as I suppose, once his natural annoyance at the news of Cytheris' infidelity left him, would see what an excellent subject he had for more elegies, perhaps a whole book of them. Suppose them written, and a copy sent off to Vergil in Italy, from Greece or wherever Gallus was at the time. Can we suppose it not accompanied by a letter, and is not the main content of such a letter very easy to guess, apart from enquiries after common acquaintances or Vergil's fortunes? "Here are my new poems, written after Cytheris broke with me; I think them not too bad, considering that I have my military duties to perform. Have you written any more pastorals of late, and did you ever try your hand at a subject like mine in your style? There are several things in Theokritos about unfortunate lovers, and you imitate him beautifully." Vergil would take a suggestion of this kind from Gallus much more readily than one from Varus, for example, that a panegyric or an epic on the late wars would be acceptable. One can imagine him turning it over in his mind, and seeing how excellent a subject it was, and how featly it could be put into a sort of semi-pastoral poem, with hints and suggestions of the amatory elegiac about it. Once begun, the poem would almost of necessity contain allusions, verbal especially, not only to the Greek classics from which some of the material and most of the framework were taken, but also to the author who had given the hint for the whole.

And so, with yet another suggestion added to the long list, and with full knowledge that it may be as completely wrong as I think most of the former to be, I conclude with one more word of thanks to the earlier writers who, by putting forward their opinions of what Vergil meant, have provided us with more reasons than ever for learning exactly what he said and how he said it.

CHAPTER VI

VERGIL AND ALLEGORY

For some time we have been studying the *Eclogues* in general obedience to Servius' precept[1] that they should not be given an allegorical interpretation unless the business of the Mantuan territory and its assignment to the veterans is concerned. We have, for instance, gone on the assumption that when Vergil says Gallus was in Arkadia, Gallus really was at least somewhere near there, and to imagine him talking to its inhabitants was no wild flight of poetic fancy but tolerably close to reality. It so happens that there is a very fine poem in our collection which enables us to put this principle to an acid test. The fifth Eclogue has much to say of Daphnis; does it mean Daphnis or someone else?

If it be decided that a certain amount of allegory in a very mild form is present in this poem, no one, I take it, will suppose that we must unsay all that has hitherto been said and look for allegories of the most pronounced type everywhere. We may allow a poet his tropes and his figures, with a moderate amount of riddling language added, and yet not be disciples of the too ingenious Mr. FitzSimon, who is of the opinion that Vergil, and apparently all the poets of antiquity, were perfectly acquainted with the chief dogmas of Christianity, handed down to them from a primal revelation and kept secret from the profane, and disclosed these to their fellow initiates through a cryptogram of more than Baconian ingenuity, whereby most letters could at will be most others and practically anything could signify something else.[2] We may see faces under the masks of pastoral, and yet neither side with Professor Herrmann[3] nor hold, with Mr. "R. W. R.,"[4] that Vergil, Gallus, and Octavian alike belonged to a highly select and very private

---

[1] Notes to chapter vi will be found on pages 245–247.

literary and dramatic society, whose performances, kept hidden from the public because of the Roman prejudice against acting and actors, lie behind sundry episodes in the poems. Here as so often in scientific or literary investigations (and the examination of ancient poems is both) we must keep an open mind, judge each case on its merits and not assume that, because a certain technique is used in one work, it must be employed in another, nor yet that, if it is missing in the one, the other cannot have it. A great writer has his style, but he is not tied to one procedure; Tacitus, for instance, was not prevented from imitating and improving on Sallust in his historical works because he had written the *Dialogue on Orators* in the Ciceronian tradition, nor St. Augustine from employing popular Latin in his sermons when he did not do so in the *De Ciuitate Dei*. It is perfectly possible that Vergil sedulously avoided allegory in most of his poems, yet used it in two or three. Let us look closely at the crucial example.

The fifth Eclogue, according to the regular rule,[5] is dramatic in form. Two shepherds, Menalcas and a younger companion, Mopsus, have just met, and Menalcas suggests that they should sit down in a grove of hazels and elms which stands hard by. Mopsus is quite willing, but points out a cave a little farther on as an even better place. As they walk towards it, Menalcas says, "Amyntas is your only rival hereabouts," and Mopsus, who is somewhat piqued, answers that Amyntas might as well try to rival Apollo and be done with it. By this time they are at the cave, and Menalcas asks Mopsus to sing, suggesting a number of subjects, to which we must return presently. Mopsus prefers to sing a new song which he has just composed, words and music, and written down on what is apparently the country substitute for paper, beech-bark;[6] let Amyntas try to rival it. Menalcas hastily soothes his feelings by assuring him that Amyntas is hopelessly inferior to him, and Mopsus begins with a lament for the death of Daphnis. Menalcas praises him highly, and answers with a song of his own, celebrating the apotheosis of this same Daphnis. With many compliments, they exchange presents, Mopsus giving Menalcas a very fine sheep-hook and Menalcas giving him the pipe on which the second and third Eclogues were composed.[7]

This poem, which in itself and quite apart from all literary and historical associations is singularly beautiful and melodious, even for Vergil, at once smacks of allegory, or at least of the using of a conventional pastoral name for a real person. Menalcas, as we have already seen, is in all probability Vergil himself. The natural corollary would be that Mopsus is some friend, personal or literary, of Vergil, and indeed more than one attempt has been made to identify him. Herrmann thinks he is Domitius Marsus,[8] not an impossible idea in itself, since Marsus lived to write some lines on the deaths of Vergil and Tibullus, but the theory lacks anything which could be called proof; Phillimore[9] ingeniously defends an old opinion that he is Aemilius Macer, and sets out to prove it as follows. Menalcas suggests that Mopsus may have something composed on the subjects of *aut Phyllidis ignes aut Alconis laudes aut iurgia Codri*. It so happens that the interpretation of these words is none too certain; does *Phyllidis ignes* mean the passion someone feels for Phyllis, or the passion she feels for someone else, and is Phyllis simply a country girl, as she is for instance in III, 76 and 78, or the mythological heroine of that name? If the latter, the story of her love for the faithless Demophon is well known enough[10] and might well interest Macer, for it is a learned sort of theme, treated by Alexandrians and their pupils the neoterics. Besides, in the form of the story which Servius gives[11] she turned into an almond tree, which for the first time put forth leaves when Demophon remorsefully threw his arms about it; Macer was not without interest in stories of metamorphoses, for he seems to have written a poem on the subject, the *Ornithogonia*, although the people in it were turned, not into trees, but into birds. Alcon might be the famous Cretan archer, the Greek William Tell, who was especially renowned for shooting a snake which had coiled about his little son, without hurting the child.[12] Codrus is rather more complicated, whether the *iurgia* are pieces of abuse uttered by or against him. Servius[13] thinks that Kodros, king of Athens, is meant, and the "abuse" is that by which, in the well-known story, he incited a Peloponnesian soldier to kill him when he was disguised as a poor man. But I fear that all such theories, ancient or modern, attractive though it might be to recognise another literary acquaintance of Vergil in this poem, must be abandoned. Bucolic poetry has its own rules, and one of them is that the ordinary mythological stories are not told by the shepherds, however conventionalised. For instance, Polyphemos, as we have seen, is a pastoral figure and he is also Homeric; but pastoral poetry does not tell of his dealings with Odysseus, save for a passing reference,[14] keeping to what I suppose to have been the local Sicilian or Aitnaian legend of how he loved Galateia the sea-nymph. A pastoral which told the story of Kodros' heroism would simply not be a pastoral at all; Phyllis and her woes belong to romantic poetry, elegiac or other, of the amatory type. In other words, however wild and savage we choose to make the scenery in which her unhappy story is placed, the telling is of the city and not of the country. Alkon might just, at a pinch, come into a bucolic poem at the price of becoming some kind of herdsman. So at least two of the three themes vanish from the list, and with them the name of any poet of Macer's type. Macer might well be mentioned, as Varius, Cinna, and Pollio are,[15] regardless of the sort of works he composed; he would not be asked to sing in a pastoral, for the same reason that an organist, in real life, would not be invited to be first violin in an orchestra, though every member of it might greatly value his skill and knowledge.

But Codrus is not yet dismissed. The name turns up in another Eclogue, the seventh, as that of a poet of high rank. There Corydon, the winning singer, asks to be given poetical talent like that of Codrus, if he is to continue in the art at all; his rival Thyrsis asks for a crown of poetry which shall make this Codrus burst with envy.[16] Here Daniel's Servius adds the vague information that "Codrus was a poet of those days, as Valgius mentions in his elegies." The Verona scholiast[17] is more definite. "Many," he says, "understand Codrus to be Vergil, others suppose he is Cornificius, some Helvius Cinna, of whom he [Vergil] thinks well. In like manner Valgius in his elegies has a complimentary mention of this Codrus, and in a certain eclogue [*ecloga;* it cannot be a pastoral poem, for that is never in elegiacs; but there seems no reason why *Eclogae* should not have been Valgius' title, since an elegiac writer is as well entitled as a bucolic poet to put forth "selections" from his unpublished works] he says of him,

> And Codrus sings as, Cinna, thou didst sing,
> And with thy numbers makes his harp-cords ring.
>
> Codrusque ille canit quali tu uoce canebas,
> atque solet numeros dicere, Cinna, tuos.

Valgius Rufus, whom Ovid knew,[18] was certainly in a position to judge of this Codrus, and when he says that he sang with Cinna's voice and numbers, he means, no doubt correctly, that Codrus was a learned poet of the type of Helvius Cinna, thus ridding us of the identification with Cinna himself and with Vergil, who, though learned enough, wrote a very different style. But still we are no nearer understanding who Codrus was. The name would be a very easy disguise of Cordus, but the only writer we know who had that cognomen was Cremutius Cordus, a historian and not a poet at all, besides being too late for Vergil at thirty years old or so to have known his works; he came to a tragic end under Tiberius.[19] Thus, if he is anyone of whom we know anything, Cornificius, the friend of Catullus, remains the most probable person, and we shall see presently that it is far from certain that Vergil would want to rail at Cornificius. Or, if we take the genitive *Codri* as subjective, we do not know that the hypothetical Cornificius railed at any person, at least in his poems. It would of course be easy to imagine him writing a work of learned abuse in the style of Euphorion's *Chiliades* or Kallimachos' *Ibis*, as Ovid did later, being in the same tradition; but we have not a scrap of evidence that he ever did anything of the kind. Besides, Mopsus is invited to sing one of his own poems, not an extract from another's. Furthermore, we have no warrant that the Codrus of the fifth Eclogue is the Codrus of the seventh, and finally and most conclusively, Vergil himself tells us that he, Vergil, and no one else, wrote Mopsus' song for him,[20] in other words, that Mopsus is a purely imaginary figure, not Aemilius Macer or anyone else, and therefore contemporary allusions are not to be assumed in the framework of the poem.

But now let us come to the songs which the two shepherds sing to each other (in plain English, to the two short poems), one of lament and the other of triumph, which Vergil has seen fit to insert in the pretty framework of a friendly meeting near a cave somewhere, perhaps, in those hill-pastures to the north of the Mantuan territory which, as we have already seen, provide the background for so many of the Eclogues.

Mopsus, to whom his courteous friend gives first place despite his tenderer years,[21] sings for just two dozen beautiful lines of the universal grief at the death of Daphnis. The lad's mother clasped his body and railed on the gods and the stars (astrology was in vogue then, though less of a universal craze than it later became) for their cruelty. No herdsmen took their cattle to water on that day of mourning, for the beasts would not drink nor touch their pasture, for sorrow that the great herdsman[22] was gone from them. Even the wild things, the very lions of northern Africa, wailed for his death, nay, the inanimate objects, the rocks and hills (if hills are quite inanimate in ancient poetry, which seems dimly to remember the times when a mountain was also a mountain-god or daimon) bear witness to the universality of the lamentation. For Daphnis was a Dionysiac being, one who, like the god himself, could drive tigers for his team, and he introduced the cult of his deity. After his loss, the very gods of the country-side departed and husbandry perforce ceased. There is now nothing left to do save to make a place of shade and fountains and there carve above the burial-mound the epitaph which Daphnis himself would have.

Having listened to this dirge, which even for Vergil is beautiful, Menalcas takes up his parable. Daphnis is not dead, but glorified. Milton took a hint here and worked it out in his own original and magnificent way for the ending of *Lycidas*. All the country-side, says Menalcas, and all its deities rejoice; nature is at peace, for Daphnis is kind and loves quiet. Wolves no longer hunt the flocks, nor men the deer, and even the wooded hills, which formerly testified to the lamentation of all nature, now lift up their voices to the very stars for delight, till every bush cries in the singer's ears that Daphnis is a god. So Menalcas will institute his cult and continue it summer and winter, with rustic sports and mirth, and this shall last for ever, alongside of the worship of the older deities of the corn and wine.

Once more, so far as the mere getting at the sense of the words is concerned, the poem is easy enough. Any tolerable Latinist could make a translation which should produce, in his vernacular, some portion of the effect of Vergil's original. But, and this again is usual, when this is done, all is yet to do. "Vergil," says Cartault in another context, "is a very careful writer, who says only what he wishes to say, a writer whom it is essential to read very closely if we would plunge down to the depths of his thought, and it is this thought which we must grasp, while the commentators [he adds "on the fourth Eclogue," but it is not only of this that it is true] seem especially bent on thrusting each his own thought upon him."[23] Let us look for a few moments at the thoughts which commentators, right or wrong, have somewhat zealously thrust upon the fifth Bucolic.

Servius,[24] who as we have seen is not very fond of allegorical interpretations, is nevertheless fair-minded enough to mention them. "Many," he remarks, "suppose that in this passage the literal Daphnis is lamented, a certain shepherd. Others assert that Julius Caesar is meant, who was killed in the Senate by Cassius and Brutus with twenty-three wounds, wherefore, they will have it, the words 'by a cruel death' (20) are used. Others think that Quintilius Varus is meant, a kinsman of Vergil, concerning whom Horace also [here he cites a few words from one of Horace's Odes, I, 24]. But after all, 'cruel death' could be used of anyone." This does not exhaust the ancient ideas about this poem. Donatus,[25] giving an account of Vergil's family, says, "He did not lose his parents till he was full grown, by which time his father was blind; he also lost two brothers, Silo, still a child, and Flaccus, then a grown man, whose death he bewails under the name of Daphnis."

Of these, I think, Quintilius Varus need not detain us long. That he was a kinsman of Vergil is absurd, and he died in 730/24 or 731/23, a full decade and more later than anything in the *Bucolics* can possibly be.[26] Vergil himself outlived him but five years. The theory is the blundering construction of some ancient sciolist who imagined that the

Varus of Eclogues VI and IX was Quintilius and not Alfenus. Flaccus, Vergil's brother, is a most misty person and his cognomen highly suspicious. Brothers, it is true, had not necessarily the same cognomen in that age, and because another son of Vergil's parents (or of his mother remarried after his father's death, a purely arbitrary supposition) might be Vergilius, must be if he was the poet's full brother, he need not also be Maro. But it is at least curious that the cognomen should be that of Vergil's friend Horace, as we call the poet Q. Horatius Flaccus. My conjecture is simply that someone somewhere spoke of the two poets metaphorically as brethren (so a very different pair, Bavius and Mevius, are called brothers by Domitius Marsus),[27] and a literal-minded reader accepted this at its face value. Silo, dying early and entering into no literary context, may perhaps be a real person; at least it is not very apparent why he should have been invented. So, I think, though in itself the story is not incredible or nearly so absurd as some ancient and modern fictions about Vergil, we may safely let Flaccus sink back into his native nothingness.

But Julius Caesar, at least, is a solid historical person, and that a poet who favoured his cause and elsewhere wrote glowingly of his star[28] should write a lament for his death and a hymn to his godhead is nowise impossible or even unlikely. This is perhaps especially true of a Transpadane poet, for that was one of the regions which had most decidedly liked and supported the great Dictator. Moreover, it was in Octavian's time and at his wish that the citizenship had been extended to Hither Gaul,[29] and to compliment his adopted father was to compliment him. Caesar, then, remains on our list, and we must return to him after considering whether any other candidate appears for this poetical election.

One of the most acute biographers of Vergil, Professor Tenney Frank, whom I have had occasion to quote already more than once, is strongly of the opinion[30] that Daphnis is no other than the poet Cornificius. His arguments are in substance as follows. Of the two traditions concerning Vergil's attitude to Cornificius, that he liked him and that they were enemies, the former has been shown to be the earlier and better.[31] Hence there is nothing out of the way in his complimenting a poet of some eminence belonging to that same neoteric group which had certainly had some influence, though how much is perhaps a matter of opinion, on himself. This is even more likely because Cornificius was the last survivor of the school. Now Cornificius ended his days a republican and was murdered, probably early in 713/41, holding Africa on behalf of Brutus and Cassius. It would not, therefore, have been politic to praise him too openly (indeed his name never occurs in the *Eclogues*, unless the Codrus of No. VII is he). But a disguised panegyric would pass; Octavian was not a man of such petty jealousies as to pry into every allusion in poetry, especially one like this which, as we shall show presently, might, rightly or wrongly, be taken quite literally as a lament for and apotheosis of a harmless mythological figure. The dates would fit well enough; Vergil wrote No. V before No. IX,[32] that is to say, earlier than sometime in 714/40, whence 713/41 is a perfectly possible year for him to have composed it.

The objection to this attractive theory is, as I think, mainly the lack of any positive evidence for it. In the first place, it is necessary to make it at least probable that Vergil always has some real topic in mind for the more elaborate of his bucolic songs, when they profess to refer to someone by name; that, although Mopsus and Menalcas may be figures of the poet's imagination, at least the former of them, the people of whom they sing should have some historical existence. But no such thing can be made probable; we remember, for example, the elaborate song of Corydon to a phantasmal Alexis[33] and the energy with which a nonexistent Mopsus is attacked and a fictitious Daphnis charmed in No. VIII.[34] There is, then, no reason in Vergil's general technique why another Daphnis who owes his existence to fancy or reading should not be lamented and then exalted to the gods. It may be worth while to look closer at the two songs and their framework, to see if we can find anything which fits the little we know of Cornificius particularly well.

I confess I can find very little. Most of the language of both songs is vaguely general, and cannot help us in an identification. However, it might be held that it is particularly appropriate for "Phoenician" or "Punic" lions (*Poenos leones*)[35] to be said to lament the death of one who died in Africa. That Daphnis yoked Armenian tigers to his car and taught the rites of Bakchos[36] would fit in very well with a poet if we knew that he wrote some kind of a Dionysiac poem, even one in which the god plays as large a part as he does in Catullus' *Peleus and Thetis;* for it is a common figure of speech to say that a poet does that which he describes someone as doing. Unfortunately, we know so little of Cornificius' work that we cannot say whether or not he ever thought of writing such a poem. Again, the description of the tomb which Daphnis[37] ordered for himself might well be an allusion; it would be neither unlikely, unpoetical, nor un-Alexandrian if Cornificius had written somewhere, "I hope I may be buried, when I die, near shade and water, with a line or two over me to tell men who I was." It would also be quite in keeping with the sort of poetry his school wrote if he put such a wish into the mouth of one of his characters. Again, we are without evidence. Then, the association of Daphnis with Apollo[38] suits a poet excellently, and to say that Daphnis loved peaceful leisure, *otia*,[39] is not to contradict the character of a man of letters, however stormy the end of his life. Lastly, the fact that Daphnis taught Mopsus to sing[40] might be urged in Cornificius' favour; it would be at least conceivable that Vergil took this way of saying that he himself owed something to the dead poet's technique or the like. But all these are the merest threads of gossamer, not enough to uphold the lightest of theories, and are broken by one stubborn fact. Daphnis, whoever he may be, is represented as young, *puer*,[41] a very odd thing to insist upon if he stands for a man who had left youth well behind him and held a magisterial position of some importance. Of the scene in which Daphnis' mother bewails him we shall speak in a moment.

One of the strongest reasons for preferring to take Daphnis to be Julius Caesar is perhaps that in that case the second song, proclaiming him a god, is not extravagant compliment but simply official fact; Caesar had been deified some time before any date at which Vergil was likely to be working on Eclogue V. If Daphnis is Cornificius, Octavian might perhaps have stomached the exaltation of his opponent to the skies, if he read the riddle, with some such comment as that made by one of the worst of his successors, *sit diuus dum non sit uiuus*,[42] "let him have his heaven, only not here on earth." But if Caesar is meant, it would be a compliment after his own heart to the adopted father for whom he presumably felt real admiration and respect, and whose prestige was the very mainspring of his own machinery of state. It would be a pendant to the declaration in Eclogue I that he himself was a god, and due proportion would be kept, for in that Eclogue the new god receives a private cult from a single deeply obliged and humble man, a compliment which, if all tales be true, had been paid ere that to lesser people without any sort of formal deification,[43] whereas Daphnis is to have regular and formal feast-days, along with the greatest of the established gods of the country-side, attended apparently by all the rural population. Now it is notorious that Octavian, even after he became Augustus, would not hear of being personally worshipped by Italians; but he encouraged the cult of his deified nominal father. To show one peasant unofficially making sacrifice to Octavian and the whole country-side doing so to Julius would be to hint very strongly that the latter was one of those whose transcendent merits had earned them godhead, the former on his way to the same goal.

The matter must again be examined in the same way; do the songs show Daphnis the sort of god whom any skilled courtier or subtle flatterer would represent Julius Caesar to be, or ascribe to Daphnis, while still on earth, anything which could reasonably be said of Caesar, either literally (with or without friendly or respectful exaggeration) or through a metaphor tolerably likely to be understood? I have put the questions in this order because I think the crucial points concern rather the still living than the dead and deified Daphnis.

The new god, then, after two splendid lines which show him in his heavenly abode, is one at whose exaltation the country-side rejoices. This may pass; if Julius Caesar is meant, then he is presumably a god powerful in the whole world, or at least the Roman world, one whose will for good may be taken for granted in a hymn written to do him honour, and so the country and town alike will share in the benefits he bestows, but only the former is in place in a pastoral setting. But the next two lines are harder, when we remember that the greatest conqueror of that age and the greatest general since Hannibal is spoken of; they describe universal peace brought about by his wish:

> Nor wolf for sheep nor hunter's net for stag
> Plots mischief now; kind Daphnis loveth peace.
>
> nec lupus insidias pecori nec retia ceruis
> ulla dolum meditantur; amat bonus otia Daphnis.

Still, they are not indefensible. To anticipate for a moment what I shall have to discuss later,[44] we may suppose Vergil to mean this. The old *saeculum* came to an end when Caesar's star appeared,[45] and its wars and tumults with it. A new order of things is now arising, no other than the Golden Age, for in what other would wolves cease to prey on flocks and men to hunt stags, that is, both alike become vegetarian in diet? The picture agrees well enough, for instance, with Ovid's Golden Age,[46] when the "care-free nations dwelt in gentle peace" (the same word, *otia*, as in Vergil) and the only food was such things as grew of themselves, acorns, berries, and the like. We have here, it might be said, an anticipation of perhaps the grandest tribute ever paid by a loyal subject to a monarch not undeserving such exalted homage, the prediction of Augustus' reign of peace in the *Aeneid*,[47] and the praise of Julius earlier in the same poem.[48] The rest of the hymn merely gives some details of the new cult, and has nothing that makes for or against any identification of Daphnis with which I am acquainted.

But if we come to the lament, it seems to me that there are features in it which tell very strongly against Julius Caesar. Agreeably to the mention of Daphnis as a boy, which assuredly Caesar was not at the time of his death, we are told that his mother clasped his dead body and railed on the cruelty of the gods and the stars. It is of course a commonplace bit of historical knowledge that Julius Caesar's mother long predeceased him in the ordinary course of nature. Therefore those who still maintain the identification of Caesar with Daphnis have to suppose that the mother in question is the mother of his line, Venus. Mr. D. L. Drew, the latest thorough-going upholder of this view against Professor Tenney Frank who is known to me,[49] appeals to the literary parentage of the lament itself, which, as he rightly enough remarks, goes back not only to Theokritos' first Idyll, but also to the *Lament for Bion* and Bion's own *Lament for Adonis*. There,[50] Aphrodite behaves much like the "mother" here:

> When she beheld, when she was ware of Adonis' incurable wound, when she saw the red blood about his wasting thigh, she opened wide her arms and wailed, "Stay, Adonis, stay, hapless Adonis, that I may touch thee for the last time, that I may embrace thee and join my lips to thine. Rouse thee a little, Adonis, and give me back one last kiss; kiss me as hard as there is life left in thy kiss, till thy spirit flow from thy soul into my mouth and my heart, and I suck forth the sweet love-charm from thee, drink all thy love, and keep this kiss for Adonis' self, since thou, unhappy, escapest me, escapest far away, my Adonis, and goest to Acheron and its grim, savage king, while I, woe worth the day, live and am a goddess and cannot follow thee. Take my husband, Persephone, for thyself art far mightier than I, seeing that all beauty flows down to thee."

Save that Aphrodite does not rail upon the stars, astrology not being yet much in favor in Greek lands, she may be said to do what Vergil briefly describes his unnamed "mother" as doing. This point, then, may be conceded to those who maintain the Daphnis-Caesar equation. And it might be added that we could fancy Vergil moved to call Venus "mother," simply and without addition, by way of a sort of allusion to the opening words of Lucretius' poem, *Aeneadum genetrix*. We might also call Ovid[51] into the witness-box and notice that his Venus, terrified at the thought of the coming murder of Caesar, vainly implores the gods to intervene and, once the crime is under way, makes the usual sign of lamentation by beating her breast till she is consoled by Iuppiter. What Ovid says at great length, Vergil might be supposed to say briefly in treating of the same event.

But a few lines further on we meet a difficulty which I think insuperable. This is the passage which we used (p.

127) as an argument in favour of Cornificius, albeit a feeble one:

> Daphnis et Armenias curru subiungere tigris
> instituit, Daphnis thiasos inducere Bacchi
> et foliis lentas intexere mollibus hastas.

> Armenia's tigers yoked to draw his car,
> 'Twas Daphnis taught us Bakchos' revel-bands
> And pliant thyrsos-wands enwrapped in leaves.

How can this apply to Caesar? Servius indeed[52] boldly says that it does; "this," he tells us, "manifestly has to do with Caesar, for it is well known [*constat*] that he was the first to introduce the rites of Liber Pater into Rome." But, although many modern books repeat this after Servius,[53] I know not a scrap of independent evidence that Caesar ever did anything of the kind, and it seems to me most unlikely. Caesar was apparently quite uninterested in religious reforms, despite his position as Pontifex Maximus; he certainly was not himself a fervent worshipper of Dionysos, nor of any deity, but an Epicurean, if he can be said to have belonged to any school of philosophical or religious thought. I would credit the statement to the combination of some grammarian, who, knowing that Dionysiac rites were common and popular in Italy[54] about that time and believing that everything said of Daphnis must apply to Caesar somehow, put the two scraps of information together and made out the statement that Caesar was responsible, in some unknown way, for the flourishing of the cult. The most desperate attempt, it seems to me, to find something Dionysiac about the historical Julius is that of Mr. Drew, who produces from Pliny[55] a statement that elephants were used in Dionysos' triumph when he conquered India, and another from Suetonius[56] that Caesar had forty elephants in his Gaulish triumph. It is true that the elephant is a Dionysiac beast in some rather late accounts of the god and his eastern adventures;[57] but the very passage of Pliny which he adduces proves that the thing had been first done by Pompey at his African triumph, which agrees ill with the statement that Daphnis introduced the Dionysiac rites, if Daphnis be Caesar.

But let us make what assumption we will about the Dionysiac ritual; let us imagine that Caesar, as a measure for securing more popularity, took steps to make some form of the cult which looked doubtfully legal into a *religio licita;* let us fancy that it is all figurative, and that Vergil really means Caesar was a great civiliser and therefore implicitly compares him to Dionysos, the prototype of civilising conquerors;[58] let us suppose that he is equating him, through Dionysos, with Alexander, the model of so much late Dionysiac mythology; the rock upon which the Cornifician hypothesis split is still full in the fairway, for Caesar at the time of his death was anything but a boy, and there is no shadow of a reason why he should be called one for the sake of the allegory, if allegory it is. And, since there is no reason, why accuse Vergil (under the pretext that his allegories are "partial" only, or the like) of not knowing how to handle a figure perfectly familiar to him as a student of rhetoric and poetry? We know what he makes of allegory in passages where beyond all doubt he does use it; for instance, when he personifies Rumour,[59] though there are touches in the picture which are not necessary to it (it was not essential that Rumour should be the daughter of Earth, her youngest-born, produced in revengeful wrath against the Olympians, after the slaughter of the Giants, but it is appropriate, for Rumour is shown as a monster and Earth is the mother of monsters), yet there are none which are out of keeping with the idea the allegory is meant to illustrate. To get a parallel to a "partial allegory" in which Caesar at the time of his death is called a boy, we should have to find a poet who went out of his way to make Rumour resemble something very quiet and inconspicuous or notoriously good at keeping secrets. Add to this all the other difficulties, the curious passage about the mother already discussed, the quite unnecessary insistence on Daphnis as the music-teacher of the shepherd who laments for him[60] (unnecessary, that is to say, if he stands for anyone whose life was spent in pursuits so far removed from pastoral piping and singing), and the implication that both the lament and the apotheosis are stock subjects,[61] not suddenly thought of nor made up under the inspiration of the moment, and I think we must conclude that to make Daphnis equal Caesar it should be shown that the passage will not make sense if not allegorical and that no other identification will hold water.

Let us therefore try the old interpretation of Servius and Cartault,[62] who suppose that Daphnis is simply Daphnis, the mythological figure. Presumably he has nothing to do with the two persons of that name who appear elsewhere in Vergil, the Daphnis who in Eclogue VII calls Meliboeus to listen to the singing-contest[63] (although at a pinch this might be the same, seeing that Daphnis of the lament and of the myth is a skilled musician) and the vagrant husband or lover whom the girl in the next Eclogue draws home by her spells.[64] Aware though Vergil always was of the realities of the country-side, in the *Bucolics* he throws over the actual fields and woods the vague and romantic atmosphere of a world of Theokritean poetry, as seen through the eyes of Theokritos' imitators rather than that writer's own. It is a world in which the rough and ever-present necessity to make a living by continuous labour has yielded to what is incidental to the real country-side of the south, the native love of and skill in simple music and the unhurried atmosphere of the pastures. In such a world, ordinary shepherds might very well be named after the mythological originator of their genre of poetry, as after a kind of patron saint; and chronology is very vague, making it quite possible for this legendary figure to be known to persons one of whom is a contemporary poet in a pastoral disguise.

Looking now at the best-known picture of Daphnis, that given by Theokritos,[65] we find that he was a victim of the wrath of Aphrodite. What the precise quarrel between them was and what form her vengeance took, we can only guess; in Stesichoros[66] it would appear that Daphnis was one of the many mythological figures who married a fairy bride and suffered for it. We learn that a nymph loved him, but made the condition that he should accept the favours of no one else; that a princess, being enamoured of his beauty, won him to her desires by making him drunk, and that the nymph blinded him. No such tale lies behind Theokritos, who seems to imply that Daphnis refuses to love at all, being a kind of pastoral Hippolytos, and that Aphrodite, to punish him, inflicts on him a strong passion for someone perfectly willing to reciprocate it, so that in the end he dies of the yearning which, to spite the goddess and her son, he will not satisfy.[67] It is a strange tale enough and we do not know where he found it, but it is a not impossible prelude to Vergil's two songs. This Daphnis was young and handsome; there is no reason why his mother should not have been there to lament him, the more so as she was a nymph and therefore long-lived if not immortal; that she should rail on the cruelty of the gods (Aphrodite and Eros, who had killed her son, the others, who had permitted it) was most natural, and the stars, that is to say Fate, would come in for their share of the blame with equal propriety. That the very lions mourned for him is Theokritos' own statement, and Vergil, in making them Punic, may have already been moved by the doubts of a literal-minded commentator on Theokritos, who points out that there are no lions in Sicily and suggests an emendation to get around the difficulty.[68] It is not known how Vergil came by the next detail, that Daphnis introduced the rites of Dionysos, but the legend seems to have ramified in all manner of directions, and may somewhere have touched the wide-reaching mythology of Dionysos, as it certainly did that of Herakles.[69] Or again, there seems to be no reason why Vergil should not have invented it for himself; Dionysos, as already mentioned, was popular in Italy, and it may have seemed to him an especially appropriate deed for a benefactor of the country-side to bring in his rites, nay, the more appropriate since, to him at all events, they were closely connected with the old rustic mummeries to Liber Pater which interested him alike as an antiquarian and as a country-bred boy.[70] If Daphnis is really Daphnis, it is easier to see why the country-side became barren and deserted by its gods when he died;[71] and the mention of Apollo in such a connection is particularly neat, for Daphnis was a herdsman, therefore under the protection of Apollo Nomios; he was also dear to the Muses,[72] therefore to their Leader. The rustic grave might well be a rustic hero-shrine.

The real Daphnis also might by a quite easy transition be declared a god, and a celestial one, for Daphnis was the son of Hermes, and when he lost his sight, he called on his father for aid, and Hermes came and snatched him away to heaven.[73] Vergil does not follow this form of the legend exactly, for his Daphnis is dead and not blind, but he may well have known and deliberately modified it. The details, such as they are, of his cult do not tell for or against any theory, for it does not appear that Daphnis was ever really worshipped,[74] hence they are imaginary details of a supposed rustic ceremonial, with the usual libations, feasting, singing and dancing, such as took place on hundreds of occasions all up and down the ancient country-side, Greek and Roman.

We seem therefore to be left with nothing that tells against the supposition that Daphnis is simply Daphnis save the apparent declaration that with his departure to a new and higher life the Golden Age has revisited the world. But it is to be noticed that Vergil never makes Menalcas say that the peaceful state of things he describes will last for ever, or even for any length of time. Menalcas is answering Mopsus' lamentations, that at Daphnis' death the beasts were too woebegone to eat or drink, by the assurance that at his apotheosis they were so joyful that the fiercest of them spared their natural prey and men ceased to hunt them. One, like the other, might be due to a passing emotion.

Finally, if we suppose that Vergil, when he speaks of Daphnis, means simply that which he says, we have in the two songs a recognisable literary and religious type, the lamentation for the dying god followed by the rejoicing at his resurrection (in this case his translation to heaven). It was a type of ceremonial perfectly familiar to Vergil, from reading if not from observation, a little modified from the ritual of Adonis. It seems to me but a small assumption to make that, knowing of that cult, he amused himself by imagining one something like it, the worship of another deity once mortal and, in this life, handsome, young, and unfortunate, as Adonis was, but, unlike him, apparently gone permanently and not temporarily away from this world. I have already suggested, what is not at all obscure, a resemblance to the Euripidean Hippolytos; it may be added that in at least one version of the story Daphnis, like Hippolytos, was a favourite of Artemis,[75] and it is even conceivable that Theokritos had before him some working-out of the legend which turned upon the rivalry of the two goddesses, on the lines of Euripides' play. It is to be remembered that Hippolytos also had his cult,[76] and that to Vergil it was a cult shared by Italy, in the grove of Diana at Nemi, where antiquarian fancy saw the son of Theseus in Virbius.[77]

We have therefore but little ground for assuming that Vergil allegorises in this Eclogue, for there is next to no real difficulty in interpreting the poem without supposing a hidden meaning. No more can be said for the allegorical interpretations than that they are not impossible in principle; that the equation, for example, of Daphnis with Cornificius has nothing absurd or inconceivable in it, but merely suffers from lack of positive evidence and one real difficulty, already seen, that Cornificius was far past his boyhood.

And having so far gone through seven of the ten poems, including six of those said by Servius to be properly bucolic, let us look back for a moment and see what part allegorical or figurative language plays in them. All are agreed that Nos. I and IX are in a sense allegorical, though the exact meaning is in some doubt. Nos. II and III are by almost common consent simply sketches of country life, that and no more, with such departures from realism as are called for by poetical conventions easily understood. No. X, we have seen, owes a certain amount to the admiration of Vergil for his friend and fellow poet Gallus, taking the shape of actual imitation of the latter's works. No. VI is not without traces of the same influence, though its exact nature and extent are far from settled to everyone's satisfaction. Neither contains anything which could be properly called an allegory, though both have a certain amount of conventional and therefore, if we like to say so, figurative language, a walk by Permessos for example meaning the beginning of a poetical career. On the whole, then, there is in the Eclogues rather less than one might expect of hidden meaning, and especially of figurative allusion to the author's own circumstances and the troubled times in which he lived. The student who has not much detailed acquaintance with the history of that age, even the specialist who knows how many are the gaps in our knowledge of the period, may enjoy them with a clear conscience, as knowing that what they tell us is not so very different from what contemporary readers found in them.

CHAPTER VII

SOME THEOKRITEAN IMITATIONS

To THOSE who like poetry better than puzzles, it is a relief to leave the group of Eclogues we have been discussing for the less controversial company of the seventh and eighth. To decide who Daphnis is or the relation between the joys of Tityrus and the woes of Vergil has something of the stimulus of a detective story; but even Miss Sayers is not the whole of English literature, excellent though she is, nor Phoebe Atwood Taylor the only name to give American fiction a place in the sun. So also there are other interests in Vergil besides the following of clues, too often to dead ends, and it is these other interests which seem to have been nearest the poet's own heart. This study will raise no questions save those of literary criticism pure and simple; where did Vergil get his material, how did he use it, to what extent is he original, what is the precise point of some of the brilliant lines he puts into the mouths of his characters?

For Eclogue VII the question of source is fairly simple. There is a pretty little poem, containing some of the sweetest and most delicate lines in Alexandrian verse, which has come down to us under the name of Theokritos (it is conventionally numbered VIII among his Idylls), but most certainly is not his, if only because it makes an occasional blunder in its Doric,[1] which a native speaker, such as Theokritos himself was, could not have made. Two shepherd-boys, one of them an otherwise unknown Menalkas, the other Daphnis, apparently the very Daphnis of Theokritos' first Idyll and Vergil's fifth Eclogue, meet and challenge each other to a friendly but serious duel of song. A casual goatherd comes in answer to their shouts and consents to act as umpire. They cast lots, and Menalkas begins. He

[1] Notes to chapter vii will be found on pages 248-252.

sings a little poem, two elegiac couplets, gracefully asking the woods and rivers to tend his lambs and also to treat Daphnis well. Daphnis, who now has the more difficult task of answering (more difficult, because the first singer may take what subject he pleases and handle it how he will, while the second is constrained to follow his lead, paralleling or contrasting everything in his song with as nearly as possible the same arrangement and rhythm),[2] utters a similar appeal. Now the match begins in earnest. It is spring everywhere, sings Menalkas,[3] and all flourishes where the lovely Nais treads, but if she should depart, everything, the herds and the herdsman, will dry up. Daphnis answers with exactly similar lines, in which the coming and going of Milon (who Milon is, does not appear and matters not in the least) have the same effect. Menalkas appropriates this Milon for himself and bids his he-goat go and summon him from where he sits in the wood, to remind him that a herdsman's life is no low thing, seeing that Proteus himself, who is a god, yet herds the cattle of the sea. Daphnis departs from Menalkas' pattern rather widely, but with a charming result; he sings of the joys of herding in Sicily, where the action naturally takes place, but that part of Sicily where the real business of life in the country is love-making:

> μή μοι γᾶν Πέλοπος, μή μοι χρύσεια[4] τάλαντα
> εἴη ἔχειν, μηδὲ πρόσθε θέειν ἀνέμων,
> ἀλλ' ὑπὸ τᾷ πέτρᾳ τᾷδ' ᾀσομαι ἀγκὰς ἔχων τύ,
> σύννομα μᾶλ' ἐσορῶν τὰν Σικέλαν ἐς ἅλα.

> Not Pelops' realm nor store of gold I choose
> Nor swiftest feet, with swiftest winds to vie,
> But, thou beside me, gazing on our ewes,
> Towards the Sicilian sea to look and lie.

Daphnis has scored, but it was by cheating and the umpire should have pulled him up; his verses do not nearly correspond to those of Menalkas in the position of their pauses and the distribution of their subject, and but roughly in the subject itself. But the author was too fond of his own pretty creation to disqualify it. Menalkas goes on with another quatrain, on the inevitability of loving when Zeus himself is a lover of women, and no doubt Daphnis answered with another on the charms of the youth of a man's own sex, with a like illustration from mythology,[5] but by some misfortune that is lost. Now Menalkas begins another section of the contest, with a comparatively long entry (eight lines), bidding his dog be watchful and his sheep feed lustily and make plenty of milk. Once more Daphnis answers off the point; a girl has looked at him and said "How pretty!" when she saw his heifers, but he paid no attention to her, for (this seems to be the connection, if any) there are better things than exchanging compliments in the country where the heifers low sweetly and smell sweetly and one can lie at ease under the open sky by the waterside. Here the goatherd, who is grossly partial, for Daphnis has really not kept to the rules (perhaps the author did not know them, or they were made stricter between his time and Vergil's) declares him the victor and asks for lessons at a fee which he names, a fine she-goat that is a first-class milker. Daphnis exults, Menalkas mourns, and from that day on Daphnis prospers till on growing old enough he marries a Naid.

It is a delightful little poem, despite some fairly obvious defects, and despite, what the author could not help, the miscopyings of some stupid scribes; I say nothing of the mishandlings of some stupider editors. Vergil evidently liked it, whether or not he anticipated Valckenaer in seeing that Theokritos was not its author. It seems worth while to spend a little time in seeing what he made, in his more formal and yet more natural Latin (after all, he was writing his own language conventionalised, while the Greek was using a dialect he had learned out of books) of this pretty artificiality of an unknown date.

Perhaps by way of bowing his acknowledgements to the original, perhaps merely because he liked the name, he introduces a Daphnis in the first line of his seventh Eclogue. This is not one of the competitors, and whether or not he is the Daphnis of the other passages we have discussed, or of the Greek original, is neither knowable nor important. He seems to be acting as judge, or at least a sort of master of ceremonies, and he hails Meliboeus (probably not the Meliboeus of Eclogue I, though again it is no matter) and invites him to leave searching for a he-goat which, Daphnis assures him, is already found, and come to listen to the competition between Corydon and Thyrsis. Meliboeus' conscience is uneasy (a touch of the *facetum* which we found Vergil possessing peeps through here), because he knows he should go home and shut up the young lambs before they suck the ewes dry and leave no milk to make cheese; but he yields to the invitation, for such a match is no everyday affair. The preliminaries are all settled before he arrives; Vergil never imitates slavishly and he had used the little squabble between the pseudo-Theokritos' shepherds as to what they should wager in another place already.[6] But the competitors are described in a paraphrase of the Greek introduction of them,[7] and it is added that they were both Arkadians, despite the fact that the Mincio is in sight.[8] In other words, although he may use descriptions of his native scenery for the background, Vergil is going to take us into the same sort of Italy as the Sicily of his original, the pastoral world which remains undisturbed by economic changes, settlements of intrusive veterans, and all the other distresses which befall the Mantuas of this too solid earth. Here, if we like, is not exactly an allegory, but a recognised convention; an Arkadian may be simply a pastoral poet, a literary figure. The two young men, having, we may say, something of a Roman sense of law and order despite their literary nationality, play their game very strictly in accordance with the rules, and one of the many good things about the poem is its originality. Corydon begins with an appeal to the Muses, or, as he calls them (for he is a learned goatherd, as befits one so purely of literature which has said good-bye to realism for the moment), the Nymphs of the fountain Libethros, an ancient place of their cult in Boiotia. He is a modest but ambitious young poet;[9] if they will make him as great as Codrus (whether Codrus is Cornificius or not),[10] so; if not, he will simply abandon poetry. Thyrsis appeals, not to the Muses (he is confident of them), but to the shepherds of Arkadia to garland him and make Codrus burst with envy. This ends the first round of the contest; both have used four-line stanzas, but in hexameters throughout, Vergil not caring to follow his model in putting elegiacs into a pastoral. So far, the two are pretty equal, the difference in tone being part of the game. Now Corydon scores. He makes a poetical vow to Artemis in the name of one Micon, a little hunter (a typically Vergilian use of his original; there is no huntsman in the Greek, but Menalkas appeals to the wolf to be merciful and to his dog to be watchful, because he is so little, μικκός, to have charge of a flock, and the name Micon with its epithet of *paruus* doubly echoes this). Micon dedicates his spoils, a boar's head and a deer's antlers, but if the skill which won them is no accident,[11] but the abiding gift of the goddess, she shall have a marble statue. Thyrsis tries to outbid this and does it badly; he represents himself as a gardener making a vow to Priapos. So far, excellent, the peaceful pursuit against the more adventurous, the lustful god against the chaste goddess. But he does not go on so well; the gardener, though he complains of his poverty and can promise but a small offering, has a marble Priapos already and is going to give the god a golden (or at least gilt) statue if the flock which he also possesses increases as it should. The next pair of quatrains is evenly and beautifully balanced. Corydon sings to Galatea; whether or not he is the Corydon of Eclogue II, he is Polyphemos as well as himself for the moment, for he calls her a Nereid, *Nerine Galatea*, and brings in a graceful reminiscence of Theokritos' eleventh Idyll. He bids her, however, come to him, not to Cyclops, when the day is over and the cattle come home. Thyrsis rises to the occasion excellently, and sings Galatea's reply. She hopes Corydon will despise and cast her off if she does not think this endless day as long as a year. Will the cattle never be done feeding?[12] Corydon makes a fresh and promising attempt; he begs some of the lovely things of summer, the mossy fountains and the soft grass, *somno mollior herba*,[13] which surrounds them, the strawberry-tree which casts a flickering shadow over all, to shield his flock from the heat of the dog-days. But Thyrsis is ready for him and replies with a jolly picture of winter, perhaps a trifle injured by a not fully appropriate comparison at the end.[14] The next quatrains are even better fitted together; Corydon declares that the beauty of the landscape at its best would vanish if Alexis were to depart; Thyrsis answers that a scene of drought and desolation which he conjures up will be replaced by glorious rain if Phyllis will come. The two singers form a sort of chiasmus with each other,[15] loveliness to desolation in Corydon's song, drought to rain and plenty in Thyrsis'. Now Corydon has a pretty conceit. Every god has his favourite tree, but Phyllis has a fancy for hazels. If she keeps to this preference, he will acknowledge that the hazel is the finest tree in wood or orchard. Thyrsis cannot think of anything quite fitting the occasion, but he makes a brave effort; several trees are each the finest in its own place, ashes in the woods, pines in parks, and so on; but if Lycidas will come to see him oftener, then Lycidas will be handsomer than the handsomest of them all. It is a little forced, and Vergil means it to be so. Therefore, perhaps after more songs,[16] it is Corydon who wins the contest, and is acknowledged (here is a Vergilian figure which has more than once given trouble to commentators, expecially the kind who measure a poet's possibilities by their own ways of expressing things) to be—Corydon; there is no higher praise.[17]

As with most poems of this sort, there has been disputation among the learned as to why Corydon wins; indeed, it is not over-easy to write a satisfactory poem involving such a contest in which the reader shall be convinced that the verdict is just. The poet, if he is true to his art, will not put bad verses or poor sense into the mouth of the loser, and if he does not, how shall he be sure that his taste and even that of a sympathetic reader will coincide? W. Baehrens, for instance, is sure that Vergil has simply given the victory to the singer whose character he prefers,[18] the proud but shy Corydon against the self-confident and materialistic Thyrsis. The poet was himself much more like the former than the latter in temperament. But I think there is more art in the poem than this. Thyrsis sings well, as he should, for Meliboeus implies[19] that the two were evenly balanced and the competition between them keen; therefore to make Thyrsis sing any but good poetry would be especially out of place. Nor does Corydon win by the near approach to cheating which gains Daphnis his victory in the Greek original, for he is the leader (an advantage in itself, as already pointed out) and so has no forms which he must imitate on pain of disqualification. Thyrsis plays fair and follows Corydon's lead closely, but Vergil has allowed him some very slight departures from good taste and formal perfection, as has been well pointed out by Mr. F. H. Sandbach.[20] First, there are some tiny metrical lapses, hardly to be detected by an ear less attuned to the finest Latin rhythms than the poet's own, and discoverable by moderns only at the cost of examining his works under a critical microscope and seeing what rules he himself follows. Thyrsis ends a line (35) with a spondee, *at tu*, immediately preceded by a strong pause in the sense. Vergil does not do this except under quite elaborate restrictions, which are not obeyed here. Elsewhere, in 41, he elides the second syllable of *tibi*,

> immo ego Sardoniis uidear tibi amarior herbis,

and that in the fourth foot and before a word to which it does not closely belong. Vergil's regular practice is, when he elides the word at all, a proceeding of which he is not fond, for it is very short and he does not much like slurring over half of it, to do so in the second foot or before a word closely connected with it in grammar. Vergil perhaps is hinting to some of his less careful contemporaries that there are some things it is not well to do in the hexameter, even though they are in agreement with its general laws, because they lack the acme of euphony which a poet should aim after, unless he is deliberately harsh for some special reason. But to discuss the minuter rules of that most complicated verse with its seeming simplicity would take us too far afield and quite outside my competence. I have already mentioned Thyrsis' somewhat inconsistent offering to Priapos, which seems to come at once from a man very poor and fairly well off; he has at least one other turn at which the judge might cavil. In our warm winter quarters, he says, we care as much for the chilly north wind as "the wolf does for the numbers of a flock, or rivers in spate for their banks." Now as a vigorous simile, this is not without its merits, or Vergil would not have put it into Thyrsis' mouth; but that it is the best simile may be doubted. The original is in a little pseudo-Theokritean poem, where yet another Menalkas (but he might be the same one as in the eighth Idyll, for he and Daphnis sing each a song) is once more pretending to be Polyphemos, this time safe in his cavern and defying the weather; the lusty giant, wrapped about with sheepskins and sitting at a roaring fire which cooks his dinner, minds the winter no more "than a toothless man does filberts when he can get fine meal."[21] To my thinking at least, this is a good rustic comparison. The Cyclops will not even turn his head to see what kind of weather it is out-of-doors; the rain and wind are simply no concern of his, any more than a kind of food which he could not possibly eat is the concern of a man who is already well supplied with what he wants. But in Vergil, is the wolf quite the right animal? He is not on the defensive, as the man in the song is, against anything; the sheep would not in any case attack him and could not hurt him. The well-protected man is made safe against something which might in other circumstances hurt him seriously, the chill of the winter with a howling north wind coming off the Alps. And certainly the banks (not dams) would not interfere much with the river in any case. I have already said that Thyrsis' last quatrain is not so perfect as it might be. So we may say that the umpire gives a proper and fair decision; while as for Vergil's preference of one character to the other, that probably is true, but he also was artist enough (when was he anything else?) to make his less likable shepherd, whom he would have lose, the less able poet, though by no means a bad one.

A more elaborate poem than this very delectable trifle of a contest in song is the eighth Eclogue, one of those in which Vergil, so far as we can judge, moves furthest away from his Greek models and ventures deepest into originality. Even in form it is a little strange; though, being narrative, it fits its even number well enough,[22] still it is practically dramatic, for the narrator, having introduced the two characters, Damon and Alphesiboeus, has no more to say, not even Meliboeus' *haec memini*, but lets them have all the rest of the poem to themselves. They are not competing; after the interpolation of Vergil's compliment to Pollio, which is in effect the dedication of the poem,[23] Damon, leaning on his staff,[24] begins to sing for, apparently, his own pleasure and that of Alphesiboeus. Both are skilled poets, local reëmbodiments, one might almost say, of Orpheus, for the beasts stop feeding and the rivers flowing to listen to them.[25] Damon's song is of the nature of those *iurgia Codri* which Menalcas would have liked to hear,[26] for it is a virulent attack upon an imaginary Mopsus, evidently not the singer in Eclogue V, who has carried off the affections of one Nysa, to whom Damon represents himself as deeply attached, and is to marry her that very day. Incidentally, he attacks Nysa herself for her pride in rejecting all other suitors, himself of course included, and exults over the mean match she has at last made of it. Finally he despairs poetically, rails on love, and declares that he will kill himself. It is all in the Theokritean tradition, though not precisely bucolic in its origins; behind it lies something of the flavour of the twenty-third poem attributed to him, though his it is not, the lament of the ill-treated lover who comes to hang himself at his love's door. But there is no close imitation of this or of any one passage in Theokritos or his imitators, but, in Vergil's usual manner, a number of adaptations of what seemed fitting to him for his subject. If he wanted a motto for it, which was not fashionable in those days, he might have taken Catullus' words *odi et amo*.[27] The song is divided by a refrain into a number of stanzas of irregular length, each having a more or less distinct pause at the end, unlike the lament for Daphnis in Theokritos' first Idyll, which lets its refrain break into the middle of a sentence.[28] Vergil's refrain is meant to suggest that of the Greek poet by its general sense and its rhythm:

> incipe Maenalios mecum, mea tibia, uersus.
> Begin with me, my flute, th' Arkadian lay.

> ἄρχετε βουκολικᾶς, Μοῖσαι φίλαι, ἄρχετ' ἀοιδᾶς.
> Begin, dear Muse, begin the herdsman's song.

The first stanza is of four lines and introduces the subject; the singer fits his song to the time of day it actually is[29] and calls on the morning star to rise, that his plaint may begin. Like a good Arkadian, he devotes his next stanza to praise of Mount Mainalos:

> Ever the pine-trees whisper and never silent the grove,
> On Mainalos, for ever it hears some shepherd's love,
> Or pipings of Pan, who roused the reeds that erstwhile silent lay,
> Begin, my flute; of Mainalos our song shall be today.

Now the sweetness of his note changes to hate and sarcasm; if Nysa marries Mopsus, anything may happen to a lover now; griffons will mate with mares and in another generation hunting-dogs and deer will come down to drink together. Now the portentous state of things must be carefully explained to Mopsus himself, he is reminded that it is his wedding that is toward, and bidden go and cut the torches which will be needed for the ceremony.[30] Then comes a more fruitful subject, for Nysa is addressed, in the most characteristic style of Vergil with Theokritos in his head:

> O fitting is the marriage, since you despise us all,
> And love not the pipe I play on nor the kids that come at
> > my call,
> And these my shaggy eyebrows and the beard that
> > clothes my chin,
> And fancy heaven can never be wroth at mortals' sin.

Whereupon it occurs to him that he has another Cyclopslike figure. It needed less than that to make Vergil think of his favourite eleventh Idyll, and he devotes some of his most delicately beautiful lines to a close imitation of one of its best passages. By the usual paradox of first-rate imitation, he does not produce a copy of the original, but something new and as good. Incidentally, he copies two passages at once, this and a stray line from the second

Idyll which in its context has nothing at all to do with Polyphemos or his Galateia, still less with Damon and Nysa.[31] I feebly tried to render the Greek in the first of these lectures;[32] here is a like libel on Vergil:

> It was between our hedges, the apples were wet with the dew.
> A child with your mother you picked them, and I was
> > guide to you.
> Eleven years I numbered, the twelfth had just come round,
> And I could reach the tender twigs as I stood on the
> > orchard-ground.
> Oh, it was see and perish, and madness from that day.
> (Begin, my flute, I prithee, begin th'Arkadian lay.)

The Cyclops now ends, and another desolate Theokritean lover begins, the serenader of the third Idyll, who can get no reply from his hard-hearted Amaryllis. We shall have a little more of him later, but here, in the Greek, he says,[33]

Now I have learned to know Love; he is a hard god. Surely he sucked the dug of a lioness and his mother reared him in a thicket, him who burns me and pierces me to the very bone.

It is characteristic of Latin that it cannot be at once simple and elegant after the manner of Greek, the peculiar charm of which died with its passing out of the classical form. Vergil is as good in his way as Theokritos in his, but the beauty of his imitation is achieved by suddenly lifting the tone of the lines. This is not a dramatic loss, for anyone who knows common men and their language is aware that emotion will sometimes take them to a plane of speech above their wont and above what one would think to be the limits imposed by their education. But a genuinely Theokritean shepherd would not be so learned as this:

> Nunc scio quid sit Amor; duris in cotibus illum
> aut Tmaros aut Rhodope aut extremi Garymantes
> nec generis nostri puerum nec sanguinis edunt.

Now know I what Love is; on hard rocks has Tmaros or Rhodope or the remotest Garymantes reared him, no child of our race or blood.

The second line, by the way, is Theokritos again, but not sung there by a simple swain, but by Lykidas, who pretends to be a goatherd but is so obviously one of the author's literary friends that no one was ever intended to be taken in by so thin a disguise.[34]

The fact is that Vergil is held by the conventions of pastoral, such as they were, just as much or as little as he pleases. This is one of many touches, especially perhaps in the later Eclogues, which show that he was beginning to feel himself rise above the bucolic level. This poem is shown by its reference to what Pollio was doing after his Dalmatian campaign to be not earlier than the end of 715/39, and thus later than No. IX, which, as we have seen,[35] refers to No. V and that in turn to Nos. II and III. It must also be later than No. IV, since that dates itself as of the year 714/40.[36] It certainly is later than No. VI,[37] and probably No. VII, with its untroubled reference to the country near the Mincio, is earlier than the poems relating to the seizure of Vergil's or his city's land. So we are quite safe in saying that it is one of the last three pastoral poems its author ever wrote, without going into the thorny and somewhat futile question of the precise order in which the ten Eclogues were composed.

I have said that this is a learned shepherd; he shows it by growing mythological, and that without reference to pastoral legends, in his further attack on Love. It is an indirect one, for the real cause of the crime to which he alludes is Love's ill-contriving congener, Jealousy, and not the great god himself. But if Medeia had not loved Jason, madly and far more than he deserved, she would not have been so bitterly jealous. This rustic bard, then, has read Euripides and knows that early masterpiece of his in which a loving woman is turned by jealousy into a revengeful fiend.

> Oh cruel Love, to stain erstwhile a mother's hands with gore
> Of her own children; cruel she towards the babes she bore.
> Say, which was worse, the mother or the wicked, wanton boy?
> His was the guilt, yet cruel she, her children to destroy.

Now comes the final outburst of artistic despair; the singer, having given us a flavour of the dying Daphnis, comes back to him, from his excursions after the Cyclops and Medeia, yet does not forget the disconsolate serenader of Idyll III. Daphnis, as he lies dying, wishes that the whole course of nature may change, "let briars and thorns bear irises and the fair narcissus put forth its flowers on the junipers; let all things be upside-down, and the stone-pine yield pears, since Daphnis is dying; let the hart drag the hound and screech-owls from the hills vie in song with nightingales." Vergil keeps the figure, but deliberately changes every one of the contrasts. "Now let the wolf undriven fly from the sheep, the hard oak bring forth golden apples, the elm blossom with the narcissus-flower, gouts of amber sweat from the bark of the tamarisks; let screech-owls vie with swans, let Tityrus be Orpheus, aye, Orpheus in the forest, Arion amid the dolphins, let all things, if they will, become mid-ocean."[38] Damon has nothing more to do in life; he will go drown himself, like the nameless serenader, but with a little more pomp and circumstance, as befits the more elevated tone of the whole song, which is throughout such as Theokritos might have assigned to a more refined Polyphemos, not to a mortal herdsman. The intending suicide in the Greek will thriftily take off his sheepskin coat, go to the top of a rock from which old Olpeus the fisherman watches for shoals of tunny, and thence jump into the sea; Damon will hurl himself headlong from "some towering hilltop's peak," *praeceps aërii specula de montis.* The serenader is not so far bent on suicide that he has no hopes of surviving the leap from this improvised Leukas, but if he does die, no doubt that is just what Amaryllis wants. Damon is quite determined to kill himself, and his death is to be his last love-gift, a touch borrowed from the twenty-third, pseudo-Theokritean piece, in which the lover tells the loved that the noose shall be his last offering.[39] And so the song closes, with a variant of the recurrent line:

> Now end, my flute, I prithee, now end th'Arkadian song.

Since the limits of this genre were beginning to gall Vergil a trifle, it is not remarkable that in the rest of the poem he does not write on a genuinely pastoral subject at all, but takes a theme from the city and gives it a slightly countrified twist. His model is still Theokritos, and Theokritos at his very best, but not dealing with the country and its ways. That Idyll which in our conventional numbering is called the second[40] deals with the troubles of a girl living in a great city, in all probability Alexandria; certainly it is large enough to have more than one wrestling-school and therefore a considerable Greek community,[41] also rich enough to indulge in a fine procession including a show of captured or tame beasts of prey.[42] Her name is Simaitha and she is in great distress. A while ago a friend had asked her to come to see the procession, and she had gone, dressed in her simple best; she remembers how she borrowed a cloak from someone to make her look finer. On the way she met two young men and fell in love at first sight with one of them. After some days of fevered restlessness,[43] she sent her maid Thestylis to invite the youth, by name Delphis, to visit her, which he did readily enough, protesting that he too was much enamoured. They at once became lovers and for some time were happy; but of late he has been neglectful, and she is told that he has another love. Now she tries to win him back to her by magic, and the poem details her rites. With much bustling and an occasional loss of temper with Thestylis, she sets going her magic wheel, *iynx*, on which the bird of the same name, a wryneck, would be spreadeagled.[44] The turning of this, as she explains,[45] was meant to make the object of the sorcery restless, or, as she picturesquely puts it, whirling before her door. The magic is as strong as she can make it; she has a little fire into which Thestylis throws barley-meal, saying the while that it is Delphis' bones. That love is a fire is of course a commonplace, ancient and modern, and the object of the ritual is clear enough. Then she burns laurel, which, being oily, burns completely, leaving no ash; so may Delphis' flesh consume. Now comes the universal tool of witches, the wax doll, which she melts before the flame; later she says that in the paroxysms of her love-sickness she looked like such a doll herself.[46] The next offering is bran, which somehow is to attract the attention of her goddess, Artemis-Hekate, and does so, as she thinks, to her extreme terror, for she hears dogs howl and takes it as meaning that the terrible deity is at her favourite haunt, the cross-roads. She bids Thestylis sound the gong, to drive off evil things, and silence comes—everywhere, as she complains, but in her own heart.[47] The fright over, she pours libations and makes prayer, and, full of hope in the help of the goddess who has come so near, she tries another spell. There is a plant called hippomanes which grows in Arkadia;[48] as its name implies, it drives horses mad, and specifically, it would seem, mad with desire. She has none, so I interpret the text, but pretends to have some; perhaps the dread powers will take the will for the deed and send Delphis to her as raging as ever a stallion was for the mare. This tried, without result, she has one more resource; she has a scrap of his clothing, an οὐσία, to use the technical language of her art, and this she now burns, but without the charm that should accompany the action, a symbolic and magical burning of the wearer of the garment; instead, she wails pitifully that Love has sucked all the blood out of her like a leech. There is but one thing left to do, except the last resource of all, which she intends to try the next day, pounding up a lizard to make poison, whether for herself or him. She sends Thestylis to his house with certain drugs, which she is to rub on the threshold, saying, "I rub Delphis' bones." Being thus left alone, she tells her troubles to the Moon in a long complaint, which at last leaves her quieted for the time being, as the Moon is quiet.[49]

This, then, was Vergil's model, and he handled it as freely as he usually did his originals. Probably every woman he knew believed more or less in magic, and it is highly likely that all the countrywomen did, especially in love-magic, which still flourishes all over the Mediterranean region. Therefore, he did not have to go to any Greek for his materials, although he was always willing to take hints from them and to learn the best and most effective arrangement. His own knowledge of magic was not profound, for he was an educated man, not a sorcerer, and had been trained by Epicureans, not by Stoics, who were impressed by the *consensus gentium* and ready to see a measure of truth in any belief if it was sufficiently universal. But he knew enough to write a little scene of amateur conjuring, or on occasion[50] to hint at such a scene without going into small details which would have shown him no expert. For this scene, he wants a happy ending, to balance the lamentable song of Damon, which ends with gloom and intended suicide. Obviously, then, a mere translation of Theokritos' poem, even if it were rustic in character, would not do; he must have a less tragic witch and a less hopeless love. The scene is sketched in a hint or two; we are in a country house,[51] the habitation apparently of a man, his wife, and a maidservant. The man is away and the wife sorely afraid that he has found a new love somewhere, in the town where he has been staying an unconscionable time. So she and Amaryllis, the maid, busy themselves with a ritual to bring him home again in his right mind, in other words, not in love with any strange woman, but with his own wife. The materials are simple; there are herbs, a little incense, a fire on the house-altar, and the inevitable wax doll, with some clay and a few other trifles. The whole tone is lighter than in the Greek, and the refrain, instead of the monotonous appeal to the *iynx* which divides Theokritos' poem into stanzas, is a hopeful address to the charms themselves:

Good charms, bring Daphnis, bring him home from town.

The first of the stanzas into which this divides the wife's song is nothing but a series of directions to Amaryllis to get water—no doubt needed by both the officiants for washing their hands ceremoniously,—deck the altar with a fillet of wool, and burn holy herbs and "male frankincense," the best quality and so the fitter for a serious rite like this,[52] which is to cure madness, or what she regards as such.[53] But exactly what the charms would be like is probably more than Vergil could have told us, and so, instead of reciting them loud enough for readers of the poem to hear, the amateur witch proceeds, in quite proper style, to praise magic in general:

Charms can bring down the very moon from heaven,
With charms Odysseus' oarsmen Kirke changed,
Charms burst in twain the chilly meadow-snake;
Good charms, bring Daphnis, bring him home from town.

The only weak point is that she should add something about her own skill in charms, claiming to be Kirke or to have brought down the moon or burst a serpent or so herself. It is, in fact, pretty clear that she has little knowledge of the subject, but has been to the local expert, exactly as a Louisianian negress in like case would go to the local hoodoo doctor for advice,[54] or a Welsh girl to the nearest *dyn hysbys*. It was a man she consulted, as appears later. At all events, he had taught her well and she has remembered her lesson. The next thing she does is to bring to bear the magic values of the number three. Three times she binds the altar about, each time with three strings of different colours, and three times she carries around it a waxen image, explaining learnedly to Amaryllis that the god likes odd numbers. Now she hands the maid nine more threads, to be tied in three knots, each of three colours, Amaryllis to say the while, "I tie the bonds of Venus." Thus the first part of the rite, the binding of Daphnis fast, is accomplished; it remains to reduce him, and herself, to the right frame of mind, and this is that he should be eager, she hard-hearted (the whole poem shows that hardness of heart is not her usual weakness). She has two dolls instead of one, a waxen image for him and a clay figure for herself; both are put before the fire, and as the wax softens and the clay hardens, so she prays that love will affect him and her.[55] Now Amaryllis, at her bidding, throws *mola salsa* on the altar, the usual sacrificial material of coarse-ground meal mixed with salt, and sets laurel on fire, one of the few coincidences with the Theokritean witch's technique, though even here there is a difference, for Vergil's lorn wife uses bitumen to make it blaze better and explains that she burns it against Daphnis because he "burns" her with love for him or vexation at his neglect. Then, instead of more charms, her wish for the success of this one is elaborated into a simile at once very Vergilian and very Lucretian. The latter describes, in one of his finest and best-known passages, the grief of a cow which has lost her calf and vainly seeks it everywhere.[56] The poor creature becomes human under his pen, and appropriately, for the point of his argument just there is that beasts no less than ourselves have individual differences of shape and appearance and therefore can recognise each other as we do. The calf has been sacrificed, so

> His childless mother wanders the green glades,
> Tracking the prints his cloven hooves have left
> Upon the sward, and ever turns her eyes
> This way and that, still seeking for the lost,
> In hopes to find him, while her piteous cry
> Fills every leafy grove, and oft she turns
> Back to the byres, in longing for her calf.
> Nor tender willow-shoots nor dew-fresh grass
> Nor rivers brimming to the topmost banks
> Can please her now nor soothe her sudden pain,
> Nor sight of other young about the leas
> Divert her, nor distract her in her grief,
> For aye she seeks her own, the one she knew.

Vergil applies this to the distracted lover that the witch would make of her Daphnis, for by now she is working herself up into a nearly convincing rage against him; the poet's *facetum* is not idle, and she says more than she means.

May such desire hold Daphnis as when a cow, poor thing,[57] worn out with seeking her calf through the groves and the lofty woods, drops down on the green sedge at the side of a waterbrook, quite despairing, and never thinks to give place to the late night;[58] may such desire hold him, and may I never trouble to cure it.

So far, her charms have had no visible effect; indeed, it is hard to see how they can have had any, since the town is presumably some distance away and Daphnis coming, if he comes, on foot. But at all events, he is not home yet, and it is the correct thing to proceed to really strong measures against him. He, like the Theokritean lover, has left some of his clothing behind, naturally enough, since it is his own house, and some of this is now taken, not to burn but to lay under the threshold, buried in the earthen floor. These pledges, as she calls them, "owe" him to her, *debent haec pignora Daphnim*. Put into the ground, they will make the ground pull him, and that particular bit of ground is inside the house, therefore he will come home. The threshold is a rather unchancy place, too full of magic (like all entrances) to be treated lightly, which is why neither a Roman bride nor a Yorkshire one whose husband has any regard for old ways must tread on it at the first arrival in the new house. To bury charms under it is pan-European, and their nature and purpose vary widely. But her great effect is still to come. She has some very special herbs, imported from the Black Sea (foreign magic is always more efficacious than home-grown),[59] given her by Moeris, no doubt in return for his fee. He is a past master of the Black Art, not simply ordinary homely magic; she has herself seen him turn into a wolf, bring up ghosts from their graves, and make the standing crops leave one field for another. These are the three stock performances of the worst kind of wizard. "It is supposed," says Daniel's Servius,[60] "that certain men can by certain arts be changed into wolves," in other words, the very wide-spread belief in the werwolf was shared by the ancient civilisations of Europe. How it was done, appears from the story in Petronius,[61] the teller of which took a moonlight walk with one of his acquaintance and was much frightened by what happened; for, passing near a burial-ground, his companion proceeded to strip, performed some indelicacies around his clothes, and went off in wolf-shape, leaving the garments turned into stone for the time being. Arrived at his destination, the narrator heard of a raid on the stock by a huge wolf, which had been hurt by one of the farm-people, and next day of course discovered that his uncanny companion had a bad wound in the corresponding place. Either the woman was getting desperate about her husband's conduct, or Vergil did not realise how black such magic was. For the evocation of ghosts, it is so common that examples need hardly be given; but the business of the crops was clean against Roman law and Moeris might have got himself into serious trouble by it. Once more the ancient commentators are of help; Servius quotes the regulation of the Twelve Tables, although in a modernised phrasing,[62] "thou shalt not entice thy neighbour's crop," and Daniel's Servius adds that Varro and other authorities vouch for the reality of such an offence. One would gladly know more about it, whether the process resembled the milking of a rope by more recent witches, whereby the milk of a neighbour's cow was made to flow into the offender's pail, and if it was the actual crops, straw and all, which came from their proper place and planted themselves in the operator's field or merely the grain which came into his barn, leaving the empty husk growing, or even the "goodness" of the grain which passed, leaving a show of corn behind which would not satisfy hunger. In any case, it was no light offence in a community of peasant-farmers or small yeomen, such as the early Romans were.

From this expert, then, she has got the necessary herbs to use for her last and most dangerous experiment. First, all remnants of the other charms must be cleared away;[63] Amaryllis is told to take the ashes to running water and throw them in over her head, without looking back; it is the usual way of getting rid of uncanny stuff, and was already familiar to Aeschylus.[64] New magic and old must not be allowed to mix, or they may interfere with each other. The operator is now screwing her courage to the sticking-place and telling herself that Daphnis is really past forgiveness; "he cares not for the gods nor any charms."[65] Moeris' prescription is in all probability a deadly one. But the refrain has hardly been repeated in preparation for the actions, whatever they are to be, which shall produce the final effect when the altar-fire, before which she stands hesitating to throw on the new materials, suddenly flares up of itself.

This must mean something, and she stops to look and listen. Promptly comes the barking of the watch-dog, and it needs no more magic to tell her that she has succeeded and Daphnis is just entering. A hurried reversal of her ritual ends the poem:

Have done, my charms, for Daphnis comes from town.

We have thus examined nine of the ten poems, leaving to the last that which is by common consent the most difficult of all and the most overlaid with comment, ancient and modern. Before we proceed to it, I think we may with profit consider one result of our enquiries hitherto. We have found reason to suppose, with Servius and the sanest commentators generally, that apart from poetical diction and the metaphorical language which goes with it, Vergil generally says simply what he means; fiction is common, as is to be expected, but allegory we have not found, unless the occasional masking of a real person under a pastoral name out of Theokritos be called allegory. When he paints us a picture of two shepherds talking, railing at each other, holding a contest of song, or simply entertaining each other with specimens of their skill, he is inviting us to contemplate that pleasant scene and not darkly hinting at a literary quarrel or a political transaction. It may therefore not be wholly unjustifiable, when we come to the fourth Eclogue, with its puzzling story of the child that is to be born and the Golden Age that is coming, to keep in mind the possibility that there really was a child for whose birth Vergil hoped, or said he did, not one already born nor an abstraction or personification, and that he entertained either genuine or poetical hopes of a bettering of the parlous state in which the world of his day found itself.

CHAPTER VIII

A CHILD IS BORN

THE FOURTH ECLOGUE has never ceased to give rise to debate, controversy, and more or less plausible and intelligent theorising since, at the latest, the generation after the author's death.[1] If I venture once more to discuss so well-worn a theme, it is not with any vain hopes of presenting the final, canonical interpretation or even of saying anything very new, but with the more modest expectation of presenting the case as it now stands, clearing away some suggestions which seem to me wholly devoid of foundation and recording my vote on some of the crucial points. To do this, however imperfectly, I think it necessary to begin by asking exactly what Vergil says in this puzzling poem, as a preliminary to asking what he means; therefore bear with me if I give the substance of some of the finest verses ever written in Latin through the distorting medium of very prosaic modern prose.

Vergil begins by asking the Muses of Sicily to let him sing something a little loftier, *paulo maiora*, than the usual pastoral strains, for "not all are delighted with bushes and low-growing tamarisks" and the "woods" of this song are to be good enough for a consul. The consul in question, he explains a few lines lower down, is Pollio, and therefore the poem dates itself within a very few months; it must have been composed either while Pollio actually held that office or shortly before he began to hold it, that is to say, in 714/40 or the concluding months of 713/41.

After this prelude begins the real matter of the poem, a message of hope and consolation to a sorely troubled world. The last age of the "song of Cumae," usually taken to be the prophecy of the Cumaean Sibyl,[2] is come; the *saecula*

[1] Notes to chapter viii will be found on pages 253-265.

are recommencing, and with their new beginning, the Virgin, Justice, who quitted mankind long ago and is to be seen in the heavens as the constellation which bears that name,[3] is returning and bringing the Golden Age, *Saturnia regna*, the good old times when as yet Zeus was not and mild, kind Kronos was lord of all the universe. The beginning of this new age of gold is to be marked by the birth of a child, and that is near at hand, for it needs but the favour of Lucina, the goddess who makes the baby see the light for the first time. In Vergil's theology, she is the same as Eileithyia and Eileithyia the same as Artemis; therefore she is encouraged to show her kindness to the expected infant by the reminder that her brother Apollo is now ruling. Pollio, while still consul, is to see the beginning of this glorious time, and under his leadership, whether by virtue of his office or of his prominent position in the state generally,[4] the traces still left of wickedness, or ill luck, for *scelus* can mean both, shall become so impotent (*irrita*) that they shall rid the world from its burden of unrelieved fear, *perpetua formidine*, a phrase which we have learned to understand in our own times all too well. But the child, once born, shall "receive the life of gods" and gods and heroes shall be revealed to him; he and they shall see one another face to face. The world in his days shall be at peace, and he shall rule it. Either the pacifying or the ability to rule is due *patriis uirtutibus;* that is, either the peace was brought about by the noble qualities his father displayed, or else he shall govern it worthily by his inheritance of those qualities.[5]

However, all this is not yet to be, for the child's infancy and growth must precede the great consummation of peace and innocence. While yet he lies in his cradle, the earth will grow her loveliest plants for him to play with, while the country-side (it is to be remembered that, though in higher mood, this is still a pastoral poem) prospers around him. The goats shall need no leading home, but come of themselves with full udders; the cattle shall have no dangerous lions to fear (clearly, the blessings of the coming age extend beyond Italy, which had no lions), snakes and poisonous plants shall die, and rare spice-plants, no longer confined to the East, shall grow everywhere. When his boyhood comes and he is old enough to read of the great deeds of his father and receive his first ideas of what excellence, moral and other, *uirtus*, means, the fields shall bear corn of themselves, the vines shall grow of their own accord on brambles, and the oaks shall sweat honey. But all is not yet done. There will yet be left traces of the "ancient sin," *priscae fraudis*, prompting men to tempt the sea with their fleets, to wall their towns against one another, even still to thrust their ploughshares into the bosom of the earth. But at least theirs shall be a noble time, for there shall be new Argonauts and the warfare shall be a second War of Troy, with its own Achilles to make it great. It is the last remnant of the old leaven; after this, when the child whose birth is now looked for is grown to full manhood, the sailor shall quit the sea, "give place to it," as Vergil picturesquely says, for there shall be no more ships to go a-trading, and no need for them, since everything is to grow everywhere. The farmers and vine-dressers shall give up their useless toils, and even the dyers shall have no more to do, for the wool on the backs of the sheep shall be of all manner of brilliant colours.[6]

The Parcae, the old deities of birth and destiny, who in Vergil's time had been fully equated with the Greek Moirai, have already spoken to their eternal spindles and bidden this age hasten, for they know the unchanging decree of Fate, whose servants they are,[7] and are glad thereat. Let the coming child but begin his career, for he is no mortal infant but a child of the gods, of Zeus himself; let him look and see how all the universe awaits his advent. Vergil hopes that he himself will live long enough to sing, in his old age, of the newcomer's deeds; if he can have such a theme, he

A CHILD IS BORN 165

will excel all poets and even Pan himself. Therefore let the babe hasten and be born, and let him show himself from the first moment a wonder-child, by smiling[8] at his mother, who for his sake has endured these ten (we should say nine)[9] weary months. For so and only so shall he become worthy to feast with gods and wed a goddess.

So much by way of synopsis of the poem; it is but sixty-three lines long, but has nearly as many disputable points as it has verses. I have merely mentioned the right interpretation of a few of them, small matters for the most part, which can be understood by no more recondite process than learning Latin and not remaining content with a smattering thereof. The real puzzles remain, and are such that no scholar, not even the best, need be ashamed of confessing that he finds them too hard to allow him to come to a final decision. But they vary in difficulty, and some of them, I think, admit of solutions so reasonable that we may come to an approximate agreement at all events. Let us begin with the easier.

All the difficulties may perhaps be classified under four heads. The first is formal; to what species of composition does this poem belong? The next is, broadly speaking, historical; is Vergil depending on Western or Eastern themes for his inspiration and the content of his work? The third is harder; why does Vergil expect the Golden Age just then? The fourth is the hardest of all; why does he foretell the birth of the child, and what child does he mean? I have arranged these points in what seems to me the ascending order of hardness; I believe that a pretty satisfactory answer can be given to the first question, that one can at least take sides on the second and do no violence to a philological conscience, which is, properly developed, a delicate and scrupulous form of love for truth, but that on the third and fourth the investigator is fortunate if he can thoroughly satisfy himself, and lucky beyond all precedent if he can convince any considerable number of readers or hearers.

A good deal of research has been devoted to the quite legitimate problem of Vergil's formal models. For this is a classical poem of a good period, and it would have been completely contrary to the spirit of the age and the traditions of his art if the poet had set out to write a work such as no one had ever attempted before. The best classical writers sought to weld together form and content into a perfect whole, and for all surviving authors (we have not the absolute beginnings of any literary genre) the form was given, as completely as paint or marble, or bronze, are the given materials of painter or sculptor. As it would never have occurred even to the rebel Euripides to write a tragedy in which there was no choral part, nor to the highly original Plautus to compose a play in which the last scene saw hero and heroine finally separated, so Vergil would not have been the craftsman he was, nor a craftsman at all, if he had tried to write on no model whatever. To vary and recombine his models, however, was what he could and on occasion did do. As the *Aeneid* is formally the product not only of the *Iliad* and *Odyssey*, but of the *Argonautica* of Apollonios of Rhodes as well, so it may be that our Eclogue is due, not to any one schema of composition, but to two or three, homogeneous enough to be blended together into a single and new whole.

Now since a poet of Vergil's day was of necessity also a rhetorician, investigators have quite rightly turned their attention to the surviving manuals of rhetoric,[10] to see if any of them contain directions for a composition at all resembling this one. That they were written for the benefit of those who would produce speeches, not poems, need not disturb us, for the show-speech, the epideiktic oration as it is commonly called, tended more and more to intrude into the domain of poetry, taking into its scope, for example, matter so obviously poetical as the hymn. It will therefore not be at all surprising if somewhere we discover rules laid down for a kind of speech which shall resemble our poem. Nor is it relevant that the rules we find and the very few apposite specimens of works composed in accordance with them are dull and poor. A good craftsman and a bad one may use the same tools, materials, and techniques, the possession or lack of native genius making the difference between the botched work of one and the masterpiece of the other. No one in his senses would say that *Arden of Feversham* and *Macbeth* were plays of equal value; it is none the less true that they are both Elizabethan dramas, and the technique of one may throw light on the composition of the other. So let us see if Menandros the rhetorician, a very dull dog, and the made-to-order loyal sentiments of an Augustan official a little later than Vergil's death may not help us to understand what sort of work the greatest poet of Augustus' principate set out to compose nine years before the Battle of Actium.

Among the speeches which, so Menandros tells his pupils, may be in demand for special occasions is the birthday oration,[11] and for this he gives directions and hints which do not now concern us. But the very end of the chapter is of some interest. Suppose, he says, the birthday is that of a very young child, obviously one can but express bright hopes, for the subject has as yet done nothing to be praised for. Then come some banal expectations which one may put into flowery language; it is "likely" that the baby will, when older, distinguish himself at manly sports, take a creditable part in the life of his community, and so on. It all savours of the small Greek town under Roman domination, and is damp with the wholesome but unexciting waters of the parish pump.

Let us turn to another variety of the same theme, the birthday of a very distinguished man indeed, no other than

Augustus himself, and see what one of his servants had to say about it. The author is the proconsul of Asia, Fabius Maximus Paullus; he is writing a circular letter to the cities of his province, proposing a calendar reform by which all shall adopt the Julian system (or the misapplication of it which was at the moment in force; the date is not later than 745/9, when Augustus saw to it that his great predecessor's scheme was carried out properly). For the new beginning of the reformed year, he proposes the Emperor's birthday, which happened to come at a fairly convenient date, the 22d day of September, that is, practically at the autumn equinox. This is what he says of it (the sense of a few words at the beginning must be supplied by conjecture, for the official copy on stone which is preserved to us is broken at that point).[12]

[I cannot say] whether the birthday of the most divine Caesar is of more delight or of more profit; we may justly reckon it equal to the beginning of all things, if not in nature, at least in utility. For it set right everything which had fallen asunder and changed to misfortune; it gave a new face to all the universe, which would gladly have undergone destruction, had not Caesar, the common blessing of all, come into being. So a man may fairly count as the beginning of his lifetime, nay, of his existence, that event which is the end and limit of regret that one was ever born. Now since there is no day from which one could make a better beginning for each man's profit, in matters public or private ...

Then follow the proposal concerning New Year's Day and, by way of appendix, the comments of the city which publishes this particular inscription, loyally agreeing with the governor's sentiments, and freely complimenting both him and "Augustus, whom Providence, to benefit mankind, has filled with virtue" and apparently, for the text is very battered here, has sent with the express purpose of making wars to cease and putting all things in good order. A similar compliment had been paid to Julius Caesar in 706/48,[13] but without reference to his birthday:

> Erected by the cities and peoples of Asia to Gaius Iulius Caesar, Pontifex Maximus, Dictator, consul for the second time, the descendant of Ares and Aphrodite, god made manifest and common saviour of the life of mankind.

It became common form, when any event took place which called for loyal rejoicings, not only a birthday or a visitation from the great man to be honoured,[14] but also an accession, as the following decree of Assos[15] shows:

> Since the answer to all men's hopes and prayers, the principate of Gaius Caesar Germanicus Augustus, has been announced, and the universe knows no bounds to its joy; and since every city and every people has made haste to see the god, knowing that the most desirable age for mankind has now begun; it is therefore decreed...

and then follow the usual oath of allegiance and other proper measures to show respect to one whom, to borrow Suetonius' expression, it was still possible to regard as an emperor and not as a portent.[16]

We see, then, that at least in Asia it was not unusual to hail a ruler both as a god and as a saviour-god, the bringer, at least sometimes, of a new era to the world, a Golden Age of peace and prosperity. It is not necessary to follow the later history of the commonplace, as it became; Rome experienced a series of official "golden ages," the gilding on which was often very thin indeed. Our business is with the early period, in which it was still possible to attach a meaning other than courtly and hollow compliment to such phraseology.

It is very clear that the rhetorical models I have been adducing all differ in one very serious respect from Vergil's form; they deal with a person, young or old, who has actually been born, and most of them refer to adults. Let us look for a moment at another class of speeches, popular about the same time, marriage orations. The greater part of their contents, it is true, need not trouble us, for it deals with the numerous good qualities which it was courteous to attribute to the married pair, their families, and all about them; but one of the commonplaces in use was to wish them children and go on to dilate on the advantages of having a family. It does not seem impossible that even a mediocre disciple of the rhetoricians might have thought of combining the two sets of instructions and expressing his hope that some distinguished couple would have children who should prove a blessing to the state and to humanity in general as well as their parents. It was regular to compare the bride and groom by implication to Menelaos and Helen, or Peleus and Thetis;[17] are we to imagine that no one ever remembered to add in prose, as Catullus did in poetry,[18] that the latter pair had for their offspring the greatest hero of the greatest of traditional wars, Achilles?

But even so, we have not yet found Vergil's model, for he says not a word of anyone's marriage, though he implies that such an event has taken place, for his wonder-child is assuredly not illegitimate. May we not, however, find an explanation which allows the poet that sort of originality which has already been described, a skilful blending and modifying of his models to produce something new by their composition? If anything is certain about the poem, it is that he assumes the tone of a prophet; the Golden Age is not yet come, but is coming; the child is not born, but will be; the sins and evils which have so long afflicted the world are still there, but their time is now short. It seems fair to understand him as using the commonplaces of rhetoric, whether in prose or in verse, not, as usual, to celebrate a marriage, a birthday, or the arrival of some important person, but to tell of the glories which yet shall be. So we may perhaps say that we have before us in the fourth

Eclogue a glorified version of a poem of congratulation and welcome, cast into the future and not the present.

If we can agree so far, it is time to attack the next point, which is much harder. Is the "Cumaean song" a real Sibylline oracle, and if so, was that oracle the product of Eastern imagination? Here we are badly handicapped by the nature of the oracles in question. Sibyls in abundance had existed, or were said to have done so, in the ancient world; the official list, as Vergil knew it from Varro, extended to half a score.[19] One of these, the Sibyl of Cumae, was the reputed authoress of the original set of oracles, in Greek verse, which the Romans had treasured, according to a tradition very likely based on fact, since the days of the Etruscan kings. But that collection had perished more than forty years before Vergil wrote his poem,[20] in a fire which destroyed the Capitol, and the Senate had sent out emissaries to gather oracles from all manner of places: Tacitus specifies Samos, Ilion, Erythrai (the homes of three of the traditional Sibyls), Africa (in the Roman sense of the word, roughly the Barbary States of our older geographies), Sicily, and the Italian colonies. These, judiciously sifted and officially recognised, after inspection and rejection, as genuine, were the Sibylline Books of Vergil's day, cared for by the Quindecimuiri, the college which had charge of all non-Roman rites.[21] These men did not as a rule publish, but consulted the mysterious (and, to judge by the few specimens we have, very poor) Greek verses of the collection, and that only by direction of the government. So far as we know, there was no opportunity whatever for any private study of them, and we know little of the principles on which their custodians judged of their genuineness, of the appropriateness of any one of them to a given situation, or of the correct interpretation of obscure passages. One thing may be taken as fairly certain, that official forgery was rife; but what is proved absolutely by the evidence we have is that many private books of oracles, Sibylline or other, existed.[22] We do not, therefore, know whence Vergil got any knowledge he may have had of a Sibylline prophecy, whether it was official or not, or whether he had ever seen the text. Certainly there existed about his time some forged oracles which had been heavily coloured by Jewish propaganda, probably emanating from Alexandria, one of the greatest centres in the ancient world of that people's intellectual, religious, and missionary activities.[23] The collection which we still possess contains large remnants of this older stratum of forging, though contaminated with later additions, including Christian workings-over.

But our old friend Servius professes, on what authority we do not know, to be acquainted with the contents of the oracle to which Vergil refers. Commenting on the words *ultima Cumaei carminis aetas*,[24] he says:

That is, Sibylline, for she was of Cumae and divided the ages by metals; she also told who was the ruler of each age, and would have it that the Sun was the tenth and last. Now we know that the Sun and Apollo are the same, wherefore he says "Thine Apollo now reigns." The Sibyl also said that when all the ages were ended, they began again anew, which statement philosophers also arrive at by the following argument. They say that when the Great Year is finished all the stars return to their rising-places and pass once more on the same course. Now if the movements of the stars are the same, it follows necessarily that all things which have been are repeated, for it is perfectly clear that everything depends on the movement of the heavenly bodies. Following this, Vergil says that the Golden Age is returning and everything which has been is coming again.

I have quoted this much-discussed[25] passage in full. If anything is clear about it, it is that there exists profound confusion either in Servius' own mind or that of his authority. Three possible schemes of world-ages, at least, are conceivable. There might have been (I know no proof that there ever was)²⁶ a system of planetary ages, or chronokratories, to use the technical term of the astrologers, in which each period should be governed by a planet and distinguished by the corresponding metal. In this, we should have, it may be supposed, a Golden Age ruled by the sun, a Silver Age governed by the moon, and ages of copper (Venus), iron (Mars), quicksilver (Mercury), tin (Iuppiter), and lead (Saturn). But Servius speaks of ten ages, and our supply both of planets and of common metals known to the ancients has run out; they were ignorant, for example, alike of the planets Uranus and Neptune and of the metals zinc and aluminium. Ten, moreover, is not a number of much significance in astrology, although there is a division of the zodiac into decans, or groups of ten degrees (one-third of a sign) each and a few other instances of decades. Seven (the planets) and twelve (the signs of the zodiac) are much more prominent figures. And such a system as we have imagined is put out of court by Vergil himself when he tells us that Apollo (by whom he may mean the sun) is ruling and also that the Golden Age has not yet come.²⁷ For there is no succession of the planets known to ancient or other astronomy in which Saturn follows the sun immediately, as in Vergil he must, if Vergil is talking astrologically at all. Saturn is the outermost planet of the ancient system, the sun being regularly in the middle of the seven, with the earth imagined to be centre of the whole.²⁸

Since we can add that Vergil nowhere shows any interest in astrology, of which Horace has some knowledge, but not very much,²⁹ we may I think safely reject any theory which supposes an astrological scheme for this poem. Let us now turn to the rest of what Servius says, that the Sibyl distinguished ten ages, abandoning the metals as a hopeless piece of confusion. Here at least we have something which we know to be a real, and an Italian, belief; it is the Etruscan theory of *saecula*. According to their experts,³⁰ a *saeculum* is an indeterminate space of time, somewhere about a century, measured by the date of death of the longest-lived person born on a given day. In or shortly after the time when Vergil was writing, the period was fixed by Roman opinion at a hundred and ten years.[31] It would seem that a nation, at all events the Etruscan people, lives ten *saecula*, and not long before the date with which we are dealing a certain Vulcanius or Vulcatius, an Etruscan diviner or *haruspex*, had proclaimed openly that the comet which, as we have already mentioned, shone at the games celebrated in honour of the dead Julius, marked the end of the ninth *saeculum* and the beginning of the tenth. The Sibyl, at all events an Italian Sibyl, might have got hold of this doctrine, and even have added the gods to it, if they were not there already (we have no proof that the Etruscans did or did not assign a divine ruler to each of their *saecula*). For we know that Nigidius Figulus, that strange scholar-mystic who was contemporary with Cicero and the most learned man of the time after the incomparable Varro,[32] did have a system of world-ages, each with a god to govern it, which he said was found in several authors, among them Orpheus;[33] in other words, it belonged to that medley which we call neo-Pythagoreanism. But his gods are little help to us here, for they are Saturn, Iuppiter, Neptune, and Pluto, to whom, says Nigidius, some people, including the Magi, add Apollo, meaning perhaps the Stoic ἐκπύρωσις, the recurrent victory of fire over the other elements, after which all things begin again. This is certainly not what Vergil means, for he has no catastrophe in mind, but rather a gradual bettering of things, which in some thirty or forty years (the thirty-year-old poet hopes to live to see the consummation)[34] will bring the world to innocence and perfection. However, he may have taken a hint from Nigidius' system, if the sequence of gods is really Saturn, Iuppiter, Neptune, Pluto, Apollo, and then Saturn again; Daniel's Servius seems to imply that this is so, and if it is, we are rid of a great difficulty which cuts across many calculations of modern scholars.³⁵ If every god has an age to rule over, and Apollo has recently begun to rule, as Vergil's phrase *iam regnat* seems to imply, how can the Golden Age be so near? But if Apollo does not rule an age, like the other gods, but merely has a transitional period to look after, his accession might herald the closeness of the time of perfect happiness when not he, but Kronos, shall be lord.³⁶ And that this may be so is suggested, though far from proved, by Nigidius' theory that the ἐκπύρωσις is meant, for that is not an age of the world but the process which puts an end, in the Stoic system, to an age, a Great Year. As a further argument for some connection between the two authors, in other words for the correctness of the ancient commentator's view, we may remember that Nigidius was then a recent and celebrated writer, by no means unlikely to attract the attention of so studious a man as Vergil; whereas if we suppose Alexandrian prophecies, Oriental doctrines, or the like, as in some of the theories to be discussed later, we have to answer the question how Vergil came to know of them, since they would for the most part be foreign to the sort of reading likely to be indulged in by a poet of the time, who was under no obligation to be a polymath and probably confined himself to works of literary importance with some excursions into handbooks of philosophy, mythology, and history. Incidentally it is to be noted that the name of Nigidius is not introduced vaguely by the scholiast, for an exact reference is given; the statement occurred in Book IV of his treatise *On the Gods*.

But here we must stop for a moment and once more ask what *Cumaeum carmen* means. The commentary attributed to Probus³⁷ has a note on the phrase which cannot be thrown aside as worthless. He says:

Either from the Sibyl, because she was of Cumae and prophesied that after four ages there should be a new generation, or else

Cumaei carminis means Hesiod, from his father, Dios, who was of Cumae, and Hesiod in his books makes mention of four ages.

By the second "Cumae" he means Kyme in the Aiolid, from which it is perfectly true that Hesiod's father came, as we know from Hesiod[38] himself. Nor does "Probus" stand alone in his interpretation; Filargirius[39] has a note which, together with some false literary history, contains the same opinion:

Some understand *Cumaei* to refer to the Sibyl, because she was of Cumae and foretold the future. But the poet follows a truer account. By *Cymaeum* he means Hesiod's poem.

Finally, the Berne scholia give preference to the same theory:[40]

But it is better to take it of Hesiod's poem, he being called *Cymaeus* from Kyme, a city of Asia. . . . Others more truly explain it of Hesiod, who lived in Kyme, a city of Asia, and, like the Sibyl, wrote the succession of the reigns of the gods and said that there were diverse heavenly sovranties; first came that of Saturn, which was golden, then that of Iuppiter, which was of silver, next of Neptune, which was bronze, and finally of Apollo, which was of iron.

It is of course clear that these notes all go back to a common original, and also that the later ones grow somewhat confused. Hesiod never lived in Kyme; he lists five, not four ages, and his poems say nothing of reigns of Poseidon and Apollo, unless, which is unlikely, the reference is to some lost passage in a work falsely ascribed to him. There has been contamination between the views of the real Hesiod and those reported by Nigidius from "Orpheus." But in itself the explanation, warmly supported in recent times by L. Herrmann,[41] has nothing in the least impossible. To call Hesiod, or Hesiod's poem, "Cumaean" when his father came from Kyme and he himself was therefore a native of that place, at least at second hand, is not at all beyond the freedom of Alexandrian epithet. Vergil himself elsewhere[42] calls the Sibyl the Amphrysian seer, because she was the servant of Apollo, and Apollo, when he was Admetos' herdsman, tended his cattle along the banks of the river Amphrysos in Thessaly. But there are, I think, fatal difficulties in the way.

In the first place, the phrase *ultima aetas* makes against Hesiod. To say that the last of that poet's ages has come is extremely stale news, for he himself had said it seven hundred years or so earlier.[43] If one age only were in question, we might take the words to mean "the end of the age," as *summus collis* means the top of a hill, *nouissimum agmen* the rear of a column on the march; but *summus collis*, *nouissimum agmen*, cannot mean the top of the highest of a number of hills, not the rear-guard of the last of several columns. *Vltima aetas*, then, cannot mean the last part of the last period of time, but only the last one of several periods. Next, Vergil implies, or rather says practically in so many words, that there is a recurrent series of ages, and the end of the last means the return of the first. Hesiod, if we press his words, might be taken to say the same; "I would," he writes,[44] "that I were never one of the men of the fifth age, but either had died earlier or been born later." The idea that after the Iron Age is at last over the Golden Age will come again might just be read into these lines; but nothing else in the *Works and Days* hints that the reign of Zeus is ever to have an end or that Kronos and his times are coming once more, in however distant a future. The poet, I think, merely means, "I wish I did not live now, but in some other time, for no other could be so bad"; it is a rhetorical expression of deep discontent, not a doctrine of cosmic changes nor anything reminiscent of the Stoic ἀποκατάστασις, the repetition of the history of the world between one conflagration, or deluge, and the next. And thirdly, Vergil's words, "thine Apollo now reigns," seem very decidedly to allude to something definite, whether a phrase in a Sibylline oracle or not. Let us see if the most ingenious of all efforts to solve this riddle, that of E. Norden, can be accepted.[45] Put very briefly, it is as follows.

Whatever else the poem means, it is partly one of compliment to Pollio on his consulship. Now consuls came into office on January 1; and this is about midway between two festivals of the sun, those which have passed gradually into Christian use under the names of Christmas and Epiphany. So, if Apollo is Helios, it is literally true to say that he is reigning when the poem is written; it is his especial time of the year. But not only is it a festival time for Helios; it is one for Aion also, that curious abstract god of time whose cult was growing in popularity during the early centuries of our era. Indeed, the festivals of which Norden speaks are, at least one of them is, a festival of the birth of Aion. It may well be that the celebrators of the festival meant no more than that the new period of time which we call a year was born, the winter solstice having come; but it would be no difficult feat for a poet to glorify that into the coming of a new epoch, if it suited his theme. As to the reason why two similar feast-days should come so close, it is historical, or rather astronomical. January 6 (Epiphany) was once the winter solstice, in the days of Amenemhet I, 1996 B.C., and they kept the feast duly on the proper date. But the solstice changes infinitesimally every year, and by about the fourth century B.C. our Christmas (now several days too late for the sun, whose feast it properly is) was the correct date; so, it would appear, the time of celebration changed to the extent of keeping both days.

This is, as usual with Norden, both ingenious and learned, and is urged in the most persuasive manner. Yet I cannot think it true. Suppose we set aside all the difficulties inherent in the construction, such as the rather hazardous conclusion about the time at which the annual festivals were established (they are not directly attested till much later),[46] and assume them to have existed in Vergil's day. Let us also assume that Vergil really did compose his poem in time for New Year's Day; I think he did, but the matter is far from certain. It has been strongly urged by Carcopino[47] and others that Pollio was by no means sure of becoming consul until quite late in the year, for he was not on the best of terms with Octavian until after the Treaty of Brundisium between the two great rivals had been signed, largely through his instrumentality, and that was about October of the year, not January. Therefore, it is argued, Vergil, who was a tactful man, would say nothing about his consulship until it was certain, for a poem congratulating anyone on an honour which he never receives is apt to fall flat, to say the least of it. But I think this has been sufficiently answered, not so much by Norden, who urges[48] that all known poems in honour of a consulate are written for the beginning of the official year, that is, for January 1, but by R. Syme,[49] who points out that the *consules ordinarii* for that year, the men by whose names it was dated, were Pollio and Cn. Domitius Calvinus, so that whether either of them actually took up the duties of his office at all, they were nominally and, so far as anything about it was legal, legally consuls from the first moment of the year. At any rate, Vergil, with an eye to Pollio's favour and perhaps living in a part of the country where Pollio's influence was considerable, would express no doubt on the matter. We may add that there had been no revocation of the arrangements of some years earlier[50] by which the consuls for some time ahead, including Pollio and his colleague, had been appointed in advance, and therefore in general opinion the pair were consuls in default of notice to the contrary. Such things as elections and the performance of the usual formal duties with which consulships began in less troubled times must have been largely in abeyance in 714/40. As it is, we do not know that Pollio ever entered Rome during the year which bore his name, though he may have done so some time after Brundisium.

Granting, then, that the poem was written for January 1, that is to say, that it was composed late or fairly late in 713/41, Norden's theory still is faced with a grave difficulty. How could Vergil know, or expect his readers to know, anything about the two rather obscure Alexandrian festivals to which he is here supposed to allude? For it is not enough that the author of the Sibylline oracle should have known them, and that he may have been an Alexandrian, whether Jew or Gentile. That would merely tell Vergil that Apollo, or Helios, was somehow prominent, if it told him even that much; for obscure though the oracular style regularly was, the specimens we possess usually set riddles fairly easy to read, and if we suppose that the oracle mentioned the festivals, we must conclude that it said something like "when Helios (or Apollo, or Phoibos) is born at his feast-day, this and that shall come to pass," which, if it were understood at all by a Westerner, would mean a certain time of year; now what the oracle might be reasonably expected to say is not that, but to define, more or less accurately, one year or period from the rest, whether by specifying the number of generations which should elapse after some other event or by foretelling a portent of some kind which would make it plain that a critical time had come.

But, if we remember how fond the East was and long had been of doctrines according to which the history of the world was divided into great epochs and there would inevitably and fatally come a good age to succeed the bad one in which, it was generally declared, men are now living,[51] it does not seem at all impossible that some such prophecy was really current in a form which had reached Vergil, and presumably other people in Italy, for he seems to refer to it as a thing fairly well known, in the form of a Sibylline oracle. It is also not absurd to suppose, with Jüthner,[52] that something like Nigidius' doctrine appeared in the prophecy, not through the influence of the Stoic theory, but rather as a last and very attenuated reflex of the Zoroastrian tenet concerning the end of the present age, the stream of fire which shall in due time destroy the evil but leave the good unharmed, preparing the ultimate triumph of Ahura Mazda over Ahriman. I would not be dogmatic on a point which involves so much conjecture concerning documents quite lost to us; but that there was some prophecy current and that it was slightly tinged with Oriental notions are quite reasonable hypotheses. It was a disturbed time, and we may be fairly sure that vaticinations of all sorts were as common and as much attended to as they had been at the outbreak of the Peloponnesian War;[53] moreover, propaganda was rife, and Mr. W. W. Tarn has made ingenious suggestions regarding the sort of thing which may very likely have been concocted in the East about then.[54] I do not, it is true, accept his views in their entirety,[55] but he has drawn attention to an important aspect of the popular literature of that day and shown where, quite possibly, we may still find remnants of it. These are certain oracles of the Sibyls, as we now have their alleged works, to the effect that Rome shall be overthrown (this may be Alexandrian propaganda in favour of Kleopatra VII, but I think it far more likely Jewish) and then a glorious time of prosperity and justice shall visit the world.[56] An Italian loyalist like Vergil manifestly would not deal with the former aspect of the prophecies, if it existed and he knew of it; but the second might attract him.

Whatever the authorship of the Sibylline oracle which he used, it is by no means unlikely that it in turn made use of Hesiod's world-ages. The poems of the great Boiotian had long been a sourcebook for forgers of many kinds, including those who manufactured Orphic poems at sundry dates from about the sixth century B.C. onward .This is of course a commonplace, and a few minutes' examination of Kern's *Orphicorum fragmenta* and the texts of the *Theogony* and the *Works and Days* will provide abundant examples. But Hesiod was a very well-known author, and the works which stole from him had their public; it is therefore perfectly possible that a Sibylline forger would go directly or indirectly to the *Works and Days* for material, and far from incredible that he should seek to improve on it by additions from other sources.[57] Certainly in the time of Juvenal there was some kind of system extant which added four more ages to the old list, apparently making each worse than the last.[58] If this is so, there may have been another of ten, although that is not a number of which the existing oracles, at all events, are particularly fond;[59] but it would be fairly characteristic of these forgers to lengthen the original, doubling the number as tastelessly as one of them expands Apollo's two-line exposition of his own omniscience into fifteen verses, which he puts into the mouth of Yahweh.[60] There may, then, be elements of truth in the confused statement of Servius with which we started.

I would therefore suggest that Vergil really is using an oracle which he believed, or for poetical reasons professed to believe, to be Sibylline; that this contained some slight tincture of specifically Oriental doctrine, though in a Hellenised form; and I would add that this is the only contact with things Oriental in the whole poem. For if there is in this Eclogue any considerable knowledge of the East and its thought, and especially if Vergil had the comparatively wide acquaintance with such matters presupposed by the theories of Norden and what I may term the Judaising interpreters, to be discussed presently, how is it that he never shows in any other part of his work more understanding of anything east of Greece than he could have got from reading the most ordinary works in his own tongue and in Greek? Elsewhere he is entirely of the West; why, if he had this supposed knowledge, did he neglect the many picturesque themes and episodes which it would have furnished him, and which he could have introduced quite legitimately into the *Aeneid*, for example? And in particular, why, when he generally shows no reluctance to come back upon a theme already touched and develop it anew (as when, again in the *Aeneid*, he improves upon the praises of Octavian in the *Eclogues*), does he not make more of such rich material in any later work, and content himself with some five dozen lines here?

With these negative considerations goes a positive one; Vergil's working out of the description of how the Golden Age shall come is purely Greek, and suggested by a picturesque passage in one of the best-known of Hellenic writers, Plato himself.[61] This seems to me evident if we but look at the order of events as described in the poem. The child and the good new time are to grow together; that much is perfectly plain. At first, while he is still a baby in the cradle, the earth will begin to show a greater fertility by producing various sorts of flowers and other plants, some not native to the West, and the domestic animals will be more tractable,[62] for wild beasts shall frighten them little or not at all. As he grows to school age, old enough to learn to read,[63] food-plants such as wheat shall begin to grow wild, not enough to make agriculture unnecessary, it would appear, for there are still farmers and vine-dressers later in the development, but sufficiently to lighten their task. But things are not yet to be Paradisal, for men go on ploughing and sailing.[64] Next come two important events, another voyage of an Argo, that is to say, an adventure for something precious into distant and unknown countries, and another Trojan War. When this is at an end, the Golden Age shall be fully come.

Now if we look once more at Hesiod's account of the degeneration of the world, it is not hard to see that Vergil is giving it, very briefly, in reverse order. Hesiod tells us of a Golden Age far in the past, when men lived like gods, never grew old, but at length fell into a gentle death-sleep and were turned into supernatural beings who wander the earth still by the will of Zeus and report the doings of mankind to him. In their day the soil needed no tilling to make it grow crops; they had but the trouble of gathering them in. Next came the Silver and Bronze Ages, progressively worse, yet the former of them good enough for its people to become a somewhat inferior kind of supernaturals after their death, living under and not on the ground. But now came a better time, that of the heroes who are also called demigods;[65] all the men of that day fell in the great wars at Troy and Thebes, but they live happily now on the Islands of the Blessed. Last came the Age of Iron, in which to our sorrow[66] we live. Vergil does not describe a Silver or a Bronze Age through which the world shall pass; he is writing a short pastoral poem, not a long one concerning agriculture and the philosophy of the farmer, and he has therefore no room for a hundred-line excursus like that of Hesiod. He confines himself to three crucial ages, and they are, in order, the Iron, the Heroic, and the Golden. In his system there is not only a cycle, with the times recurrent in circular order, as Golden, Silver, Bronze, Heroic, Iron, Golden again, but also a rectilinear movement, first forward and then backward. We have come from Golden through Heroic to Iron; now we must go backward through Heroic to Golden and so begin again *ab integro*. And we do not have to search long in the best-known of all philosophers (one familiar, it should be remembered, to rhetoricians also) to find the source of his idea. It is the myth of the *Politicus*.

Plato there[67] puts forward a strange theory of the way the world wags; whether it is his own or not is a matter foreign to our present subject. According to this doctrine, the material universe, though living and in a sense divine, yet cannot, because it is material, enjoy the perfect and eternal sameness of deity. It is subjected to the least possible change, however, namely, reversal of its motion from time to time, after certain fated periods have elapsed. Hence it alternately moves in the divine direction and in the opposite one. Therefore, at regular intervals God intervenes to move it in His direction once more, and when this occurs, everything that we regard as normal development is reversed, men growing younger instead of older, till they return once more to babyhood, while the race is kept up by the dead returning to life and starting at once to grow younger like the rest. This process brings the world back to the reign of Kronos, during which men are the immediate care of deities, and so live a life of bliss and, since it is Plato speaking, of profound philosophy. Now it is evident that not all of this myth, acknowledged by its author[68] to be half playful, is suitable for a poem of such grave tone as Vergil's. He never, as we have seen, imitated slavishly, and he deals in poetical imagery, not in the subtleties of philosophy. To foretell an age in which people would grow backwards, as Plato logically says they do when God takes a direct part in the affairs of the universe, would be too grotesque here, and directly contrary to his main theme, which is that during the normal life of a human being from infancy to maturity the great change will come about. But such parts of the Platonic scheme as are suitable he adopts: not only the reversal of the ages, but also the familiar converse with supernatural powers. For Plato assures us that under the rule of Kronos, which was and again shall be:

as to men . . . a god in person was himself their ruler and shepherd, as nowadays men, being more divine animals than the rest, are the herdsmen of other and baser kinds than themselves. Now under that god's rule there were no governments nor marriages and families, for all returned to life out of the ground, remembering nothing of what had been before; all such things were absent, and they had in abundance the fruits of trees and many other growing things, not produced by husbandry but sent up unbidden by the earth. And for the most part they lived in the open without clothes or covering, for their weather was without discomfort and temperate, and they had soft beds in the abundant grass which sprang up out of the earth.[69]

Further, since all living things and not men alone were under immediate divine supervision, the gods dividing among themselves the care of the different species,[70] men and beasts could talk with one another and join in the common search after wisdom and exchange of ideas.[71] It is basically the conventional picture of the Golden Age, adapted by Plato to his own ends, the mythical introduction to a discussion on statesmanship; now Vergil readapts it to his purposes, the description of a world of perfect peace and happiness, ruled by a king yet to be.

So we may give an answer, I think, to our enquiry as to the kind of doctrine Vergil teaches concerning the ages of the world. His is not an astrological scheme, the resemblances thereto being few and superficial. It is not the orthodox Etrusco-Roman arrangement of *saecula*, though he uses the word *saeculum* for his world-ages, along with *magni menses*, which implies the astronomical or astrological *magnus annus*. It is not the Hesiodic scheme unmodified, for the reign of Apollo, to say nothing of other matters, is quite foreign to that. It is not Plato's myth in all its details. It is not, I feel fairly confident, entirely derived from a Sibylline oracle, though I am very ready to admit there may have been such a prophecy, which said that the Golden Age would return soon. It is a typically Vergilian blend of elements from all or most of these sources, and the inspiration is neither Eastern nor Western, but rather Hellenistic, that is to say, a compound of both; while the handling is simply the poet's own, like that of everything else that he wrote, from the *Alexis* to the *Aeneid*.

We must now attack the kindred and even more difficult problem of the poet's reasons for saying, with whatever use of figurative language we choose to suppose, that the good old times of Kronos were soon to revisit the world. No one, I suppose, imagines that he literally believed that before the end of his own life everything, good or bad, which characterised the culture of his day was going to vanish and man to return to a state of innocence and simplicity comparable to that which, in the Hebrew myth, Adam enjoyed before the Fall. But this is a serious poem, not a cry of despair under the disguise of a plea to the better elements of Rome to come out from a world of sin and trouble and seek some happier land, like Horace's famous sixteenth Epode,[72] nor a joke, like the many caricatures of the Golden Age whereof the fragments of Greek comedy show us something. We have seen that he likes and uses poetical, even highly poetical, phraseology, but does not allegorise much, if at all; and so I think it only fair to suppose that he wrote this Eclogue because he had some reason, good or bad, sound or fanciful, to think that his age had seen the worst and might expect better things in the near future.

Not a few commentators[73] have an answer ready; 714/40 was the year of the pact of Brundisium, which for the time being brought some kind of accord between the factions of Octavian and of Antony and sealed it, as was hoped, by the marriage of the latter to Octavia. But there are grave difficulties in the way of such an explanation. Either the poem was written in, or rather before, January of that year or it was composed some nine or ten months later.[74] In the former case, Vergil must have had more knowledge of the intentions of the leading men in the Roman state than we have any reason to suppose he would have opportunity to acquire. Even if we postulate, what I think has already been shown to be very dubious,[75] that he was really intimate with Pollio, it seems hardly likely that the latter, unless we suppose him extraordinarily loose of tongue and imprudent, would have let his plans for a reconciliation between his own chief and Octavian be noised abroad so soon; and though he certainly was a vain man and of less importance and ability than he fancied himself to be, I know of no evidence that he was a fool in his political measures. But although we make such hazardous assumptions, we have still to suppose, what is surely beyond the bounds of possibility, that a man possessed of as much good sense as Vergil would proclaim, even by allusion, the success of a measure which had not yet been openly begun at all. If, on the other hand, he wrote the poem about October, he surely wrote it very quickly for so finished a composition, and that too in a year far from empty of other literary activities; also, he speaks as if a good deal of Pollio's consulship was still to pass, and Pollio, it is well known, retired before the year was up.[76] Besides, it is by no means plain that the pact, when signed, was greeted with much enthusiasm, since it did not result in the peace that had been hoped for, at least in the most welcome effect of peace, a fall in the price of food in Italy, for the activities of Sextus Pompeius went on as vigorously as ever.[77] The most, I think, that can be said for this theory is that some rumours of a proposed reconciliation might have circulated about the end of 713/41 and Vergil have heard them. Let us once more take an imaginary modern parallel and see if a reasonable man would have acted as, on this theory, he did. At the moment when I wrote this, September 14, 1939, a rumour was appearing from time to time in the newspapers that Mussolini intended to try once more to bring the belligerent powers to a conference. Can we imagine a writer of the day, though the most convinced Fascist and the warmest admirer of Il Duce, sitting down to compose a panegyric on his hero in which he hailed him, then, as the bringer of an age of peace and predicted that there would never be another serious war in Europe? Can we even suppose a tolerably well informed man, on the strength of such tales as I have mentioned, venturing on the vaguest prediction of that kind, the expression of a hope that in a few months or years a better and more rational mode of settling differences will prevail? Yet, on the theory we are discussing, Vergil does this and more than this, with no better warrant than some piece of gossip, which afterwards turned out to be true, that his patron was going to negotiate between the two real sovrans of the world.

It is far more likely that the other type of interpretation is correct, that which supposes, to quote S. Reinach,[78] that Vergil spoke *sur l'autorité d'une prophétie courante ou d'un calcul mystique*. He prudently adds *que nous ignorons*, but others who think as he did have tried to deduce what this calculation may be, whether embodied in a Sibylline or other oracle or current in some different form to which Vergil might reasonably be imagined to have access. It seems worth while to mention one or two of the types of "mystic calculation" which have been postulated from time to time.

Since Vergil says that a new series of ages, *saecula*, is beginning, it is very understandable that several have tried to bring at least this part of his poem into line with the Etrusco-Roman system of secular years. It is well known that that system included ritual to mark the end of a *saeculum*, with all the ill luck or pollution which it had acquired, or, to speak more correctly, beneficent magic intended to bury (*condere*; so the Romans said *fulmen condere* when they enclosed and marked a place where lightning had "gone to ground")[79] that ill luck or pollution. We know one of the rites employed, the solemn driving of a nail into a temple wall by the supreme magistrate,[80] but it seems improbable that on so important an occasion nothing else was done. The purpose of the nail no doubt was to fasten the evil down, so that it could not get about and do more harm, and the wall of the Capitoline temple was chosen because the strong and good *numen* of that holy place would further weaken the evil thus rendered inactive and presumably destroy it altogether in the end. But this old system, which seems to have governed the years 291/463, 391/363, and 491/263, gave place to a new, Greek arrangement, dating from 505/249, in the First Punic War, when the Sibylline Books were consulted. This was an elaborate offering to the underworld powers, and should have been repeated in 605/149; it was actually not celebrated again till three years after that date. We are not concerned with the purely fictitious series of secular celebrations alleged to have taken place in 298/456, 408/346, 518/236, and 628/126; they are the product of the free fancy of the Quindecimuiri, reckoning back from the actual Secular Games which Augustus, for reasons best known to himself, saw fit to celebrate in 737/17, and are the ones which ought to have taken place if his calculations had been based on anything real.[81] This figment did not exist when Vergil wrote, and was too glaring to deceive that learned if dull potentate the Emperor Claudius in later days.[82] But it is quite possible that the idea, already referred to,[83] that a *saeculum* was 110 years, was current as early as the writing of this Eclogue; if it was, then 715/39 should have been a secular year according to it, and with the common Roman (and Greek)[84] confusion between inclusive and exclusive calculation, the notion may have won favour with some that 714/40 was the real date of the beginning of the new and end of the old era. The objection to any such theory is that it is pure conjecture, and we have no sort of positive evidence for it; all that can be said is that it is in accordance with the sort of ideas which we know were then prevalent.[85]

Allied to this, but not the same, is the suggestion of H. Wagenvoort.[86] Like most scholars, he supposes that Vergil

A CHILD IS BORN

really had seen an oracle thought to be Sibylline; this, as we have seen, is likely enough, and is in keeping with the fairly numerous references to the existence of vaticinations of one sort or another which foretold all manner of extraordinary happenings about the time of Vergil's youth and early manhood.[87] He then argues that the style of such an oracle would be, "when such-and-such an event takes place, this and that will result,"[88] and this is certainly in accordance with what we know of oracular style generally, from fairly early times on. Now it is far from unlikely that the particular prophecy Vergil read was a recent forgery, and the event which it used to warn its hearers of coming change was no other than the famous comet of 710/44, of which something has already been said.[89] This, as Augustus himself tells us,[90] appeared during the funeral games of Julius Caesar and was accepted as proof that the murdered Dictator was become a god. But Augustus himself, says Pliny, secretly rejoiced to think that it was a sign meant for him, and (whatever these words may mean) that it was created (literally "born") for him and he in it. Therefore, if he really had such thoughts and allowed anything of his ideas to leak out, in other words, if Pliny is giving us anything more here than his own fancies, it might have been known among his supporters that he took the portent seriously. If so, in those days of propaganda disguised as prophecy, there is nothing incredible in such an oracle as that postulated.

But, as Wagenvoort honestly recognises, there are great difficulties in the way of any such theory. The poem is dedicated to a supporter of Antony, not of Octavian; it never mentions the comet nor Octavian himself; and the date is some four years wrong. The first is a point which we must come back to later; for the moment, let us imagine it disposed of. The second Wagenvoort counters by saying[91] that Vergil left it to his readers to find out for themselves what he meant, an assumption which must indeed be made on any explanation of the poem, with the corollary that apparently few if any of them succeeded, at least after his own lifetime. For the third, there is a very ingenious answer. The interval between the comet and the poem (if we date the latter about January 1) is not four years, but three and a half, from July 710/44 to January 714/40, that is to say, the "time, times and an half" so familiar to Jewish and Judaising apocalyptic.[92] But I rather doubt if even Horace's credulous Hebrew Apelles would have faith enough to accept this Hebraism.[93] Granted the existence of the sham oracle, it must have been produced either in the East or in the West. If the former, it was probably Alexandrian, and Jewish influence there is far from impossible, though not certain. But in that case the Roman interpretation of the comet as heralding something advantageous, in all probability something highly advantageous, for Rome would hardly be found in it. On the other hand, an Italian or other Western forgery might indeed make the most of the comet, as Vergil himself did, but would certainly not Hebraise either in diction or in its themes. I cannot, therefore, think that the *Iulium sidus* will help us here, although the underlying proposition, that its appearance heralded a better age, is one not without support.

I fear therefore that we must, with Reinach, resign ourselves to ignorance[94] concerning the oracle, whatever it was, which Vergil took as his text; but I see no reason to doubt his own assurance, expressed in so many words, that it existed. If we accept this, we must, I think, also accept it that the most puzzling figure in the whole poem, the child, was mentioned therein. Let us look at the words which first mention him, and at their context. Once more I use the plainest of modern prose to shadow forth Vergil's rich poetry:[95]

The last age of the Cumaean song is come, the great series of the ages is coming into being anew. Now returns the Virgin, now returns the reign of Saturn, now a new race is sent down from high heaven. Only do thou, chaste Lucina, show thy lovingkindness to the child at his birth,[96] by reason of whom the Iron race shall first end and the Golden arise over all the universe. Thine Apollo now rules.

The child, a figure to whom I can find no parallel in any classical document, is thus introduced without a word of explanation, not even a parenthesis like "for born he must be ere the new age shall begin," as if he were the most familiar thing in the world. I do not see how to avoid the conclusion; he is thus introduced because the oracle, supposed known, spoke of him. But this does but push the difficulty one place further back; why did the oracle mention a child; in other words, where did this unknown manufacturer of prophecies get the idea? We may be fairly sure that it is of the East, but that is a wide enough district and its civilisations miscellaneous enough to leave us a broad field in which to search.

For Christian commentators of the first few centuries of our era, indeed up to the Revival of Letters, when historical sense and a feeling for chronological possibilities were born anew, it was of course obvious that the Messianic prophecies of the Old Testament had somehow made their way to Vergil, or the Sibyl, or rather, that the latter was inspired to proclaim the coming of a religion still of the future and foretell its Founder's birth. It is hard, save perhaps for those who have come into contact with the remnants of such a mentality which still linger here and there under the labels of Fundamentalism or the like, for us today to realise that the following passage, typical of many, proceeds from the pen of the high-minded and comparatively skeptical St. Augustine, one of the keenest intellects of the last days of the Roman Empire:[97]

For there were also prophets not of God Himself, and even in them are to be found some things which they had heard and uttered concerning Christ. So it is said of the Sibyl among others; which I would not readily believe but that a certain one of the poets, the most famous in the Roman tongue, before saying of the renewal of the age things which seem to fit and agree with the kingdom of our Lord Jesus Christ, prefixes a verse in which he says, "The last age of the Cumaean song is come."

A few moderns still fight a rearguard action for this sort of explanation in a modified form; they contend that Vergil may have had some slight acquaintance with the Old Testament, and even point to a possible line of communication between him and it, in the form of some rather vague Jewish connections of Pollio.[98] They try to strengthen their case by drawing attention to certain resemblances between Vergil's Golden Age and the descriptions of a like time in the future contained in Isaiah.[99] But this view is worth mentioning only as part, so to say, of the history of the case; the resemblances, which really exist, resemble also well-known and common classical details of the traditional and conventional Golden Age.[100] If we like to suppose that these and the descriptions of the Hebrew prophet have a common origin, the case is arguable;[101] but it does not justify us in drawing any such conclusion concerning Vergil as that, having his curiosity aroused by Pollio or some Jewish acquaintance of his, he dipped into the Septuagint and saw its poetical possibilities through the mist of its uncouth Greek. His immediate source, unless extremely strong proof to the contrary can be adduced, as it cannot, must be assumed to be the Greek and Roman authors whom he knew and imitated.

Much more to be regarded is the wide-spread Oriental belief, found for instance in Egypt,[102] that a bad age shall be succeeded by a good one, ruled over by an enlightened monarch. There was a popular tale to the effect that a wise man appeared at court and told the king that there should arise a great Pharaoh under whom all the ills of the land should disappear.[103] And this was not confined to Egypt by any means; indeed, its most striking form is Persian. The followers of Zarathustra expected that at the end of the age a virgin, bathing in a certain lake, should be impregnated by the holy seed of the reformer himself, preserved there through the ages. Her child should be Saoshyant, the Saviour, who should do battle victoriously against the powers of Ahriman and so bring about the end of all things and the coming of *frashokereti*, the renewal of the universe.[104] Apart from serious eschatological doctrine of this kind, which it is by no means impossible might have spread far enough west to influence an Alexandrian or other manufacturer of Sibylline verses, it was and for some time had been correct to speak of kings as gods made manifest,[105] while, if we like to suppose Jewish influence present by some route, there exists to this day a Sibylline promise, not of course of a divine king begotten by Yahweh, as Egyptian kings were on occasion by Re,[106] but of a God-fearing world-conqueror whom God shall "send from the sun,"[107] whatever exactly that may mean. And that hopes of a better age under a good ruler had reached Rome is evident enough from the coins struck by several mint-masters late in the career of Caesar,[108] with such emblems as a globe surmounted by a cornucopia between a steering-oar and a sceptre (i.e., there shall be or is a strong governor who brings plenty), the head of the Sibyl, or again a globe surmounted by a double cornucopia (this seems to be a piece of Egyptian symbolism, like their double crown) and on the other side of the piece a child, whether he be Aion or some other figure. That Aion does appear on Roman coins for a time is certain; and some of these emblems are combined with Caesar's star, while one series is decorated with the sun, moon, and planets, perhaps indicating the coming of a new Great Year. On the whole, I think we are not rash in once more assuming that Vergil means what he says, and that he really had hold of a prophecy which said that better new times were coming, indeed a revolution of all things for good, and that somehow and somewhere a child was to be born who should have a part in it.

This leaves us, supposing agreement reached so far, face to face with the most troublesome problem of all. Who was the child Vergil refers to? Was he ever born? Was he a real child at all, that is to say the infant whom some actual human couple either did produce or might have hoped for about the time the poem was written? We may perhaps start with the list given by the Christian grammarian whose commentary lies behind the confused and rambling note of the Berne scholia.[109] Condensed, his explanation runs thus:

> This Eclogue is written in honour of Asinius Pollio, or, as some say, of his son Saloninus, who was named after the city of Salonae in Dalmatia because Pollio begat him after being appointed proconsul of Dalmatia. The "new race" is either Saloninus, Augustus, Christ, or Marcellus, son of Octavia.

This, however, does not exhaust the list of ancient conjectures. If we consult Daniel's Servius, we are told [110] that

> Some understand it of Saloninus, son of Pollio, others of Asinius Gallus, brother of Saloninus, who was born earlier while Pollio was still consul designate. Asconius Pedianus reports that he heard from Gallus that this Eclogue was composed in his (Gallus') honour.

Moderns have made a few additions to this list. The chief ones are a child of Antony, or the expected child of Octavian and Scribonia, who turned out to be the notorious Julia,[111] and an abstract and allegorical infant, either simply a representative Roman of the new and blessed generation,[112] a reborn Zagreus or some similar Dionysiac-Orphic figure,[113] or a kind of incarnation of the new epoch.[114] Let us consider whether any of these candidates is possible[115] and, if so, which of them. If we find none of them satisfactory, we may perhaps look further and see whether any more additions can be made to the already long catalogue.

We have already discussed the natural misapprehension which made the Eclogue into a prophecy of the Nativity of Christ, and need go no further into the matter.[116] It is more profitable to discuss Saloninus, for he is readily disposed of, seeing that it is extremely improbable that he ever existed.[117] In the first place, Saloninus would not be a natural cognomen for a person born at Salonae, for it is derived, not from the name of the town, but from the gentile name Salonius, by which indeed the Berne scholia once or twice impossibly call him; impossibly, because though a son need not have the *cognomen* of his father, he must have the same *nomen* unless he changes it by adoption. Secondly, the whole authority for the connection of Pollio with Salonae and the birth to him of a son there is shaky. The historians and the *acta triumphalia* say nothing about it, only the scholiasts on Vergil and Horace[118] seeming acquainted with the matter. And they are a mass of confusion. Daniel's Servius gravely states that Pollio, at the head of the army of Germany (*Germanicus exercitus*),[119] won a triumph before he was consul (his campaign was in 715/39, while he was governor of Illyricum). What he would be doing at Salonae, which is not in his province at all, it is hard to say, still less why he should have taken it, as the scholiasts say he did,[120] for it was a loyal place with a population largely Roman. On the whole, the modern equivalent of this remarkable perversion of ancient history would be an account of Sherman's march to the sea which began by saying that, putting himself at the head of the Canadian Expeditionary Force, he stormed and occupied Washington before entering Georgia. The tales of the life and death of Pollio's alleged son are the most obvious fiction; he was born amid all sorts of portents, laughed the first day, had the power of speech and twenty fingers instead of ten, and finally, exhausted no doubt by these precocious efforts, died on the ninth day. That a baby should have a cognomen not hereditary in his family is almost as hard to believe, and if he really was born and lived but nine days, he never had a name at all.[121] The fact is that he seems to be a reflex from a real Saloninus, the son of Asinius Gallus.[122] But even if we like to assume, quite gratuitously, that Pollio's wife, for some reason of convenience or safety, did visit Salonae while her husband was on campaign, and there was delivered of a son (who must have died young, whether after eight days of life or some other period, for no one but the scholiasts has heard of him), we have not only to confront all the difficulties which attend the assumption that any child of Pollio is meant, but also to accuse Vergil of the cruelty of publishing a poem which would remind bereaved parents of their grief, and that in the most poignant way, by immortalising bright hopes never to be fulfilled.

Asinius Gallus has at least this advantage over his brother, that he did live and found some to credit his assertion about being the wonder-child of the poem. St. Jerome in his *Chronicle*, under the year of Abraham 2030 (A.D. 14), says, perhaps on the authority of Donatus, that at that time "Gaius Asinius Gallus the orator, son of Pollio, of whom also Vergil makes mention, was put to death with horrible tortures by Tiberius." Taking the relative clause to refer to Asinius Gallus and not to his father, the only mention Vergil can be supposed to make of him is in this poem; hence it would seem that by the time the *Chronicle* was compiled, there were some who believed his boast to Asconius. But there is no evidence that Asconius believed it, or that it was generally accepted in less credulous times or by scholars of more skeptical minds than either the good Father or his unknown authority. We must weigh the assertion on its merits, first noting that Gallus was the vain son of a vain father, not likely to be too scrupulous in claiming distinction for his own family.

The difficulties are twofold. In the first place, Vergil speaks of a child soon to be born, not of one already born, and whatever Gallus' birth-year was, it was not 714/40,[123] but earlier. In the second place, Pollio, although Vergil speaks of him with the respect and admiration due to a patron not unworthy, despite his shortcomings, of such courtesies, could hardly, even in his own opinion of himself, merit such praises as the father of the mysterious child receives. That the boy, when of school age, will read of his father's exploits, *facta parentis* (26), in itself proves little, for Pollio was certainly important enough for his name to be mentioned in any history that might be written, though it is somewhat flattering to speak of his doings in the same breath with *heroum laudes*. But line 17 is the strongest of evidence against Pollio. It runs

>pacatumque reget patriis uirtutibus orbem.

That is, either the child is to govern a world "pacified" by the excellences, or valorous deeds, of his father, or else, the world being "pacified," he is to rule it by the exercise of those excellences which he will no doubt inherit. In either case the world is "pacified," and it is hard to believe that this, to a Roman of any date, would mean anything else than "conquered," "reduced to order," by Rome.[124] The father, then, is either explicitly or by implication stated to be a world-conqueror. But not only is this absurd in fact of Pollio; it is contrary to all we know of him to suppose that he ever had ambitions that way, for he seems to have been a peace-loving man, more than a little of a republican in sentiment, anxious to put an end to civil strife and not altogether unsuccessful in his attempts. Vergil, if he wanted to describe a peaceful rule with no conquest involved, knew very well how to do so; we have but to remember what he wrote later of Latinus:[125]

>rex arua Latinus et urbes
>iam senior longa placidas in pace regebat.

If, then, he had meant here that the boy was destined to a reign of peace and that the peace was due, or his ability to rule was caused, by the good qualities of his father, why did he not say, for instance,

>atque reget placidum patriis uirtutibus orbem

or

>et patriis in pace reget uirtutibus orbem?

As it is, he tells us that the child is to be heir to a world in which he will meet with no opposition, because it has already been overcome, presumably by the wars which shall precede the Golden Age and the prowess of the "great Achilles," who might be himself, his father, or some third, unnamed person, who shall do battle against the new Troy.

Finally, a point which has repeatedly been made, if Vergil meant a son of Pollio, what conceivable reason had he, in a poem addressed to the latter and speaking highly of him, for never mentioning his fatherhood?[126] He emphasises the honourable part which he shall take, as *consul* and *dux*, in preparing the way for the new era; if he is actually to be the father of its destined king, why omit this greatest of all titles to recognition?

Marcellus, although he has some modern advocates,[127] has an even weaker case. His father was an insignificant member of the great family of the Marcelli, and it is the father, not the mother of the child who is emphasised elsewhere than in the tender and beautiful lines at the end of the poem, which do not dwell upon her greatness nor any qualities which the baby shall inherit from her, but simply on her physical motherhood, its pains and its reward. If we say that Vergil is thinking, not of Marcellus the Elder, but of Octavia's second husband, the great Antony, a throng of difficulties confront us. Octavia lost her first husband sometime in 714/40;[128] therefore, if Vergil wrote the poem, as we have seen he probably did, late in 713/41, she was then a

A CHILD IS BORN

married woman and there was no reason to suppose that she was to be remarried to a more distinguished man. If he did after all not compose the Eclogue till about October, 714/40, when she was married to, or about to marry, Antony, we meet with further complications. We need not assume that she was then carrying the younger Marcellus, the date of whose birth is uncertain;[129] let it be granted that Vergil simply means that she and Antony will have a child who shall in time fulfil the promise of the poem. We then have to consider the following ingenious theory.[130]

It is granted by everyone who has read both works that Vergil owes something to the sixty-fourth poem of Catullus, the *Peleus and Thetis*. This is most evident in line 46 of the Eclogue,

talia saecla, suis dixerunt, currite, fusis,

which deliberately echoes the refrain of the Fates' song in Catullus,

currite ducentes subtegmina, currite fusi,

but, after the fashion of Vergil when he echoes another writer, completely alters the meaning and part of the context. In Catullus, the Fates bid their spindles turn and hasten to make the thread of destiny for the newly married pair and their future son Achilles; in Vergil, it is not the spindles but the ages to be which are bidden to hasten or run on. But there are other resemblances. For instance, Catullus' picture of the dealings of gods and men in the Heroic Age certainly is like the description of Vergil's wonder-child and his acquaintance with the gods. Catullus says,[131]

praesentes namque ante domus inuisere castas
heroum et sese mortali ostendere coetu
caelicolae nondum spreta pietate solebant.

For Heaven's dwellers in that olden time
Ere goodness was contemned, were wont to seek
Heroes' pure homes and meet the throngs of men.

And he goes on to explain why this is no longer so; the gods ceased to be friendly to man

> postquam tellus scelerest imbuta nefando,
> Iustitiamque omnes cupida de mente fugarunt.[132]

> When sin unspeakable polluted earth
> And covetous hearts drove Righteousness away.

This is certainly reminiscent of Vergil's description of the reverse process which shall take place during the child's lifetime, when

> si qua manent sceleris uestigia nostri[133]
> irrita perpetua soluent formidine terras.
> ille deum uitam accipiet diuisque uidebit
> permixtos heroas et ipse uidebitur illis.

> The traces of our sin that yet remain
> Shall fade, and rid the earth of endless fear.
> The child shall win a life divine and see
> Heroes with gods commingled, face to face.

And the reason, as he has just explained,[134] is that Justice is returning, and therefore the earth is once more a fit place for gods to visit in visible form, *praesentes*, as Catullus says, while Vergil says the same thing in more words, *uidebit atque ipse uidebitur*. Both poets refer to the meeting of human and divine face to face. Furthermore, Catullus lays great stress on the future greatness of Achilles,[135] with whose generation the Heroic Age passed, he being its mightiest representative. Vergil says there shall be a new Achilles,[136] plainly an embodiment or representative of the new Heroic Age which shall usher in the Golden Age. There is also a curious little point to which Mr. Slater draws attention. Vergil's poem, if we leave out the three introductory verses, which have nothing to do with his prophecy and are mere preface and compliment, is exactly sixty lines long, which is precisely the length of the prophetic song of the Fates in

Catullus.[137] This is not quite correct, for the Fates have but fifty-eight lines, one of the fifty-nine which the manuscripts give them being an accidental repetition of the refrain in the wrong place; but it is near enough correct to make it possible that some significance is to be attached to it, in a poem like this, meant for careful reading by learned or at least literary men.[138]

So much for the facts on which the theory depends; the hypothesis is that we have here something in the nature of a marriage-hymn, all formal difficulties notwithstanding. Vergil knew that Octavia was to marry Antony (so Slater), or he knew that she was expecting a child by her former, or still living, husband Marcellus; this would seem to follow from Herrmann's theory. He therefore wrote this prophecy concerning her offspring and deliberately introduced by implication Catullus' theme of the wedding of Peleus and Thetis, either because Marcellus corresponded to Peleus, the mortal who married a goddess, while Octavia, with her relationship to Octavian her brother and through him to the deified Julius, to say nothing of her own direct claim to divine ancestry through Venus and Aeneas, played the part of Thetis herself;[139] or else because her wedding with Antony was in itself an important enough event to be celebrated by a poet in what was essentially a marriage-hymn, since it marked the reconciliation between her new husband and her brother.

The difficulties of supposing that Marcellus, the husband of Octavia, was the father of the wonder-child have already been touched upon. Even the ingenious equation of him with Peleus will hardly meet them, for Peleus was one of the most distinguished of the legendary heroes, chosen as a fit husband for Thetis by reason of his outstanding goodness as well as his valour, whereas Marcellus was a man who had made but little noise in the world for any qualities, good or bad. Also, to suppose that Vergil knew, early in, or more probably before, 714/40, that she was with child argues a degree of intimacy with her affairs hardly likely in a man of mediocre social position and having, so far as we know, no channels by which personal news of this sort concerning the most distinguished families in the land could reach him. But if we suppose Antony alluded to as her husband and so in a sense her child's father, if only by adoption, we meet once more with the difficulty of the form of the poem. If it is a marriage-hymn, why has it none of the commonplaces appropriate to such a composition, neither praise of the bride and groom or their families, laudation of wedlock in general, reflections on the joy awaiting the wedded pair, or mention of any of the numerous deities of marriage? Add to this the fact that a comparatively late date for the poem, that is, one towards the end of 714/40, has been shown to be the less likely, and I think we may dismiss the theory entirely.

It remains, however, to consider whether a child, existing or expected, of Antony may not be meant. This view is vigorously upheld by H. Jeanmaire,[140] a scholar in whose commendation it may be said that he does not lose sight of the intimate connection between the politics and the religion of the Near East at that date. His views may be thus summarised. The child in Vergil is divine and of divine parentage in some sense.[141] Specifically,[142] his character is Dionysiac. His coming is foretold by a Sibylline oracle, which is most likely to be a piece of Egyptian propaganda.[143] Where, then, is it probable that Vergil would find this divine ancestry, the "new race" which is to descend (or is descending) from heaven, the hope of the return of a Golden Age and the incidence of a critical time at which such a revolution might naturally be expected? He answers, that if any actual recent event is hinted at[144] it is that which had occurred only the year before Pollio's consulship, the meeting of Antony with Kleopatra on the Kydnos.

Her dressing as Aphrodite-Isis was no wanton masquerade, but a piece of calculated "politico-theological" scheming, and he met her at least halfway by his Dionysiac claims, appropriate alike to the position of the husband of Isis, Osiris-Dionysos,[145] and to the intending conqueror of the East, or rather of that Eastern power which loomed largest on the horizon, Parthia. Vergil had at that time no reason to be hostile to this pair of incarnate deities, nor to suspect that in a few years his own leader Octavian would be Antony's mortal enemy; indeed, his mention of Apollo as now ruling suggests that he thought of Octavian as entirely friendly to Antony, for Apollo is well known to have been Octavian's favourite god.[146] It might be added that Apollo is traditionally the friend and supporter of Dionysos, with whom he shares the most famous of all his shrines, Delphoi. The poem may have actually been composed or begun before the Perusian War.[147] As to dates, Jeanmaire is of the opinion, though we are not well informed about the small details of the chronology of those times and by no means all his calculations are accepted by other scholars, that Kleopatra's twins, Alexander Helios and Kleopatra Selene, were born in 714/40.[148] Such divine offspring of a divine union would be a suitable enough subject for poetry, and he ingeniously accounts for the Golden Age by the argument[149] that a divine monarchy would bring the world back to where, by Egyptian or Graeco-Egyptian ideas, it started, namely to the rule of beneficent gods dwelling on the earth. There is even something to be made out of the words *iam redit et Virgo* for his theory, since on the Graeco-Egyptian star-map Virgo is Isis.[150] He adds a most ingenious scheme of world-ages. The Golden Age is to return by the time the child is a full-grown man, in his *firmata aetas* (37). Suppose this means the age of seven times eight, or fifty-six years.[151] Add this to 714/40, and we arrive at A. D. 16, exactly 1200 years after the traditional date (1184 B. C.) of the fall of

Troy. Are these twelve centuries the "great months" of Vergil's year?[152]

Mr. Tarn is of a different opinion concerning the personality of the child, but, like Jeanmaire, sees Alexandrian influence at work.[153] He believes that Vergil originally meant the poem to refer to no human baby at all, but a "mystical" child, an embodiment of the Golden Age itself, if I do not misunderstand him; in other words, that Norden's theory[154] would be right if we had the work as it was first composed but never published. He further supposes that, late in 714/40, when the marriage of Octavia to Antony had taken place or was about to take place, Vergil published his poem in the form we now have and that, as Slater supposes, he meant it to be an epithalamium for the newly married pair. But Antony and Octavia between them falsified the prophecy. Octavia bore a daughter, Marcella minor, and Antony, in 717/37, finally left her for Kleopatra, thus making Alexander Helios, and not the son whom Octavia never bore him, into the child of the prophecy, so far as he was able.[155] By that time Vergil also was changing his views, and had become a whole-hearted and exclusive supporter of Octavian as the one hope of the time and the true restorer of the Golden Age.[156]

These views, and any others like them, have at least one decided advantage, that they explain why the poem is dedicated to a supporter of Antony, and not, for example, to Gallus or some other avowed follower of Octavian. Yet they seem to me to have a fatal weakness. Vergil nowhere in the *Eclogues* shows the least partiality to Antony nor makes any mention of him, if we leave this poem out of account. He was an intelligent man, apparently very loyal, though without any of the meaner arts of the courtier, once he had given his adhesion; and it is plain enough from such passages as *Ecl.*, IX, 46 sqq., I, 42 sqq., that about the time he was composing this poem he was rather decidedly of the party of Octavian, despite all reserves and implied criticisms. This does not mean that he hated or despised Octavian's great rival, but it is incredible that he knew nothing of the rivalry, which surely was notorious by that time if not earlier. It is of course true that he, like all men of good will, would welcome the reconciliation between the two and the marriage which was its chief outward sign. If we had from him a poem in which, under a pastoral disguise or in some other form, he expressed joy at so happy an event and hopes of an end to strife, it would not be at all surprising. But that he should so handle the subject as to put the offspring of the marriage decidedly in the foreground and imply that the father, Antony, was the beneficent master of the world, not simply a prominent contributor to the better order of things, is so inconsistent with his known political views at the time (I say nothing of his later expressions of opinion, for his other works were not published till Antony was dead) that I cannot believe it. I would therefore reject all hypotheses of this sort, allowing only that Vergil, being neither a fanatic nor rashly imprudent, did not express himself so openly, here or elsewhere in the *Eclogues*, as to come forward a declared opponent of Antony and leave no loophole for a reconciliation with his supporters if he should in the end prove the victor. Nor, indeed, would it be expected of any admirer of Octavian at that time so to express himself; probably outspoken abuse of Antony, even implied detraction, would have been discouraged by Octavian and his ministers. We may compare the fact that Horace, writing perhaps some three years later than Vergil[157] and at a time when he was, if not exactly in the confidence of Maecenas, at least intimate enough with him to know what sort of allusions would best please both him and Octavian, mentions friendship with Antony among the good qualities of Fonteius Capito. And this same consideration, it seems to me, greatly lessens, if it does not entirely remove, the difficulty of a work which, as I with many others believe, highly compliments Octavian while being addressed to an Antonian. Pollio may already have been known, when Vergil wrote the dedication of this poem, to be anxious for a better understanding between the two leaders; therefore officially at least he would be ready to admit admirable qualities in Octavian and to hear his praises, unmixed with any detraction from the greatness of Antony, with equanimity, at all events when conjoined with the assurance that he himself was to take a very respectable, even a leading, part in the happy issue of Octavian's activities.

It is therefore time to examine that view which supposes that the child is, in Tarn's phrase, "mystic," that is, no real infant at all but some kind of abstraction. The most persuasive and learned statement of this theory is that of Ed. Norden, and because it is his it deserves quotation at some length.

The conception that χρόνος, thought of as accompanying man, is born with him and grows old with him, is current in Greek thought, but takes a new and strange shape when applied here to the motif of the ages. The child is young with the age, and with it he grows and ripens to manhood.... Peace does not come (until he is a man) ... for, being free from sin, he shall rule over children of heaven (the *noua progenies* of 7).... To feel our way into the conceptual complex which is implied by the parallel development of the time and the child is not easy for us, since in our thought time and eternity are abstract ideas. We must therefore help ourselves out by periphrases, such as the usual one that the child is the representative of the *aion*, or the *aion* is manifested in him. But for the more concrete thought of antiquity, the conceptual abstraction was easily transformed into a real personality. [Certain phrases and ideas in Herakleitos, Euripides, and Aristotle] show that the ground was ready to receive the seed from the Orient, which ripened into the Hellenistic cult of Aion....The liturgical formula of the Alexandrian festival of Aion on January 6, "This day has the Virgin borne Aion," we have already made the acquaintance of, and have learned that at the similar festival, likewise Alexandrian, of December 24-25, the statuette of a child, as a symbol of the newly born sun-god, was carried in the procession of the initiate. [Macrobius tells us that] at the winter solstice "the sun seems to be a little child, such as the Egyptians show him when they bring him forth from the inner shrine on a certain day, because then, as it is the shortest day, he appears as it were small, a mere baby. Then, as his growth increases, at the spring equinox he undergoes a change like that of a growing boy, and so is shown under the shape of a man."[168] He gives like information concerning the other two cardinal points of the year, in the summer and autumn, to bring before us the parallelism of the sun's course and the life of man. It is the same idea as the growth of the child into the age of Helios, which our poem celebrates. The ritual of that festival may be no earlier than the Hellenistic period, but how far back the underlying idea reaches is clear from the words of king Amenophis IV to the sun-god, "Thou art lifetime itself."[169]

But it seems to me that no upholder of this or a like view can explain away the concluding lines of the poem. The mother who has undergone the weariness of a long pregnancy and now awaits the smile of her new-born babe to tell her that he is no common infant but a wonder-child, the offspring in some sense of a god, is as fully human a figure as any in poetry, and has nothing about her to suggest that she is any sort of personification. Who she is we may not succeed in determining; but assuredly she is a woman, real or imaginary, and no superhuman nor abstract figment. Further, eloquently though Norden argues for the identification, here or elsewhere in classical literature, of a period of time, thought of as something concrete, with a person, I find no evidence that any Latin of Vergil's age thought so. His countrymen were Westerners and moderns, and their minds ran along much the same paths as ours; if they did think of the year, for example, as something existing independently, it was as pale a phantom as those figures of the Old and New Years which sometimes are to be found in our illustrated papers. Anna Perenna is a most shadowy goddess, and the theory (about contemporary with Vergil) that the god Ianus was the same as Aion is but one of several guesses at the nature of a god who puzzled Roman theologians, and others, because he had no Greek counterpart.[160] Their concrete time was rather a thing which a child had in small quantity, to be given more as he grew older, while an aging man was losing it;[161] not anything identified with either the child or the older person. Nor is it at all necessary to do more, for the interpretation of this poem, than to say that the change back from the Iron to the Golden Age will take about as long to complete as a new-born infant needs to reach maturity. I therefore reject all theories which do not suppose that a real child is meant, whether he is found ever to have existed as a historical figure or not.

The claims of Scribonia to be the mother of the expected infant can be briefly dismissed. At the beginning of 714/40 she was not yet married to Octavian; the marriage took place in the summer of the year. Her daughter Julia, the only child of the marriage, was born late in 715/39.[162] Hence she was probably not married to Octavian, certainly not with child by him, when Vergil wrote.

We are therefore left with the following clues to the child's identity, or rather that of his parents, for we have no evidence that he was ever born. He is not the offspring of any couple which we have considered; but his parents, at least his father, are real and the father a man of very high distinction. Since the child is in some sense divine, it would seem to follow that father, mother or both have some claim to deity, personally or by descent.[163] At least, one of them should be an outstanding benefactor of mankind. His birth is expected shortly, apparently but not certainly during the current year; therefore there was a prophecy of some kind which foretold the happy event with an indication of date clear enough for the poet to understand or think he understood it. And one of the reasons for this expectation is that Apollo is in some sense the ruling god.

Therefore, although we have not succeeded in identifying the mother and probably never shall, surely the father is not far to seek. There was a man of the highest distinction, elsewhere in the *Eclogues* referred to as a god, in the sense of a great benefactor. He claimed divine descent and had an especial devotion to Apollo. I mean, of course, Octavian. He, as we have seen, was interested in proclamations of a new age and in portents; it would thus be a reasonable expectation that he would be pleased with a poem in his honour which made such things its principal theme. He was also, at least in later life, perhaps already at that date, zealous for at all events the outward observances of the traditional religion of his country, including the Sibylline oracles and their interpretation. He did not like extreme flattery, and it would have been extreme to say then, in the midst of his struggles, that he was on the very point of bringing in an age of universal innocence, peace, and harmless prosperity. But for a poet still young and ardent to say that he was working towards that end, that the next generation would see a better world, was surely nothing more than some optimist might say of a leading general or statesman now.

I therefore take the true interpretation of the poem to be no more than this: "There is a prophecy that this year, the year of your consulship, Pollio, shall see a turn for the better, leading in the end to a new Golden Age. The change will not be very rapid, but it is sure; Apollo, who inspired the prophetess and whom Octavian honours, has the power and the will to bring it about. We have still much to do, for the earth is sinful; there are more wars to fight, and we shall see valiant champions by sea and land go forth and conquer (here it may very well be that he hints at Antony and his proposed carrying out of Caesar's plans for overthrowing Parthia and so removing the most serious menace to peace on the eastern frontier). But there shall be a return, by divine intervention, as Plato said long ago (i.e., another servant of Apollo), to the times of Kronos. Octavian himself has the hard task of bringing peace out of strife, but he will succeed, and the world his son shall see will be an infinitely better one. Let him therefore soon give the world that son, to succeed him and carry on his beneficent task under easier conditions. Happy will that woman be who bears so glorious a child; may her reward come soon."

If we accept this explanation, we have an answer to a question which haunts the other interpretations and will not be easily banned, namely, why Vergil never seems to have attempted to suppress his prophecy once it was falsified by the birth of Julia, the action of Antony in turning his back on all Western ideals, the non-appearance of a Golden Age. For, as I think, it never was falsified in the poet's lifetime. Octavian, or Augustus as he was then, survived him, and still hoped for an heir, whether actually of his body or not, to continue what he had begun. Times were bettering, little by little, *paulatim*, as Vergil had said, and the fears which for a while succeeded his optimism[164] proved unjustified. Later, when his poetical powers and Augustus' policy alike were matured, he was to hail the Emperor as the true restorer of the real Golden Age,[165] its founder if not its perfector. He did not live to see the enlightened and liberal despotism of his hero succeeded by the mechanical tyranny of Tiberius, nor could he foretell the madness of Caligula or the vagaries of Nero.

By this interpretation also we keep to the principle already enunciated of supposing the minimum of allegory in Vergil. We suppose that the child is real, that the lordship of Apollo means something, that the Golden Age is a poetical expression of the better time which really did come and the poet had the perspicacity and political judgement already to hope for. Further, we suppose that he drew, as the rest of his work indicates, largely on the ordinary literary models familiar to a man of his education, not on obscure and out-of-the-way sources not likely to be available either to him or to his Italian readers. We also suppose that his political ideals were connected with the only person we know him to have trusted and thought of as a possible or probable solver of the hideously complex problems of that time. We take his religious beliefs, or those which he assumes for the purposes of the poem, to be simply those which we know were current among educated men of that time and place, and not the dogmas of any obscure or foreign sect. In a word, it appears to me that the explanation given makes Vergil fully Vergilian, and that all the rest depart more or less widely from leading characteristics of him and his work.

Excursus: The Chronokratories

In order to see more clearly that Vergil's world-ages are not astrological, it is convenient briefly to review those schemes which are definitely such. The most abundant source of information on the subject is *C(atalogus) C(odicum) A(strologicorum) G(raecorum)*, IV, pp. 114 sqq., with the notes of F. Cumont. The document there published, or rather the two documents, representing a shorter and a longer series of excerpts from some writing now lost, is to the following effect. Astrologers (ἀποτελεσματικοί) hold as one of their most difficult and obscure doctrines that the first thousand years of the world were ruled over by the planet Saturn. Now since his is the outermost orbit and his revolution of thirty years the longest period of the whole system, it follows that in those days men lived much longer than they do now. Furthermore, their way of life was Saturnian; they pursued such things as farming, the planting of trees and the like (φυτουργία, p.116, 8), house building, and general equality. After Saturn came Jupiter, and his much shorter period of revolution, twelve years only, brought about a corresponding abbreviation of the life of man. Human beings now adopted Jovian ways, ruling and being ruled after the fashion of a monarchy, founding cities instead of single dwellings, practicing justice, goodness, and unaffected love and raising families of handsome children. Next came Mars, whose two-year revolution entailed yet further shortening of human life. His rule brought with it war, strife, and all the attendant miseries of slaughter, discord and so forth. The next thousand years were under the government of the sun, whose comparatively short revolution of a single year meant still more abbreviation of the span of life. His influence, however, was on the whole good, for it resulted in strong and glorious kings and other potentates, who practiced justice. After him, Venus had her turn;

life grew somewhat shorter yet and excessive passion with its attendant prevalence of fornication, idolatry (p. 117, 12; the document has been through Christian hands, and the constant Biblical connection of the two offences has forced itself on the scribe), feastings, and so on. Mercury followed Venus; human life grew yet shorter, and the characteristics of that age were the arts of Hermes, such as seercraft, philosophy, astronomy, philology and rhetoric in all their branches, arithmetic, and geometry. Last came the moon, with her very rapid revolution of 28½ days; the short-lived humanity of her rule became treacherous and mutable, as she is. Whether she still governs the world is not clearly stated, but it seems to be implied. Thus we have a scheme of 7000 years, which does not include a Golden Age of the sort either Hesiod or Vergil describes, although the period of Saturn has some of its characteristics, notably the general equality of mankind. But there is a much more complicated scheme in *CCAG*, V (2d ed.), 135, 6 sqq., the work of some unknown Byzantine, doubtless drawing upon an older source. When God created the world, He gave the millennia to the planets in the same order as that sketched above, but within each millennium was instituted a system of co-regency. The first century of the first millennium was governed by Jupiter, followed in the same order as before by Mars, the sun, and so on, till the seventh century found Saturn his own co-regent in this respect. The first decade fell to Mars, followed in like manner by the other planets, the first year to the sun, the first month to Venus, the first day to Mercury, and the first hour to the moon. So, in circular order, the planets have constantly succeeded one another as governors of these various periods of time, and any given moment finds all seven of them exercising more or less lasting domination. An odd and apparently defective scheme is that in *CCAG*, VIII (3d ed.), 199, 6 sqq., where the first, third, fifth, and seventh millennia go respectively to Jupiter, the sun, Mercury, and the moon, but it is not said what became of the even-numbered periods.

Passing over such documents as *CCAG*, VII, 88 sqq., which explains how the hours of the week are divided among the planets, VIII (2d ed.), 92, an excerpt from Hephaistion which describes an elaborate Egyptian cycle of ten years elaborately divided among regents and sub-regents in a way similar to the Byzantine scheme of millennia just described, and X, 156 sqq., in which each planet in turn rules a year, with various effects on the weather and other happenings (a document of the eighteenth century, but with traces of older material), we come to the curious system in Firmicus Maternus, *Mathesis*, III, 1, 11 sqq., in a passage which certainly shows Stoic influence of some kind, for it deals with ἐκπυρώσεις and κατακλυσμοί, and perhaps is ultimately Poseidonian. According to this, the moon comes into conjunction with one planet after another (the sun is omitted in this part of the arrangement), thus making him chronokrator for the time being (ut . . . temporum traderet principatum). Saturn comes first, at the beginning of human history, when all was savage; next came Jupiter, Mars, Venus, and Mercury, as before, with the result that mankind grew steadily more civilised and accomplished, but ex uariis institutis moribusque confusis creuit improbitas, which is why Mercury comes last, ut ad imitationem istius sideris intenta gens hominum plenam malitiae conciperet potestatem.

It is thus clear that the astrological schemes include no Golden Age proper, although they do suppose a time of rustic simplicity, variously estimated according to the taste of the author, while Saturn was chronokrator, and none of them has a period governed by the sun (Apollo) immediately preceding a restoration, or advent, of such an age. Vergil probably knew nothing of any such doctrine, and if he did, certainly made no use of it here.

A CHILD IS BORN

There is indeed an astrological document which formally resembles the Vergilian, or Sibylline, prophecy of the child's birth, as is rightly pointed out by Boll, *op. cit.*, pp. 12 sqq. It is in the handbook of Hephaistion of Thebes, printed in Engelbrecht's Vienna edition of 1887,* p. 65, 17 sqq. There the astrologer says that if anyone is born under the third decan of Aquarius with the planets in a favourable position, "he shall be begotten of gods and shall be great and shall be worshipped with the gods and be ruler of the universe (κοσμοκράτωρ), and all things shall obey him." As J. Weiss, quoted by Boll (p. 12, note 2) says, the resemblance to Lc. 1, 32 sq., is fairly close; so also is that to Vergil's language in the Eclogue, cara deum suboles, magnum Iouis incrementum; deum uitam accipiet; reget . . . orbem. I would conclude, not to any astrological influence on Vergil (that the author of the Sibylline oracle may have known something of astrology, however, is not excluded), but rather to a common fund of prophetic language, appropriate to any prediction, however arrived at, and therefore likely to produce like expressions in any two or more passages which foretell an illustrious birth, or the results of such a birth. With the formal likeness here goes a considerable difference in content. It is one thing to say "*if* anyone is born when the position of the heavenly bodies is such-and-such, he shall be a great ruler," quite another to predict that at some more or less definite date a child *shall* be born who is destined to govern the world.

* *Hephaestion von Theben und sein astrologisches Compendium*, von Dr. August Engelbrecht. Wien, Verlag von Carl Konegen, 1887. It is a rather rare monograph and prints Bk. I only of Hephaistion.

NOTES

Notes to Chapter I: The Pastoral Before Vergil

¹ The fragments of Sophron are mostly in G. Kaibel, *Comicorum Graecorum fragmenta* (Berlin, 1899), pp. 152 sqq. The new fragment, however, was first published in 1933 (Norsa and Vitelli, in *Studi italiani di filologia classica*, n.s., X, pp. 119 sqq.). The following text, which represents a reëxamination of the papyrus by Signorina Norsa, is taken from N. Festa's article in *Mondo Classico*, II (1933), pp. 476–484. It runs:

	τὰν τράπεζαν κάττεσθε	– ⏑ – – – – ⏑
	ὥσπερ ἔχει · λάζυσθε δὲ	– ⏑⏑ – – – ⏑⏑
	ἁλὸς χονδρὸν ἐς τὰν χῆρα	⏑ – – ⏑ – – – ⏑
	καὶ δάφναν πὰρ τὸ ὦας.	– ⏑ – – – –
5	ποτιβάντες νυν πὸτ τὰν	⏑⏑ – – – – –
	ἱστίαν θωκεῖτε . δός μοι τὺ	– ⏑ – – – ⏑ – – ⏑
	τὤμφακες · φέρ' ὦ τὰν σκύλακα.	– – – ⏑ – – ⏑⏑⏑
	πεῖ γὰρ ἁ ἄσφαλτος; – οὔτα.	– ⏑ – – ⏑ – –
	— ἔχε καὶ τὸ δᾴδιον καὶ τὸν	⏑⏑ – ⏑ – ⏑ – – –
10	λιβανωτόν · ἄγετε δὴ	⏑⏑ – ⏑⏑⏑⏑ –
	πεπτάσθων μοι ταὶ θύραι	– – – – – ⏑ –
	πᾶσαι· ὑμὲς δὲ ἐνταῦθα	– ⏑ – – – – ⏑
	ὁρῆτε, καὶ τὸν δαελὸν	⏑ – ⏑ – – – ⏑
	σβῆτε ὥσπερ ἔχει · εὐκαμίαν	– – ⏑⏑ – – – ⏑ –
15	νυν παρέχεσθε ἇς κ' ἐγὼν	– ⏑⏑ – – – ⏑ –
	πὸτ τᾶνδ' ἐπάκτ' ἁλιύσω.	– – – ⏑ – –
	πότνια, δείπνου μὲν τὺ καὶ	– ⏑⏑ – – – ⏑ –
	ξενίων ἀμεμφέων ἀντιάσασαν	⏑⏑ – ⏑ – ⏑ – – ⏑⏑ – ⏑

As to its interpretation, I differ a little from the best commentary I have seen, the article by S. Eitrem in *Symbolae Osloenses*, XII (1933), pp. 10 sqq., but have learned much from it. The table presumably has on it offerings of some kind; it is put somewhere in the middle of the room, and the congregation proceeds to protect itself against the uncanny influences which the expert is going to let loose. The hearth is Hekate's own place (Euripides, *Medea*, 397), as is proper, for she is chthonian, and chthonians are worshipped at a hearth, not an altar, as being more in contact with their abode, the ground. So those present group themselves about it, sitting, as is proper for those who deal with the powers below (e.g., Althaia in Homer, when she curses her son, calls on Hades and Persephone in a squatting position, πρόχνυ καθεζομένη, I, 570). But it is, I think, a cold hearth; in line 13 I suppose that the exorcist notices one piece of wood still flickering, and bids it be quenched. Fireless offerings are the usual thing for the chthonians. The object of the rite is twofold, to coax or force Hekate to leave those whom she is troubling and to prevent her from entering into anyone else. So she is given the offering she and her kind most love, a dog (whose blood very likely, as Eitrem suggests, p. 18, is poured on the hearth), and the prayer pointedly reminds her that she has been treated with this proper respect. But appeals merely to the good feeling of such unchancy creatures

222   NOTES TO CHAPTER I

as she is are not to be relied on; indeed, no sorcerer is content merely to make polite requests. The congregation are well protected against her by contact with two things which ill-omened creatures hate like holy water, laurel and salt (see Eitrem, pp. 15-18). With the torch and (burning) bitumen the sorceress will presumably fumigate her patients; the incense may be part of the offering or part of the fumigation; cf. Eitrem, p. 21.

[2] There remain a few broken words after the last of those quoted above, but nothing out of which reasonably certain sense can be made.

[3] For Theokritos, I use the text edition of U. von Wilamowitz-Moellendorff in the *Bib. classica Oxoniensis* (*Bucolici Graeci*). See further, besides the various histories of Greek literature, the same author's *Textgeschichte der griechischen Bukoliker*, and his *Hellenistische Dichtung*, Vol. I, pp. 189 sqq., Vol. II, pp. 130 sqq.

[4] Archimedes' dedication of his *Sand-Reckoner* to Hieron's son Gelon suggests mathematical interests in the royal family.

[5] I do not go into the question of which Sosibios it was. For discussion of the poem and its subject, see E. Cahen, *Callimaque et son œuvre poétique* (Paris, Boccard, 1929), pp. 20, 318, 637.

[6] Women attend a show in Idyll XV; men talk of their private affairs, XIV; a woman practices magic, II. This last is said by the scholiast to owe something to Sophron: τὴν δὲ Θεστυλίδα (the amateur witch's servant) ὁ Θεόκριτος ἀπειροκάλως ἐκ τῶν Σώφρονος μετήνεγκε μίμων, schol. ad init. Unless the person who hands various things to the exorcist in the fragment of Sophron quoted above is called Thestylis, the resemblance between it and the Theokritean piece is negligible.

[7] Theokr., Id. V, 1 sqq.

[8] Theokr., Id. XI, 25 sqq.; the next couplet is *ibid.*, 58-59.

[9] Theokr., Id. VII, 143.

[10] *Ibid.*, 93.

[11] Hesiod, *Theogony*, 22 sqq.

[12] Servius, *comm. in Buc. prooem.*, p. 3, 20 Thilo: sane sciendum vii eclogas [of Vergil] esse meras rusticas, quas Theocritus x habet. That these ten were the first ten of the ancient editions (Wilamowitz-Moell., *Textgesch.*, p. 14), as they are of his printed edition of the poet, is now seen to be wrong by the different order in the Oxyrhynchos and Antinoe papyri (see Hunt-Johnson, *Two Theocritus Papyri*, London, Egypt Exploration Society, 1930, p. 3), but it does not follow that they were never so placed in antiquity; still less that they do not form, and were not regarded as, a group by themselves.

[13] For a good text of it, see Wilamowitz-Moellendorff, *Buc. Graec.*, pp. 91 sqq. The MSS. attribute it to Theokritos himself, which is about as correct as it would be to ascribe Shelley's *Adonais* to Donne.

[14] *Epitaph. Bion.*, 77. Hence the equation Arethusa = pastoral poetry in Vergil, *Ecl.*, X, 1: extremum hunc, Arethusa, mihi concede laborem.

[15] *Ibid.*, 80 sqq.

[16] The following are obvious enough: *epit.*, 18, ἀπώλετο Δώριος Ὀρφεύς, cf. *Adon.* (append., x, Will.), 1 etc., ἀπώλετο καλὸς Ἄδωνις; *epit.*, 67, στυγνοὶ περὶ σῶμα τεὸν κλαίουσιν Ἔρωτες, cf. *Adon.*, 80, ἀμφὶ δέ νιν κλαίοντες ἀναστενάχουσιν

NOTES TO CHAPTER I

Ἔρωτες; *epit.* 69, τὸ φίλημα |τὸ πρῴαν τὸν Ἄδωνιν ἀποθνᾴσκοντα φίλησεν, cf. *Adon.*, 14, ἀλλ' οὐκ οἶδεν Ἄδωνις ὅ μιν θνᾴσκοντα φίλησεν; *epit.*, 125, καί σε Βίων πέμψει [sc. Κώρα] τοῖς ὤρεσιν, cf. *Adon.*, 96, to which it seems a sort of answer.

[17] Theokr., Id. VI, 43.
[18] Theokr., Id. I, 25–26.
[19] Tibullus, I, 4.
[20] Bion, frag. 6 Wilam.
[21] *Epit.*, 89, οὐ τόσον Ἀλκαίω περιμύρετο Λέσβος ἐραννά· 91, σὲ πλέον Ἀρχιλόχοιο ποθεῖ Πάρος.
[22] *Ibid.*, 94, Αὐσονικᾶς ὀδύνας μέλπω μέλος.
[23] *Epit.*, 8 etc.; Theokr., I, 64 etc.
[24] Bion, frag. 12, cf. *epit.*, 58 sqq.
[25] Persius, I, 70 sqq. (we let people try to write epic): nugari solitos Graece [i.e., just beginning rhetoric under a Greek tutor], nec ponere lucum/artifices nec rus saturum laudare.
[26] The dates are: Catullus died not long after 699/55; Vergil was born October 15, 684/70, composed the Bucolics about 712/42–715/39, having lost his estate sometime after the Battle of Philippi in the former year.
[27] Vergil, *Georg.*, I, 497 sqq. (but with one faint hope; if the gods allow, Octavian may still put things right); Horace, *epod.*, 16 (completely despairing; civilisation cannot stand another generation of war, and the only thing left to do is to escape to some undiscovered paradise overseas); Livy, I, *praef.*, 10: haec tempora quibus nec uitia nostra nec remedia pati possumus.
[28] Frag. 1 Naekius (*Choerili Samii quae supersunt*, Leipzig, Weidmann, 1817), probably from the proem of his *Persika*: ἆ μάκαρ ὅστις ἔην κεῖνον χρόνον ἴδρις ἀοιδῶν|Μουσάων θεράπων, ὅτ' ἀκήρατος ἦν ἔτι λειμών·|νῦν δ' ὅτε πάντα δέδασται ἔχουσί τε (δὲ codd.) πείρατα τέχναι,|ὕστερον ὥστε δρόμου καταλείπομεθ', οὐδέ τοι ἔσται|πάντῃ παπταίνοντα νεοζυγὲς ἅρμα πελάσσαι.
[29] Molle atque facetum/Vergilio annuerunt gaudentes rure Camenae, Horace, *sat.*, I, 10, 44–45.

Notes to Chapter II: Molle atqve Facetvm

[1] *Ecl.*, VII, 45, somno mollior herba.

[2] For example, Paris is *mollis* when he runs away from Diomedes (Horace, *carm.*, I, 15, 31); a lustful woman accuses Horace of being *mollis* (*epod.*, 12, 16), meaning that he is not a vigorous lover; *mollis inertia*, *epod.*, 14, 1, is unmanly idleness; *molles querelae* are womanish complaints, *carm.*, II, 9, 17; valiant soldiers are *non molles uiri*, *epod.*, I, 10. Catullus puts *mollis* alongside an even plainer word in lampooning Thallus, 25, 1, and examples in Martial are not far to seek, e.g., III, 73, 4.

[3] *Georg.*, III, 76: mollia crura reponit, "puts his feet down springily."

[4] Cicero, *de off.*, III, 58.

[5] Catullus, 43.

[6] Plautus, *Truc.*, 355. See further Excursus I, below.

[7] I use the fifth ed., revised successively by Nettleship and Haverfield. Both these good scholars seem to have been withheld by mistaken piety from pruning the original editor's appallingly bad criticisms. For some good comments on the form of this Eclogue, see R. Maxa, *Die strophische Gliederung an der zweiten und zehnten Ekloge des Vergilius nachgewiesen*, Trebitsch, 1882.

[8] For consideration of some curious features of Vergil's prosody, see W. F. J. Knight, *Accentual Symmetry in Vergil* (Oxford, Blackwell, 1939).

[9] Statius, *Theb.*, I, 1-17.

[10] Theokr., III, 9, ἀπάγξασθαί με ποησεῖς; (so, not ποησεῖς.) Cf. in general E. Pfeiffer, *Virgils Bukolika* (Stuttgart, Kohlhammer, 1933).

[11] *Aen.*, XII, 603.

[12] Theokr., Id. VII, 22; see Rose in *C. R.*, XLI (1927), p. 100.

[13] Theokr., Id. II, 38-39: ἠνίδε σιγῇ μὲν πόντος, σιγῶντι δ' ἀῆται,|ἁ δ' ἐμὰ οὐ σιγῇ στέρνων ἔντοσθεν ἀνία.

[14] See for instance Ovid, *Amores*, I, 5, 2.

[15] Cf. Rose, *op. cit.*, p. 99.

[16] Tennyson, *Walking to the Mail*. See, for the identification of botanical names in Vergil, J. Sergeaunt, *The Trees, Shrubs and Plants of Virgil* (Oxford, Blackwell, 1920); on pp. 67 sq. the author explains the meaning of *ligustra* here and cites the English parallel.

[17] Sergeaunt, pp. 56 sqq.

[18] Cf. Propertius, III, 15, 41-42: uictorque canebat/paeana Amphion rupe, Aracynthe, tua.

[19] See Steph. Byzant., *s. u.* Ἀράκυνθος, who cites Rhianos; Serv. on *Ecl.*, II, 24.

[20] Theokr., Id. XI, 34.

[21] Hence Vergil calls it *pressi copia lactis*, *Ecl.*, I, 81; contrast, e.g., Theokr., Id. V, 87; XI, 36.

[22] Theokr., Id. VI, 34 sqq.

[23] Sergeaunt, p. 54.

[24] Theokr., Id. XI, 72 sqq.

²⁵ Rose, *Handb. of Gk. Myth.*, pp. 39 sq., note 55. The story is of course quite late and artificial, but may have been known to Vergil.

²⁶ See Excursus II, below.

²⁷ The riddles are (lines 104–107):

>   D. Dic quibus in terris, et eris mihi magnus Apollo,
>   tris pateat caeli spatium non amplius ulnas.
>
>   M. Dic quibus in terris inscripti nomina regum
>   nascantur flores, et Phyllida solus habeto.

Servius gives two interpretations of the former riddle, one that it alludes to the tomb of a certain Caelius, luxuriosi cuiusdam, qui uenditis omnibus rebus et consumptis tantum modo sibi spatium reseruauit quod sepulchro sufficeret. This is obviously a piece of scholiast's invention, made to suit the occasion, and may safely be neglected. His other solution is that it means the famous well at Syene which was said to have the sun directly at its zenith at noon of the summer solstice, or simpliciter ... cuiuslibet loci puteus, since the sky would show no more than three cubits wide from the bottom of it. This is yet more absurd, and a better than either is the modern guess (attributed in De la Rue's note to "Ciacconius et Cerdanus") that *caeli* here means *mundi* in the sense of the ritual pit, or rather pits, so called. Unfortunately we have no information of how wide they were, but it is quite possible that Vergil knew and that some of them, e.g., that dug in founding a city, were no wider than 4½ ft. Servius is much more plausible on the second riddle; the flowers are *hyacinthi*, and *nomina regum* is a rhetorical plural for *nomen regis*, the markings on the plant, by one explanation, spelling the name of Aias.

²⁸ Hor., *epod.*, 10.

²⁹ For refs., see my *Handb. of Lat. Lit.*, p. 345.

³⁰ Lines 90–91: qui Bauium non odit, amet tua carmina, Meui,/atque idem iungat uolpes et mulgeat hircos. Servius glosses by faciat ea quae contra naturam sunt; the metaphors smack of country proverbs.

³¹ Simple though Vergil's language is, the lines have been erected into a crux by certain interpreters, ancient and modern, partly because *aut* and *haut* or *haud* tended to be confused in writing as they were in pronunciation, the *h* becoming silent in late Latin. Servius explains well enough: et tu et hic digni estis uitula et quicunque similis uestri est; nam supra unus dixerat "triste lupus stabulis, maturis frugibus imbres, arboribus uenti, nobis Amaryllidis irae" (80 sq.), item aliter, "dulce satis umor, depulsis arbutus haedis, lenta salix feto pecori, mihi solus Amyntas" (82 sq.), ad cuius amatoris similitudinem pertinet "aut metuet dulces," etc. But Filargirius writes amazing rubbish: si metuet dulces, experietur amaros, sin autem non metuet amaros, experietur dulces. He apparently read *haut* for the second *aut*. Hirtzel, following Graser, reads *haud* both times; I leave the honoured shades of these scholars the task of determining what, if anything, the lines may then be supposed to mean.

³² *Catal.*, 5, 10; for the reading, see chap. iv, note 38, end.

Excursus I
(Cf. Note 6)

The phrase *molle atque facetum* has a little literature of its own, ancient and modern, with the findings of which I am partly but not wholly in agreement. Setting aside commentators on Horace himself and on Vergil, we may begin with Quintilian, *inst. orat.*, VI, 3, 2, who says truly: facetum quoque non tantum circa ridicula opinor consistere, neque enim diceret Horatius facetum carminis genus natura concessum esse Vergilio. decoris hanc magis et excultae cuiusdam elegantiae appellationem puto. ideoque in epistula Cicero haec Bruti refert [the letter in question is lost save for this quotation] uerba; ne illi sunt pedes faceti ac deliciis [?] ingredienti molles; quod conuenit cum illo Horatiano, e.q.u. Brutus' acquaintance, that is, had not exactly witty feet, but a subtle and delicate way of walking, especially under the circumstances which the probably currupt *deliciis* is meant to indicate. Among moderns, the following have all had something to contribute. L. Bayard, in *Rev. de Philologie*, XXVIII (1904), No. 3, p. 213, takes both words as adjectival, agreeing with *epos* in the preceding line (Horace, *sat.*, i, 10, 43, after discussing the merits of Fundanus in comedy, Pollio in tragedy: forte epos acer/ut nemo Varius ducit; molle atque facetum e.q.s.), but admits that, even so, Horace refers or may refer to matter as well as style. A *molle epos* might be a verse or poem which treated of *molles*, or *mollia*, certainly. R. Pichon, *ibid.*, XXXII (1908), pp. 64 sq., adds that *mollis* is especially used by elegiac poets of their own works. Going into the matter more thoroughly, Professor C. N. Jackson (*Harvard Studies in Class. Phil.*, XXV, 1914, pp. 117-137), notes the use of both adjectives in rhetoric and concludes that both are appropriate to the elegance and delicacy of the *genus tenue* affected by the Atticising writers of the day, whereof Pollio was one. This is true, but may not at once be converted into the proposition that wherever a writer, especially a master of words like Horace, uses them of literature he means no more than that; the generic sense is not swallowed up by the specific and technical. Moreover, as M. B. Ogle shows (*Am. Jour. Phil.*, XXXVII, 1916, pp. 327-332), *mollis* is used with a wider range of meaning, even in rhetoric. It was not the word his contemporaries would use of the rather harsh style of Pollio, and it is by no means employed only of the *genus tenue*. Agreeing on the whole with him, Charles Knapp (*ibid.*, XXXVIII, pp. 194-199) quotes with approval the explanation of Arthur Sidgwick and one or two others of *facetum* as "playful," which is not far from the meaning "humorous" which I incline to give it.

Excursus II
(Cf. Note 26)

I find that it is necessary to point out in more detail that Palaemon in *Ecl.*, III, 55-57, means spring and not summer, for by no means the worst of the writers on Vergil, A. Klotz in *Neue Jahrb. f. das klass. Altertum*, XLV/XLVI (1920), p. 148, still insists that the latter season is meant. Let us analyse and interpret the lines closely. I have spoken of the first, dicite, quandoquidem in molli consedimus herba. The grass is soft, therefore the weather has not been hot for long; and the shepherd-boys are near home, 34, therefore they are not in a hill pasture; therefore they are in the lowlands and yet they can sit on the grassy ground in comfort and their flocks have apparently plenty to feed upon (that Aegon's ewes are milked twice in an hour, 5, is of course Menalcas' scandalous exaggeration, but it is not the sort of joke which could be made of beasts with a poor yield of milk; cf. 30, where a young cow has milk enough for two calves and two milk-pails over). 55, et nunc omnis ager, nunc omnis parturit arbos. *Parturit*, not *parit*, so the "birth-pangs of the sheath" (κάλυκος ἐν λοχεύμασιν, Aesch., *Agam.*, 1392) are not yet come; in other words, everything is showing signs of growth, but nothing is mature yet. 56, nunc frondent siluae, the woods are leaving, nothing being said of the size of the leaves; nunc formosissimus annus, which in itself should be enough for anyone who has read the ancient authors; spring and no other season is the proverbially lovely time.

Notes to Chapter III: The Poet and His Home

[1] See p. 61.

[2] That the farm was once his *peculium* and now, on emancipation, becomes his *patrimonium* is rightly insisted upon by F. Leo in *Hermes*, XXXVIII (1903), pp. 6 sq. The story is told with dramatic confusion, to the utter puzzlement of some commentators. In 27, being asked what was the reason for his going to Rome, Tityrus answers in one word, *libertas*, which Servius rightly glosses *amor libertatis*. He then explains rather lengthily why he had not become free sooner; it was Galatea's fault. That he went to Rome to buy his freedom, saw his master there, and concluded the bargain is all so obvious to Meliboeus, and should be to readers, that Vergil does not need to mention these particulars. The two great points of his story are that Rome is a wonderful place (19-25) and that while there he somehow met the *iuuenis* (41 sqq.). That the meeting with Octavian is somehow allegorised as a meeting with his master (Conington, p. 23), or that this, or any other Eclogue, is a jumble of two themes (cf. E. Bethe in *Rhein. Mus.*, n.f., XLVII, 1892, p. 489) which Vergil was too clumsy to combine, are the ravings of bad criticism. One subtlety of the master's art here is that Tityrus' somewhat incoherent story relieves him of the necessity of imagining an occasion for the meeting with Octavian. Even F. Altheim, *Römische Religionsgeschichte*, III (Berlin, de Gruyter, 1933), pp. 31 sqq., makes too much of what is a very trifling difficulty and dramatically good.

[3] Hanc mecum poteras requiescere noctem, 79. For *poteras*, you might (and still may). P. Thomas (*Revue Belge*, VII, 1928, pp. 138-140) appositely quotes Horace, *sat.*, II, 1, 16, cf. *carm.*, i, 37, 4 (add *ars poet.*, 329); Ovid, *Metam.*, I, 678.

[4] Agent, and therefore presumably free, Servius p. 108, 15 Thilo; cf. Leo, *op. cit.*, p. 13, who supposes the two to be partners. But as Moeris speaks as if he acted under the orders normally of Menalcas and now of the soldier, he might well be either a freedman employed as a farm-bailiff or a slave in the same capacity.

[5] He says *haedos*, 6, and they are few enough for him to carry slung together, if that, the natural interpretation, is to be given to *hoc fasce*, 65. Therefore they can hardly be more than two.

[6] *Hos illi mittimus haedos*, ibid. This might mean "we [the farm-servants] are sending them *to* him" or "are sending them [to town] *for* him," i.e., to sell for his benefit.

[7] It is rightly pointed out, e.g. by J. S. Phillimore, *Pastoral and Allegory* (Oxford, 1925), pp. 22, cf. Tenney Frank, *Vergil, a Biography* (New York, Holt, 1922), p. 113, that the Mantuan estate was no longer Vergil's own home. He may no doubt have visited it occasionally, and might have spent a holiday there now and then if it had not been lost; but in or near Rome was the only place for a young man of letters at that date.

[8] Servius, p. 108, 14 sqq. Thilo.

[9] Lines 23-25 (Theokr., Id. III 3-5) and 39-43 (Th., Id. XI, 42 sqq.).

[10] Lines 27 sqq. The poem to which they are supposed to belong is incomplete (26), which I take to hint at the abandonment by Vergil of his fruitless efforts to

[228]

induce Varus to show leniency to the Mantuans. In passing it may be remarked that Varus, in the *Eclogues*, is always Alfenus Varus (see next chapter).

[11] Lines 46 sqq. Under the star of Caesar the crops and the vines are to flourish; as Servius correctly explains, Vergil means the comet which appeared at the funeral games celebrated for him by Octavian.

[12] This of course is not to say that Menalcas everywhere in the *Eclogues* is Vergil, as L. Herrmann, *Les masques et les visages dans les Bucoliques de Virgile* (Brussels, 1930), pp. 18 sqq., would have it. Even his principle that one name (granted that it is used allegorically) and one name only is used for the same person, e.g., that Vergil cannot be both Menalcas and Tityrus (p. 7), is none too certain, seeing that Theokritos is Thyrsis in Idyll I (see esp. 24, he has contended with Chromis of Libya, that is to say, entered into relations with African, i.e., Alexandrian, poets; 65, he comes from Aitna, a very easy riddle, Hieron I's foundation being put for the city in which he was tyrant), Simichidas in Id. VII.

[13] Servius, p. 4, 21 Thilo.

[14] Cf. Serv. on *Ecl.*, VIII, 55, SIT TITYRVS ORPHEVS uilissimus rusticus Orpheus putetur, etc.

[15] In the article cited above, note 2.

[16] Verse 28, candidior postquam tondenti barba cadebat; young men did not shave, and Tityrus is so far past youth that the bristles on his chin are grey.

[17] Cf. note 17 above.

[18] This much may perhaps be elicited from the tale in Donatus (*Vita Vergilii*, p. 8, 11) that he was born while his mother was on her way from Andes to the open country near it. But even if he was born in Mantua itself, that was never a large or important city.

[19] Vrbem quam dicunt Romam, I, 19.

[20] It is adopted, e.g., by R. S. Conway, in *Atene e Roma*, VII (1926), p. 179; G. Jachmann in *Neue Jahrbücher f. d. klassische Altertum*, XLIX (1922), p. 117, who is certain that Eclogue I must express the personal gratitude of Vergil to Octavian. That it was common in antiquity long before Servius or Donatus is clear from the following passages: Calpurnius, *Buc.*, V, 160 sqq.,

> qualis qui dulce sonantem
> Tityron e siluis dominam deduxit in urbem
> ostenditque deis et, Spreto, dixit, ouili,
> Tityre, rura prius sed post cantabimus arma.

The same poem has other allusions to the equation of Tityrus with Vergil. Cf. Martial, VIII, 56, 8 sqq.,

> Iugera perdiderat miserae uicina Cremonae,
>   flebat et abductas Tityrus aeger oues;
> risit Tuscus eques paupertatemque malignam
>   reppulit et celeri iussit abire fuga.
> Accipe diuitias et uatum maximus esto,
>   tu licet et nostrum, dixit, Alexin ames.

Here, incidentally, Vergil is identified with Corydon also; see next chapter.

[21] *Aen.*, I, 411 sqq.

[22] IX, 7-10.

[33] *Ecl.*, VII, 12-13.

[34] *Nuove ricerche sul paese natale di Virgilio*, in *Virgiliana*, II (Mantova, 1930/viii), p. 4.

[35] Mantuae stagnum effusum Mincio amni cruentum uisum, Livy, XXIV, 10, 7.

[36] In pago qui Andes dicitur et abest a Mantua non procul, Donatus, p. 8, 7; cf. Donatus auctus, p. 27, 5. Mantua Romuleae generauit flumina linguae, Focas 2 (p. 37, 26). ciuis Mantuanus, Servius, p. 40, 29 (p. 1, 4, Thilo-Hagen). genere Mantuanus, Vita Bernensis, p. 44, 18. in pago qui Andes dicitur haut procul a Mantua, Filargirius, p. 45, 12 (p. 1, 3 Hagen). in pago Andensi in uilla quae Andis dicitur iuxta Mantuam, Vita Monacensis, p. 45, 24. in pago qui Andes dicitur haud procul a Mantua, Vita Noricensis (from Jerome's version of Eusebius' *Chronicle*, an. Abr. 1949). The references are to the pages of E. Diehl, *Vitae Vergilianae*, Bonn, 1911 (Lietzmann's *Kleine Texte*, No. 72).

[37] *Probi qui dicitur commentarius in Vergilii Bucolica et Georgica*, p. 323, 4 Hagen.

[38] Dante, *Purgatorio*, xviii, 82 sq.

[39] B. Nardi, *The Youth of Virgil*, trans. B. P. Rand (Harvard Univ. Press, 1930), p. 118; cf. Donatus, p. 8, 2; D. auctus, p. 26, 25; Focas, 6 (p. 37, 30); V. Monacensis, p. 45, 27; V. Noricensis, p. 49, 11.

[30] St. Jerome, *Breuiarium in Psalmos*, 77 (Migne, *P. L.*, XXVI, 1046A).

[31] *C. I. L.*, V, 3827, if genuine, cf. Conway, *op. cit.*, p. 176.

[32] Nardi, *Nuove ricerche*, p. 5 (the higher levels near the Mincio) son formate, com'è noto, di terreno fluvio-glaciale, ossia di detriti della grande morena che chiude il Garda. . . . In mezzo a questi cumuli il Mincio aveva scavato un assai profondo solco, si che quelle alture, a chi le osservava dalla sponda del fiume, apparivano innalzarsi sul livello normale di Andes. He is speaking of mediaeval conditions; cf. *Youth of Virgil*, App. II. See further his article in *Class. Quart.*, XXXIII (1934), pp. 31-34.

[33] Conway, *op. cit.*, cf. his *Harvard Lectures on the Vergilian Age* (Harvard Univ. Press, 1928), pp. 14 sqq. Both of these represent revisions and enlargements of his original statement of the theory.

[34] *Ecl.*, I, 83.

[35] III, 12, 111.

[36] Cf. E. K. Rand, *In Quest of Virgil's Birthplace* (Harvard Univ. Press, 1930), p. 46.

[37] V, 6.

[38] VII, 56.

[39] Servius, Vol. I, p. 2, 1 Thilo-Hagen.

[40] This is verbally correct, for L. Antonius was Octavian's opponent and besieged by him in Perusia; but it is likely that Servius is confusing his dates and thinking of the war with M. Antonius which ended at Actium, see his comments on *Ecl.*, IX, 11, 67; Probus, p. 327, 29 Hagen.

[41] *Ecl.*, IX, 28.

[42] On *Ecl.*, IX, 7.

[43] *Ibid.*, 10.

NOTES TO CHAPTER III

[44] Rand, *op. cit.*, p. 84.
[45] Conway, *Atene e Roma*, VII, 175; *Vergilian Age*, p. 21. It is *C. I. L.*, V, 4046.
[46] Rand, *op. cit.*, p. 83.
[47] Theokr., Id. VII, 10 sq.
[48] On *Ecl.*, IX, 60, cf. *Aen.* X, 198 sqq.
[49] *Ecl.*, IX, 60–67.
[50] *Ibid.*, 57–58.
[51] *Ibid.*, 63.
[52] *Ibid.*, 60 sq.
[53] See Nardi, *Nuove ricerche*, pp. 6 sq.
[54] Ancient, quoted in note 42; Frank, *Vergil*, p. 127; Rand, *op. cit.*, p. 113 sqq.
[55] Rand, *ibid.*, p. 46.
[56] ueteres, iam fracta cacumina, fagos, IX, 9 in most of the older MSS.; ueteris . . . fagi one old MS., some later ones and Quintilian. See the apparatus of any critical ed.
[57] *Catalepton*, 8; see Th. Birt, *Jugendverse und Heimatpoesie Vergils* (Teubner, 1910), pp. 85 sqq. Cf. below, Excursus II.
[58] Initia aetatis Cremonae egit usque ad uirilem togam, Donatus, p. 9, 20; cf. Don. auctus, p. 27, 19. diuersis in locis operam litteris dedit; nam et Cremonae et Mediolani et Neapoli studuit, Servius, p. 40, 30 (p. 1, 5 Thilo-Hagen). primum Cremona ciuitate in Italia eruditus, V. Monacensis, p. 46, 13. Virgilius Cremonae studiis eruditus sumpta toga Mediolanum ingreditur, V. Noricensis, from Jerome, *Chron.*, an. Abr. 1960.
[59] *Ecl.*, I, 47 sqq.
[60] Cf. note 53 above.
[61] It is true that Meliboeus, *Ecl.*, I, 51 sqq., uses *hic . . . hinc . . . hinc* in speaking of it; but this simply means that he has just mentioned it, not that it is in sight. Tityrus, 42, uses *hic* in just the same way of Rome, which he mentioned last in 19.
[62] Varro, *de re rust.*, ii, 1, 16: neque easdem loca aestiua et hiberna idonea omnibus ad pascendum. itaque greges ouium longe abiguntur ex Apulia in Samnium aestiuatum atque ad publicanum profitentur, ne si inscriptum pecus pauerint, lege censoria committant. muli e Rosea campestri aestate exiguntur in † burbures altos montes.
[63] *Ecl.*, I, 56, and Servius there.
[64] Donatus, p. 10, 6, cf. Don. auctus, p. 28, 33.
[65] Aestate pueri si ualent, satis discunt, Martial, X, 62, 12.
[66] *Ecl.*, V, 46 sq.; VII, 45 sq.; X, 40 sqq.
[67] Thestylis (10) is getting dinner ready for reapers.
[68] See 29, 63.
[69] *Ecl.*, III, 33 sqq., 56 sq.
[70] *Ecl.*, IV, 25; cf. III, 89.
[71] *Ecl.*, V, 6.
[72] *Ibid.*, 21; see Sergeaunt, *Trees*, etc., p. 35.
[73] *Ecl.*, VII, 12 sq.
[74] *Ibid.*, 4.

232   NOTES TO CHAPTER III

⁷⁵ The olive "is too tender to grow at high altitudes, or, except on warm coastlands, in the north of Italy," Sergeaunt, p. 88.

⁷⁶ Frank, *Vergil*, pp. 114 sq.

⁷⁷ See note 57 above.

⁷⁸ Aristophanes, *Knights*, 207.

⁷⁹ Cf. *Georg.*, II, 176.

⁸⁰ Servius on *Ecl.*, VIII, 55, cf. note 13 above; Leo, *op. cit.*, pp. 12 sq.

⁸¹ Pascite, ut ante, boues, pueri, summittite tauros, *Ecl.*, I, 45.

⁸² Lucr., V, 7 sqq.

⁸³ Much the same point is made by G. Costa, *Atene e Roma*, IX (1906), pp. 246 sq.; he revives an old conjecture that this is what Vergil alludes to when he says (*Georg.*, IV, 565 sq., where see Daniel's Servius: quidam 'audax' propterea dictum uolunt quod in duabus eclogis quae sunt in bucolicis occulte inuectus sit in Augustum propter agros) that he was *audax iuuenta* when he wrote it. Cf. Cartault, *Etude*, p. 66.

⁸⁴ Servius and Daniels' Servius on *Ecl.*, IX, 1, cf. Servius p. 3, 5 Thilo, and on *Ecl.*, III, 94. The variations of the story are well summed up by Diehl, *Vit. Vergil.*, p. 58: it is left in doubt "1) ob der centurio Arrius (Don. ecl. praef. Serv. ecl. praef. ecl. 9, 1.3, 94) oder der nachbar Clodius (Serv. auct. ecl. 9, 1) oder der miteigentümer Claudius (Schol. Bern. ecl. 9 praef.) oder der primipilar Milienus Toro (Prob. ecl. praef.) das leben des dichters gefährdet 2) ob V. sein eigentum gegen den gewaltsamen eindringling Arrius auf leben und tod verteidigte (Don. ecl. praef. Serv. auct. ecl. 9, 16), oder ob der rehabilitierte dichter bei seiner rückkehr aus Rom von Arrius bedroht ward (Serv. ecl. praef.), oder ob grenzstreitigkeiten zwischen V. und seinen nachbarn nach erlangung der immunität die ursache gewesen (Serv. auct. ecl. 9, 1), oder endlich die wut der veteranen, die sich in das besitztum V.'s geteilt hatten und ihren primipilar vorschickten (Prob. ecl. praef.) 3) ob V. sich durch einen sturz in den Mincio und schwimmen ans jenseitige ufer gerettet (Don. ecl. praef. Serv. ecl. praef. ecl. 3, 94) oder durch die flucht in eine köhlerkneipe, deren wirt ihn zur hintertür hinausliess (Serv. auct. ecl. 9, 1), oder durch die flucht schlechthin (Prob. ecl. praef.) 4) ob der angriff nach V.'s rückkehr aus Rom erfolgte (Serv. ecl. praef.), oder bei der rückerstattung des landguts durch Cornelius Gallus' vermittlung bei Augustus (Serv. ecl. 3, 94, Prob. ecl. praef.), oder als der dichter immunität erlangt hatte (Serv. auct. ecl. 9, 1) 5) ob der gegner mit gezucktem schwert auf den dichter losging (Don. ecl. praef. Serv. auct. ecl. 9, 1) oder es sich lediglich um einem tätlichen angriff gehandelt (Serv. ecl. praef.) 6) ob sich V. ein zweites mal an den kaiser gewandt hat, der sodann ein kommando zur unterstützung und rehabilitierung des dichters entbot (Serv. ecl. praef.) oder nicht." In short, the only point on which there is agreement is that Vergil's life was in some kind of danger from someone, and as this is highly likely to be a mere attempt to explain *Ecl.*, IX, 16, it is a statement of little value.

⁸⁵ See esp. *Ecl.*, IX, 11 sqq.

EXCURSUS I

Chapter iii was written before I had studied the ingenious little work of Mgr. A. Besutti, *La patria di Virgilio* (Asola, Mantova, 1927). While suffering from the same weakness as the other studies mentioned, namely, the assumption that the country Vergil describes must be in the Mantuan territory and the neighbourhood of his father's estate, it is the only theory I have seen which adduces evidence for its identification of Andes that combines linguistic with topographical elements. Mgr. Besutti somewhat scornfully rejects Pietole, chiefly because (p. 40) the scenery is, as Conway declares and he agrees, utterly unlike that of most of the *Bucolics*. At most, he would admit (p. 46) that the elder Vergilius may have owned some property there and that his son visited the place occasionally in childhood. But the name alone disqualifies it (pp. 42 sqq.), for the renaming of a village for no assignable reason is a strange phenomenon; while the local legends (p. 41) are patently mediaeval or later, and of no worth whatever for proving the identity of Pietole with Vergil's home. On the other hand, Bande, on the present border between the districts of Mantova and Verona, in the commune of Cavriana (p. 17) fulfils all requirements (pp. 51 sqq.). The scenery is hilly, with streams, the Mincio in sight, and it is some distance from the town, far enough more or less to fit the "thirty" miles of Probus, which reading he unreservedly adopts. And its name is a perfectly possible corruption of Andes, by misdivision (Bracciano is said to bear a like relation to the ancient Arcenum, p. 57) of the phrase *ab And-*, very easily heard (especially in an Italian language, old or new, which invariably divides its syllables before a consonant, regardless of etymology and the ends of words) as *a Band-*. If born here (he makes great use of the story in Donatus, *Vita*, p. 8, 11, that Vergil's mother was surprised by the birth-pains while on a journey to the country and brought forth her son *in subiecta fossa*, suggesting a greater distance from Mantua than the three Roman miles to Pietole), Vergil might indeed have been said by detractors (cf. Macrob., *Sat.*, V, 2, 1) to have been born and reared in the Mantuan country-side, amongst forests and bushes, away from all culture. The monograph closes with an attempt to identify scenes from the *Eclogues* with the scenery of the neighbourhood of Bande, the *alto mantovano*.

Excursus II

When chapter iii was delivered as a lecture, an ingenious and plausible suggestion was made by one of the audience, a lady personally unknown to me, that the elder Vergil, of whose childhood nothing is recorded, may have been born at Cremona or in its territory. This contradicts no established fact and agrees with a possible rendering of the last line of the epigram, Mantua quod fuerat quodque Cremona prius, viz., "what Mantua and, before that, Cremona was to him." It is of course fully consistent with his owning property in both districts.

Notes to Chapter IV: The Poet and His Friends

[1] Reading *Caeli* in III, 105; cf. above, chap. ii, note 27.
[2] See p. 48.
[3] Servius on *Ecl.*, I, 29.
[4] *Ibid.*, 39.
[5] Servius on *Ecl.*, II, 1, 73.
[6] *Ibid.*, 15.
[7] Servius on *Ecl.*, III, 20.
[8] *Ibid.*, 96.
[9] Servius on *Ecl.*, IV, 1, 11, 13, 17.
[10] Servius on *Ecl.*, V, 20.
[11] *Ibid.*, 55.
[12] Servius on *Ecl.*, VI, 13.
[13] Servius on *Ecl.*, VII, 21.
[14] Daniel's Servius, *ibid.*, 22, cf. p. 121.
[15] Servius on *Ecl.*, VIII, 6.
[16] Servius on *Ecl.*, III, 20, after the passage quoted in note 10: sed melius simpliciter accipimus ("it is better for us to take the passage literally"); refutandae enim sunt allegoriae in bucolico carmine, nisi cum, ut supra diximus, ex aliqua agrorum perditorum necessitate descendunt. By *supra* he means his own introduction to the *Eclogues*, p. 2, 17 Thilo: et aliquibus locis (sc. intentio est ut) per allegoriam agat gratias Augusto uel aliis nobilibus, quorum fauore amissum agrum recepit. in qua re tantum dissentit a Theocrito, ille enim ubique simplex est, hic necessitate compulsus aliquibus locis miscet figuras, quas perite plerumque etiam ex Theocriti uersibus facit, quos ab illo dictos constat esse simpliciter.
[17] For a sketch of some of them, see the monograph of N. Terzaghi, *L'allegoria nelle Ecloghe di Virgilio* (Florence, Seeben, 1902), which also discusses with good sense the general question of how much figurative statement there really is in the poems.
[18] Léon Herrmann, *Les masques et les visages dans les Bucoliques de Virgile* (Bruxelles, 1930).
[19] He thinks she may be the Plotia Hieria or Heria of Donatus, *Vita*, p. 10, 12 Diehl; see *op. cit.*, p. 142.
[20] Herrmann, *op. cit.*, p. 172.
[21] *Ibid.*, pp. 47 sqq.
[22] *Ibid.*, pp. 110 sqq., 120–21, 124, 126, 131.
[23] *Ibid.*, p. 137; cf. Horace, *ars poet.*, 438 sqq.; *carm.*, i, 24.
[24] Herrmann, *op. cit.*, p. 146.
[25] J. S. Phillimore, *Pastoral and Allegory* (Oxford, 1925), p. 18.
[26] *Ibid.*, p. 6.
[27] *Ibid.*, p. 13.
[28] *Ibid.*, p. 21.
[29] For Gallus, and a refutation of the statement that he was of low birth (Suet., *diu. Aug.*, 66, 1), see R. Syme in *Class. Quart.*, XXXII (1938), pp. 39–44. Varus,

NOTES TO CHAPTER IV   235

if he really is identical with the "cobbler" of Horace, *sat.* i, 3, 130 sqq. (see Klebs in Pauly-Wissowa, *Realenc.*, I, 1472, 44), was of no better origin than Vergil himself, but we have no real proof that he and Vergil ever met, unless it was in Siron's lecture-room, cf. note 40, below.

[30] Cicero, *Tusc.*, iii, 45.

[31] Ovid, *Tristia*, IV, 10, 21. However, the difference in age between him and Vergil was much more considerable (27 years) than that between Vergil and Catullus.

[32] Donatus, pp. 9, 20–10, 4 (Cremona, Milan, Rome), cf. Donatus auctus, p. 27, 19 sqq. (Cremona, Milan, Naples); Focas, lines 41 sqq. (Ballista the brigand-schoolmaster, presumably at Mantua or Cremona; Siron at Rome); Servius, p. 41, 1 (p. 1, 5 Thilo-Hagen), gives Cremona, Milan, and Naples; under Epidius, with "Caesar Augustus" and so presumably in Rome, Vita Bernensis, p. 44, 20; Cremona, Milan, Rome, V. Monacensis, p. 46, 13; same, V. Noricensis (from Jerome, *Chron.*, an. Abr. 1958).

[33] See preceding note.

[34] Cf. Donatus, *Vita*, p. 12, 7.

[35] Frank, *Vergil*, p. 18. That Epidius did teach Octavius rhetoric is not in doubt, see Suetonius, *de rhet.*, 4. The question is whether he taught him and Vergil at anything like the same time; indeed, I would not call it certain that he taught Vergil at all, seeing that only the Berne life mentions it. Probus, p. 43, 12 (p. 323, 6 Hagen), says vaguely, *summis eloquentiae doctoribus*.

[36] He was then fifteen, see Donatus, p. 10, 1, cf. Frank, *ibid.*, p. 15.

[37] See my *Handbook of Latin Literature*, pp. 258 sqq.

[38] The poem is so difficult and its interpretation so disputable that I print it here in full with my opinions on its meaning.

>   Ite hinc, inanes, ite rhetorum ampullae,
>   inflata r(h)o(r)so non Achaico uerba,
>   et uos, Selique Tarquitique Varroque,
>   scholasticorum natio madens pingui,
>   ite hinc, inane cymbalum iuuentutis.   5
>   tuque, o mearum cura Sexte curarum,
>   uale, Sabine; iam ualete formosi.
>   nos ad beatos uela mittimus portus,
>   magni petentes docta dicta Sironis,
>   uitamque ab omni uindicabimus cura.   10
>   ite hinc, Camenae, uos quoque; ite iam sane,
>   dulces Camenae, nam fatebimur uerum,
>   dulces fuistis, et tamen meas cartas
>   reuisitote, sed pudenter et raro.

2. rore *Aldina*. 3. se liquntar quinque, se liqunt argutique, se liquit argutique, seliquir arquitique MSS., emend. Ellis, Haupt. uarioque most MSS. 10. uindica(ui)mus MSS.

The most important commentary is that of Birt, *Jugendverse und Heimatpoesie*, pp. 71 sqq., which appears to me quite wrong at several points. First, the poem does not fall into two parts of seven lines each, as he says (p. 71), nor consist merely of a farewell to rhetoric and a taking refuge with philosophy. It is divided, as I have indicated by indentations, into five little stanzas of 2, 3, 2, 3, and 4 lines respectively, and their subjects are (*a*) farewell to rhetoric, (*b*) farewell to antiquarianism, or philology, (*c*) farewell to romantic affection, (*d*) welcome to philosophy, (*e*) partial farewell to poetry.

As to (*a*), there is and can be no disagreement, the question being merely whether he is still taking leave of rhetoric in (*b*). Here the names have been badly corrupted; if the received emendations are correct, Selius is totally unknown to us as rhetorician, fellow student of Vergil, or anything else that will apply; we merely know that such a name did exist at that date (Birt, p. 73). Tarquitius and Varro coincide in name at least with Tarquitius Priscus the writer on Etruscan antiquities (cf. Macrobius, *Sat.*, III, 7, 2) and M. Terentius Varro the great antiquarian, grammarian, and miscellaneous writer. But the genitives in 4 and 5 are ambiguous; does the former mean, as Birt takes it (p. 74), "tribe of *scholastici* moist with grease," i.e., as he would have it, sleek with the contents of their metaphorical *ampullae*, or with real oil, or "tribe that is moist with the grease of the *scholastici*," and, in either case, who are the *scholastici*? Is the second to be taken as meaning that the *natio* of 4 is a cymbal—a big drum, in modern parlance—to which the younger generation listens, or one which they play? In the latter case, they are probably rhetoricians or students of rhetoric, setting out to make a great, if empty, noise in the world; but it is at least as probable that the former interpretation is right, and that the *iuuentus* is having its ears filled by the noise of the persons mentioned in 3. Now, the chances against the probability that two out of three names were by mere coincidence those of well-known scholars seem to me very considerable, and I prefer to think that Tarquitius, Varro, and a third, unknown writer are meant. Birt (p. 73) objects, "Varro, der vornehme, hochbetagte Buchgelehrte, kann damals solchen rhetorischen Unterricht in Rom nicht erteilt haben." I agree; but as I do not think rhetorical instruction is spoken of here at all, I am not impressed by the alleged difficulty. What Vergil seems to me to be giving up is learned antiquarianism, such as in fact he always loved, the sort of information which was to be had in Varro, Tarquitius, and presumably the unknown, but which must give place now to the all-important claims of philosophy. Seneca the Younger (*de breuit. uit.*, 13, 1 sqq.) later affected a like contempt for the chief subjects of liberal study and research; Vergil outgrew such fanaticism, if he ever really felt it save in a passing mood of enthusiasm for a new pursuit. The "fat" I think is illustrated for us by Horace, *sat.*, II, 6, 14 sq., pingue pecus domino facias et cetera praeter/ingenium. The whole "tribe of lecture-room haunters" is dismissed as fat-headed. That *scholastici* can mean rhetoricians or students of rhetoric no one denies, but I see no reason to assume that that is what it means here. I therefore suppose that *cymbalum iuuentutis* has the former of the two meanings suggested above. The best-known use of *cymbalum* in any such sense is its application to Apion, a man of no small learning (Pliny, *N. H.*, *praef.*, 25).

The phrase *cura curarum* in 6 sounds odd, even Hebraising Latin, but I suggest it is a sort of pun; Sabinus is the *cura*, or object of affectionate interest (like *tua cura Lycoris*, *Ecl.*, X, 22) of the author's *curae*, that is, subjects or pursuits which have engaged his attention (cf. *Georg.*, III, 384, *si tibi lanitium curae*, "if production of wool is your chief interest"). These being literary, it is natural to suppose that he had written something, perhaps a poem, perhaps an epideictic speech like that of Lysias parodied in the *Phaedrus* of Plato or the one falsely ascribed to Demosthenes, in his honour. He means, then, that he will no longer continue a romantic friendship with the unknown Sabinus nor write in his praise. In 10, since *b* and *u* are practically indistinguishable in mediaeval hands, I would read the future, *uindicabimus*, supposing that Vergil does not claim already to have achieved philosophical ἀταραξία, but only to have taken the first steps towards it; cf. above, chap. ii, note 31.

[37] The famous ex-muleteer of *Catal.*, 10. If I believed, with Birt, p. 74, that *formosi* in 5, 7 is ironical, I might understand him to be the Sabinus in question, taking the lines (construed as in the previous note) to mean that no more poems carefully written about that subject are to be expected of the versifier turned philosopher; but I suppose it to be quite serious.

[40] Servius on *Ecl.*, VI, 13: sectam Epicuream, quam didicerant tam Vergilius quam Varus docente Sirone.

[41] Frank, *op. cit.*, p. 48. Focas (above, note 32) puts him in Rome, and not a few moderns follow him; for our present purposes the question is unimportant.

[42] *Ibid.*, p. 51.

[43] Donatus, *Vita*, p. 10, 5: corpore et statura fuit grandi, aquilo colore, facie rusticana, ualetudine uaria; nam plerumque a stomacho et a faucibus ac dolore capitis laborabat, sanguinem etiam saepe reiecit... [16] et ore et animo tam probum constat ut Neapoli Parthenias uulgo appellatus sit, ac si quando Romae, quo rarissime commeabat, uiseretur in publico, sectantis demonstrantisque se subterfugeret in proximum tectum. This of course refers to him at a later date, but though his health in young manhood may have been better, it is most unlikely that he would be less countrified in appearance or less reluctant to be conspicuous.

[44] I assume, with Birt, *op. cit.*, p. 11, that Vergil wrote much else, which he never published. Like him, I reject all the Appendix Vergiliana except such poems of the *Catalepton* as may be genuine.

[45] To my mind, this is very unlikely; would an imitator, say of the age of Tiberius or Claudius, have enough historical and literary imagination to see that Vergil would be highly likely to imitate Catullus and his school and to use metres other than the hexameter? Unlike the *Culex*, those poems of the *Catalepton* which imply that they are by Vergil have a very strong claim to be considered really his.

[46] Horace, *sat.*, i, 5, 40.

[47] See Birt, *op. cit.*, pp. 66 sqq., 126 sqq.

[48] *Georg.*, I, 2; II, 39, etc.

[49] Donatus, p. 14, 6.

[50] Probus, p. 43, 17 (p. 323, 10 Hagen).

[51] Appian, *de bell. ciu.*, IV, 10 Mendelssohn (Teubner). Here I have made much use of a very lucid article by J. Bayet, *Virgile et les triumvirs "agris diuidundis,"* in *Rev. Et. Lat.*, VI (1928), pp. 271 sqq., esp. the first half, which seems to me to combine the maximum of documented fact with the minimum of hypothesis. With the opinions expressed in the latter half I am not in full agreement.

NOTES TO CHAPTER IV

[52] Appian, V, 48. This was in 713/41.
[53] Appian, V, 64–67; Cassius Dio, XLVIII, 9, 1–3.
[54] Appian, V, 51.
[55] *Ecl.*, IX, 4.
[56] Appian, V, 54.
[57] *Ibid.*, 54 sq.
[58] *Ibid.*; Dio, XLVIII, 6, 2 sqq.
[59] Appian, V, 79.
[60] Dio, XLVIII, 12, 5.
[61] *Ibid.*
[62] Cf. Dio, XLVIII, 9, 3.
[63] Dio, XLVIII, 12, 5.
[64] E.g., Donatus, *Vita*, p. 14, 2.
[65] Servius, p. 2, 1 Thilo-Hagen: Augustus uictor Cremonensium agros, quia pro Antonio senserant, dedit militibus suis. qui cum non sufficerent, his addidit agros Mantuanos, etc.
[66] See p. 179.
[67] *Ecl.*, III, 84–89.
[68] *Ecl.*, VIII, 6 sqq. The poem is described as iussis carmina coepta tuis, which may mean that Pollio had told Vergil he liked what he had seen of his work and hoped there would be more of it.
[69] Horace, *carm.*, i, 1, 9–16, with the difference that Horace mentions Pollio's career at the bar and in the Senate, Vergil his consulate.
[70] Pliny, *epp.*, VI, 15, 2. He is a little shocked at this breach of literary convention and explains that Iavolenus Priscus was *dubiae sanitatis*.
[71] Cf. Cartault, p. 28 of the work cited below, note 89.
[72] Those excited by the agreement at Brundisium were by no means over-exuberant, as Sex. Pompeius' raids did not stop (see Carcopino, *Virgile et le mystère de la IVe Eclogue*, pp. 111 sqq.), but they must have existed.
[73] Quint., *inst. orat.*, X, 1, 92, citing *Ecl.*, VIII, 13.
[74] Cf. above, note 29.
[75] See chap. iii, p. 55, and note 43.
[76] Daniel's Servius on *Ecl.* IX, 7.
[77] Cf. note 75 above.
[78] Alfenum Varum Cremonensem, Pseudacro on Hor., *sat.*, I, 3, 130, Porphyrio, *ibid.*
[79] Servius on *Ecl.*, VI, 13.
[80] Non iniussa cano, *Ecl.*, VI, 9.
[81] This, of course, by both Latin and Greek idiom, means that he had been somewhat strongly urged to do so.
[82] *Ecl.*, IX, 26 sqq.
[83] Cf. my *Handb. Lat. Lit.*, p. 358 and note 61.
[84] See Donatus, *Vita*, p. 14, 13.
[85] Propertius, II, 34, 67 sqq.: tu canis umbrosi subter pineta Galaesi/Thyrsin et attritis Daphnin harundinibus, *e.q.s.* But as he is already at work on the *Aeneid* (63–66), this proves little for his early residences.

86 It will be seen that I do not agree with H. Wagenvoort in *Mnemosyne*, LVIII (1930), p. 158, that Vergil set out to save the Mantuan territory *carminibus pangendis*, of which the first Eclogue was one; I think it more than doubtful that there was time.

87 Herodotos, II, 55 sqq.

88 *Ecl.*, IX, 39–43; Theokr., Id. XI, 42 sqq., 63 sqq.

89 See the commentators, ancient and modern, on *Ecl.*, IX, 47, and A. Cartault, *Etude sur les Bucoliques de Virgile* (Paris, Colin, 1897), pp. 17 sq., and references there; he makes the curious assumption that Vergil wrote this passage immediately after the appearance of the comet.

90 See chap. vi, pp. 129 sqq.

91 Cf. R. Waltz in *Revue Belge*, VI (1927), p. 55.

92 *Ecl.*, I, 73.

93 *Loc. cit.*

94 *Ecl.*, I, 70 sq.

95 As is shown by *Georg.*, IV, 566.

96 Macrobius, *Sat.*, II, 4, 21.

97 Waltz, *op. cit.*, p. 40.

Notes to Chapter V: Gallus, Silenus, and Arkady

[1] This seems to have been first noticed by Wagner in the fourth edition of Heyne's Vergil, which he revised. It is discussed by Cartault, *Etude*, pp. 53 sq., and by an oversight of a sort which is likely to grow increasingly common as the mass of books about books becomes more impossible to know, it is put forth as a new observation by A. Klotz in *Rhein. Mus.*, LXIV (1909), pp. 325–327. I take this opportunity of saying that if this little treatise anywhere offers old remarks for new, it is to be set down to the like unavoidable oversight and not to any desire to plagiarise.

[2] Presumably Varus' active duties would not begin till the fall of Perusia, which surrendered in February or March of that year according to modern historians.

[3] See below, note 29.

[4] VI, 82.

[5] Servius on *Ecl.*, VI, 31. Most moderns assume that Vergil was a convinced Epicurean at the time, if not later; some tend to think his Epicureanism nothing but interest in Lucretius. I incline towards the former view, but a full discussion would take too long and is not necessary for the purposes of this work.

[6] This rough translation will, I hope, make it plain that I accept none of the proposed emendations for the perfectly satisfactory reading of the MSS. (save for the blunder, *ex omnia* for *exordia*, in the codex Palatinus, anticipated at his leisure by one of the worst and most reckless of modern emendators, Peerlkamp), ut his exordia primis/omnia et ipse tener mundi concreuerit orbis. The words mean: how from (by means of) these first things (absolute beginnings) all beginnings (fundamental materials of the universe, elements) and the (still) soft sphere of the universe itself grew together. That is to say, the *semina* or atoms of the Epicurean system joined to make the four simple bodies, earth, air, water, and fire, of the earlier systems from Empedokles on. It is exactly what Lucretius teaches in I, 635 sqq., in his polemic against the various theories which would reduce all things either to one element or to the Empedoklean four. I do not give an analysis of the verbal debt of Vergil to Lucretius here, since that has been sufficiently done by Fr. Skutsch, *Aus Vergils Frühzeit* (Teubner, 1901), pp. 45 sq., cf. Cartault, *op. cit.*, pp. 269 sqq.

The idea of making Seilenos sing when caught is not in itself new, as Daniel's Servius remarks (on *Ecl.*, VI, 13). It is the old tale of King Midas and the Seilenos whom he made drunk and obliged to answer his questions (see my *Handbook of Greek Myth.*, p. 157), and has presumably some connection with the similar tale of Proteus and Menelaos in the *Odyssey* (IV, 384 sqq.). Theopompos had retold it, and between him and Vergil Theophrastos and Krantor likely enough intervene, see Skutsch, *op. cit.*, p. 29, and references there. Vergil, however, gives it a new turn by making it all a joke, with no serious questions asked or answers given, but only songs. The cosmological beginning is borrowed, as has been often observed, from Orpheus' song in Apoll. Rhod., I, 496 sqq.

[7] Cartault, *Etude*, pp. 41 sq. *Ibid.*, p. 285, he improves on this passing suggestion by supposing, what is perfectly plausible in itself, but does not explain the

NOTES TO CHAPTER V

structure of this poem, that Vergil was in the habit of turning into a few lines of striking and expressive verse anything which particularly pleased him in the wide reading in which, on Cartault's or anyone else's views, he must have been engaged at this and other seasons of his life.

[8] *Op. cit.*, pp. 28 sqq.

[9] Cf. above, chap. iv, note 30.

[10] *Iliad*, I, 234 sqq.

[11] "Sir, Addison had his style, and I have mine," Johnson to Boswell, in Boswell's *Life of Johnson*, A.D. 1750 (Vol. I, p. 260, note 2 Hill).

[12] *Aen.*, IV, 345.

[13] Skutsch, *op. cit.*, p. 47.

[14] This is assuming that Egnatius the rhetorician was also the Egnatius who is quoted by Macrobius, *Sat.*, VI, 5, 2 and 12.

[15] Anon., ἐπιτάφιος Βίωνος, 80 sqq. (the poem is sometimes numbered 3 among the works of Moschos; it is No. I of the Appendix to the *Bucolici Graeci* in Wilamowitz-Moellendorff's ed.). Propertius, see above, chap. iv, note 85.

[16] Daniel's Servius on *Ecl.*, VI, 64.

[17] *Ecl.*, X, 2, meo Gallo. One man did not speak of another as *meus* unless they were on very good terms, provided neither was the near kinsman or slave of the other.

[18] Gallus was 43 when he died in 727/27, Jerome, *Chron.*, an. Abr. 1990. If this is exact, he and Vergil were born in the same year, but as R. Syme rightly points out (in the article cited in chap. iv, note 29), such literary synchronisms were apt to be rounded off to make them more striking. We may take it that the two were about of an age, and since Gallus was born in Forum Iulii (Fréjus, not Friuli, see Syme, *op. cit.*) they must have made each other's acquaintance during the period of their education, i.e., at Rome or perhaps Milan, or not long after that. If Vergil really was personally well acquainted with Pollio, cf. above, pp. 83–84, Gallus, who was on good terms with the latter (cf. Cartault, *op. cit.*, p. 22, for refs.) probably was the intermediary.

[19] Leo in *Hermes*, XXXVII (1902), p. 29; Skutsch, *op. cit.*, p. 47.

[20] His elegies at least were widely known in Ovid's day, *Amores*, i, 15, 29 sq. To the taste of Quintilian he was somewhat lacking in polish, *durior*, *inst. orat.*, X, i, 93 (not, I think, *plus sevère*, as H. Bornecque renders it in his edition).

[21] Skutsch, *ibid.*, pp. 61 sqq.; *Gallus und Vergil* (Teubner, 1906), pp. 4 sqq. I am, on the whole, inclined now (contrast *Handb. Lat. Lit.*, p. 262) to allow that the *Ciris* is a pre-Vergilian poem, but still deny that Gallus wrote it.

[22] Skutsch, *Frühzeit*, p. 37.

[23] *Ibid.*, p. 36, citing Propertius, II, 10, 25–26: nondum etiam Ascraeos norunt mea carmina fontes,/sed modo Permessi flumine lauit Amor. This may throw some light on *Ecl.*, VI, 64, errentem Permessi ad flumina Gallum. Skutsch interprets, "der Strom des Permessus bedeutet für Properz die niedere, die erotische Poesie, die Musenquellen aber die höhere, die heroische." But Propertius uses in this connection the important word *Amor*, which shows clearly how he was employed when his poems were washed in the waters of a metaphorical Permessos,

i.e., at the foot of Parnassos, for it is a stream flowing down from the mountain. It by no means follows that everyone who is said to wander on its banks is engaged in writing amatory elegiacs, when no other hint of such a thing is given; even if we reject the view of Cartault, *op. cit.*, p. 280, "c'est une simple promenade, qui convient à un poète; il ne faut pas voir là autre chose," the most that can be fairly extracted from the words is that they tell us allegorically that Gallus had not yet climbed the heights of Parnassos, i.e., was not yet a great poet, until the inspiration came which enabled him to write his epyllion on the Gryneian grove. The meeting with Linos and the Muses is, by the way, typically Alexandrian and no doubt borrowed from Euphorion, cf. the vision of the Muses with which the *Aitia* of Kallimachos started (Schneider, *Callimachea*, pp. 113 sqq.). That it is ultimately taken from Hesiod (*Theog.*, 22 sqq.) is of course true, but the conclusion drawn thence by Cartault, *ibid.*, that Vergil is directly imitating that passage is unjustified. Much Alexandrian poetry regarded Hesiod as a great predecessor on whom it refined, cf. Kallimachos, *epigr.* 29 (27), 'Ησιόδου τό τ' ἄεισμα κτἐ.

[24] Leo, *op. cit.*, p. 22.

[25] In *Eos*, XXIV (1919–20), pp. 1 sqq.

[26] Ovid, *Metam.*, I, 381 sqq.

[27] Aphrodite, see Hyginus, *fab.*, 40, 1; Poseidon, see Rose, *Handb. Gk. Myth.*, p. 283, or any of the larger works on mythology, for refs.

[28] *Ecl.*, IX, 26 sqq., cf. p. 89.

[29] H. Flach, in Fleckeisen's *Jahrb. f. klass. Phil.*, XXV (1879), p. 792, rightly points out that the opening line, extremum hunc, Arethusa, mihi concede laborem, tells us no more than that the piece was placed last in the complete publication. It may have been added or rewritten. Therefore, no indication of the date, absolute or relative, of the poem can be gathered from it.

[30] *Ecl.*, X, 2–3, by the most natural interpretation, but it would be possible to understand the expressions (pauca meo Gallo . . . carmina sunt dicenda; neget quis carmina Gallo?) as meaning that the idea was Vergil's own. Incidentally, the words omitted in the foregoing quotation, sed quae legat ipsa Lycoris, do not mean, as Max Pohlenz supposes (*Studi Virgiliani*, publ. della R. Accademia virgiliana di Mantova, 1930, X, pp. 208–209), that the poem is to be erotic, but that it is to be of a very high order. Since Gallus' elegies were addressed to Lycoris, she is used only to the very best verses, and so these must be something above the ordinary. Love is in fact the matter of both Vergil's poem and the works of Gallus alluded to, but that is not stated in what Vergil here says.

[31] Servius on *Ecl.*, X, 46: hi autem omnes uersus Galli sunt, de ipsius translati carminibus.

[32] Skutsch, *op. cit.*, pp. 2 sqq.

[33] The idealisation took place somewhere between Theokritos and Vergil; the fact that it lay off the main tracks both of commerce and of wars, which Sicily did not, probably had much to do with it.

[34] See Leo in *Hermes*, XXXVII (1902), pp. 14 sqq. He suggests, p. 19, that it was with Antony (cf. Plutarch, *M. Antonius*, 23, 1) that Gallus left Italy, by no

means an impossibility for Octavian's man, as the two leaders were at that moment supposedly reconciled on a permanent basis. Cf. also R. Bürger, *ibid.*, XXXVIII (1903), pp. 19 sqq., who tries to reconstruct the supposed elegy from Vergil.

[35] Sollicitos Galli dicamus amores, *Ecl.*, X, 6, cf. Pohlenz, *op. cit.*, p. 210.

[36] I understand the words nunc insanus amor duri me Martis in armis/ . . . detinet to mean "as it is, mad lust after cruel warfare keeps me in arms," not, as Leo (*op. cit.*, p. 17) would have it, "love-madness has hold of me in the midst of cruel warfare." For this *amor*, cf. Eurip., *I. A.*, 1264–1266.

[37] It is that of the commentators on Vergil, especially Servius on *Ecl.*, X, 1, with nothing in any ancient to indicate that they are wrong. See Cartault, *op. cit.*, pp. 46 sqq., and to the objectors to the identification (for chronological reasons) add Bürger, *op. cit.*, p. 25; Leo, *op. cit.*, p. 19, accepts the equation.

[38] References in Cartault, *loc. cit.*

[39] *Ibid.*, p. 47.

[40] Anon., *de uir. illustr.*, 82, 2. It is a most unlikely story; were some of his poems (Tac., *Dial.*, 21, 11) amatory enough to serve as a basis?

[41] Servius, *loc. cit.*, p. 118, 10.

[42] Leo, *loc. cit.*

[43] If, that is, *Chalcidico uersu* (*Ecl.*, X, 50) does not include both; see, among others, Skutsch, *op. cit.*, p. 3.

[44] That it is at this time and not earlier that we must put her desertion of Gallus appears pretty clearly from the following considerations. (1) She was Antony's mistress till 708/46, see above, p. 108. (2) After this she had a liaison with someone else, allegedly Brutus, cf. note 40, since, for such a scandal to have got about concerning a man generally reputed serious, there must have been a period after the affair with M. Antonius when she was not notoriously connected with Gallus and Brutus (born in 669/85) was not so old as to make the tale utterly absurd. That for a while she had no lover is incredible. (3) Gallus must have been her acknowledged protector, not an occasional and furtive visitor to her when she was supported by someone else, or he could hardly have written so much about her under so transparent a disguise as the name Lycoris. (4) Supposing his association with her began as early as 709/45, leaving but a year for the alleged affair with Brutus, this will leave but four years or so (late in 45–sometime in 41) for the composition of three books of poems by a member of a school which believed in leisurely writing; for it is scarcely likely that during the fighting at Perusia and his activities in connection with the distributions of land Gallus had much time for poetry. It is to be remembered that during these same years he must have been actively bringing himself to the favourable notice of Octavian, who otherwise would not have employed him, in 714/40 and later, on such serious business. Hence, as a date for the breach between the lovers, especially if we are to suppose Gallus really in Greece, we cannot go higher than the beginning of 715/39 and may have to come lower. I would reject Leo's suggestion (note 42), for L. Antonius triumphed *ex Alpibus* in 713/41, *C. I. L.*, I, p. 478, too early a date to be probable, and think rather of some officer who went on Agrippa's cam-

paign of 716/38 to Gaul and Germany (refs. in *Prosop. Imp. Rom.*, III, p. 439). Cf. B. Nardi, *The Youth of Virgil*, pp. 101 sqq.

[45] Four books, Servius, *loc. cit.*, p. 118, 4 Thilo. Skutsch, *op. cit.*, p. 18.

[46] Leo, *op. cit.*, p. 18; Bürger, *op. cit.*, pp. 19 sqq.

[47] Schiller, *Die Piccolimini*, II, 7 (lines 1099 sq.):
> Ganz Deutschland seufzte unter Kriegeslast,
> Doch Friede war's im Wallensteinschen Lager.

This is from Seneca, *Troad.*, 323–324: et tanto in metu/naualibus pax alta Thessalis fuit. Here Pyrrhus is replying to Agamemnon's taunt about Achilles' inactivity when the Greek camp was in danger by saying that owing to the terror of Achilles' name his part of the camp enjoyed perfect peace. In Schiller this defence of Achilles has been transmuted into an attack on Wallenstein, whose defence is given in vigorous lines of Schiller's own.

[48] See, e.g., Cartault's analysis of his use of Theokritos in *Ecl.*, III, *op. cit.*, pp. 126 sqq.

[49] Cf. the preceding note.

[50] Skutsch, *op. cit.*, p. 19.

[51] It is an old observation, Servius, p. 3, 20 Thilo, that only seven of the ten Eclogues are pure pastorals; to which J. Hubaux, in *Rev. Belge*, VI (1927), pp. 603–616, adds the curious observation that only these seven have a bucolic name, i.e., one which by Theokritean convention is that of a countryman, in the first line (I, *Tityre*, tu . . .; II, formosum pastor *Corydon* . . .; III, dic mihi, *Damoeta*; V, cur non, *Mopse* . . .; VII, forte sub arguta consederat ilice *Daphnis*; VIII, pastorum Musam *Damonis* et *Alphesiboei*; IX, quo te, *Moeri* . . .).

[52] That it is humorous is maintained by Pohlenz, *op. cit.* (see note 30), p. 220; it had already been suggested by G. Gevers, see Cartault, *op. cit.*, p. 383, who himself, with Ph. Wagner, maintains that the poem is serious.

[53] Theokritos' nymphs are asked (Id. I, 67) if they were in Greece proper, since they were not in Sicily; Vergil's (*Ecl.*, X, 11 sq.), where they can have been, since they were not in their favourite haunts in Greece.

[54] Cf. *Ecl.*, II, 71 sq.

[55] *Ecl.*, X, 76; Sergeaunt, *op. cit.*, p. 64, can give no reason for this belief.

[56] *Ecl.*, II, last line, cf. p. 37.

[57] *Ecl.*, X, 72, uos [the Muses] haec facietis maxima Gallo.

Notes to Chapter VI: Vergil and Allegory

[1] See chap. iv, note 16.
[2] Vincent A. FitzSimon, *The Ten Christian Pastorals of Vergil* (New York, 1912).
[3] See chap. iv, note 18.
[4] In *Class. Rev.*, XXII (1908), pp. 40–43.
[5] See chap. v, note 1.
[6] He says (13–14) quae cortice fagi/carmina descripsi et modulans alterna notaui. That the bark had first been peeled off to serve as a substitute for paper (Vergil would remember what *liber* originally meant) seems to be certain. The words *alterna notaui* seem to mean that he had inserted the musical signs, as was usual in antiquity, between the lines of text.
[7] *Ecl.*, V, 85–90.
[8] L. Herrmann, *Masques et visages*, p. 120.
[9] J. S. Phillimore, *Pastoral and Allegory*, p. 29; schol. Bern., p. 783–784 Hagen.
[10] It is, for example, the subject of the second of Ovid's *Heroides*.
[11] Servius on *Ecl.*, V, 10.
[12] Rose, *Handb. of Gk. Myth.*, p. 294.
[13] Servius on *Ecl.*, V, 11.
[14] Theokritos, Id. VI, 22–24.
[15] *Ecl.*, III, 84 sqq.; IX, 35.
[16] *Ecl.*, VII, 21–26.
[17] On *Ecl.*, VII, 22 (p. 399, 11 Hagen).
[18] Ovid, *ex Pont.*, IV, 16, 28.
[19] Tacitus, *ann.*, IV, 34, 35.
[20] *Ecl.*, V, 40, spargite humum foliis, inducite fontibus umbras (Mopsus is singing). Cf. IX, 19–20 (if Menalcas-Vergil had died) quis humum florentibus herbis/ spargeret, aut uiridi fontis induceret umbra? i.e., who would write any more songs like that of Mopsus?
[21] He says *tu maior* to Menalcas, *Ecl.*, V, 4.
[22] He is βούτας in Theokr., Id. I, 84.
[23] Cartault, *Etude*, p. 211.
[24] On *Ecl.*, V, 20.
[25] Donatus, *Vita*, p. 12, 4.
[26] Rose, *Handb. Lat. Lit.*, p. 275, note 133.
[27] *Ibid.*, pp. 341 sq.
[28] *Ecl.*, IX, 46 sqq., cf. p. 90.
[29] Cf. p. 80.
[30] Tenney Frank in *Class. Rev.*, XXXIV (1920), pp. 49–51; *Vergil*, pp. 115 sqq.
[31] Wissowa in Pauly-Wissowa, *Realenc.*, IV, 1628, 38 sqq.
[32] Cf. above, note 20.
[33] Cf. p. 26.
[34] Cf. pp. 153 sqq.
[35] *Ecl.*, V, 27.
[36] *Ibid.*, 29 sqq.

[37] *Ibid.*, 40 sqq.
[38] *Ibid.*, 35, 66.
[39] *Ibid.*, 61.
[40] *Ibid.*, 39.
[41] *Ibid.*, 54.
[42] *Hist. Aug.* xiv, 2, 8 (Caracallus of Geta).
[43] See Plut., *quaest. Graec.*, 34 (298 F) with Halliday's note.
[44] See below, chap. viii.
[45] See Daniel's Servius on *Ecl.*, IX, 46, and cf. p. 174.
[46] Ovid, *Metam.*, I, 100 sqq.
[47] *Aen.*, VI, 792 sqq.
[48] *Ibid.*, I, 286 sqq.
[49] *Class. Quart.*, XVI (1922), pp. 57 sqq.
[50] Bion, 'Αδώνιδος 'Επιτάφιος (No. X in the Appendix to Wilamowitz-Moellendorff's *Bucolici Graeci*), 40 sqq.
[51] Ovid, *Metam.*, XV, 761 sqq.
[52] Servius on *Ecl.*, V, 29.
[53] E.g., C. Bailey, *Religion in Virgil* (Oxford, Clarendon Press, 1935), p. 189. Upholding the view that Daphnis is Caesar as one of which "there can hardly be any doubt" (p. 188), he reports Servius' dictum with the cautious modification "reintroduction," knowing well that there were Dionysiac cults at Rome long before Caesar's day.
[54] For archaeological evidence (some, to my thinking, most inconclusive) of this, see M. I. Rostovtzeff, *Mystic Italy* (New York, Holt, 1927).
[55] Pliny, *N. H.*, VIII, 4 (elephanti) Romae iuncti primum subiere currum Pompei Magni Africo triumpho, quod prius India uicta triumphante Libero patre memoratur; cited by Drew, *op. cit.*, p. 60.
[56] Suetonius, *D. Iulius*, 37, 2; Drew, *ibid.*
[57] See, e.g., Plut., *quaest. Graec.*, 56, and Halliday there.
[58] "Daphnis teaching the swains to celebrate the 'Liberalia' is an emblem of the civil reforms of Caesar," Conington *ad loc.*
[59] *Aen.*, IV, 174 sqq.
[60] *Ecl.*, V, 48 sqq.
[61] Mopsus composed his song quite at his leisure, not long before he sings it, cf. note 6 above. Menalcas' hymn is not new, but already famous locally, cf. 55. Daphnis, then, has been dead for some time, although the two singers knew him personally, and seems to be already a stock theme for songs.
[62] Cartault, *Etude*, pp. 178 sqq. Cf. A. Mancini in *Studi Virgiliani*, II (Rome, 1932), p. 345.
[63] *Ecl.*, VII, 7 sqq.
[64] *Ecl.*, VIII, 68 sqq.
[65] Theokr., Id. I, 66 sqq.
[66] See Rose, *Handb. Gk. Myth.*, p. 169, and the refs. there given (note 15); add Cartault, *ibid.*, pp. 166 sqq.

NOTES TO CHAPTER VI 247

⁶⁷ He is wasting away, ἐτάκετο, Theokr., *loc. cit.*, 66; Priapos, who cannot imagine any other distress than that caused by purely physical desire, is frankly puzzled and asks Daphnis what more he wants, when the girl, so far from shunning him, is actually looking everywhere for him, 81 sqq. Aphrodite, who apparently means no more than a rather cruel jest and expects him to yield at any moment, taunts him with having defied Love, 97; Daphnis in his reply bitterly reproaches and scorns both Love and her, 100 sqq., and especially taunts her with being unchaste, 105 sqq.

⁶⁸ Theokr., *ibid.*, 72, τῆνον κὤκ δρυμοῖο λέων ἔκλαυσε θανόντα. The scholiast produces a delightful variant, reflected in a number of our MSS., ἂν ἔκλαυσε, i.e., the lion would have lamented for him if any such beast had existed in Sicily. Our scholia are the detritus of ancient commentaries, with later additions, and this gem of criticism might be as old as Vergil's day.

⁶⁹ See Daniel's Servius on *Ecl.*, VIII, 68; Athenaios, 415 b, cf. Cartault, *op. cit.*, p. 171.

⁷⁰ *Georg.*, II, 385 sqq. For the question whether Liber Pater be not after all simply Dionysos, see Altheim, *Terra Mater* (Giessen, Töpelmann, 1931), pp. 15 sqq. For some interesting speculations on the connection between Daphnis (whom he equates with Caesar) and Dionysos, see E. Pfeiffer, *Virgils Bukolika* (Stuttgart, Kohlhammer, 1933), pp. 60 sqq.

⁷¹ *Ecl.*, V, 34-35: postquam te fata tulerunt/ipsa Pales agros atque ipse reliquit Apollo.

⁷² Theokr., Id. I, 141.

⁷³ Daniel's Servius on *Ecl.*, V, 20, p. 56, 24 Thilo.

⁷⁴ That the Berne scholia call him *deus pastoralis*, proem to *Ecl.*, VII, is of no importance, being merely an allusion to *Ecl.*, V, 64.

⁷⁵ Diodoros Siculus, IV, 84, 4.

⁷⁶ Euripides, *Hipp.*, 1423 sqq.

⁷⁷ *Aen.*, VII, 761 sqq.

Notes to Chapter VII: Some Theokritean Imitations

¹ For its inadequacies in language and metre, see Wilamowitz-Moellendorff, *Textgeschichte der griechischen Bukoliker*, p. 122.

² See Cartault, *Etude*, pp. 117 sqq.

³ Ps.-Theokr., VIII, 41 sqq. It will be seen that I do not accept any of the transpositions and other needless emendations proposed by various critics and accepted by Wilamowitz-Moellendorff in his edition.

⁴ There is an attractive, but not strictly necessary, emendation of Jortin here, Κροίσεια for χρύσεια, which balances γᾶν Πέλοπος very well.

⁵ This was nothing new; the Unjust Argument recommends its use, Aristoph., *Clouds*, 1080 sq., a passage which almost reads as if it were a parody on this much later one.

⁶ *Ecl.*, III, 28 sqq.; see p. 39.

⁷ *Ecl.*, VII, 4–5, cf. ps.-Theokr., VIII, 3–4.

⁸ *Ecl.*, VII, 12 sq.

⁹ See the excellent little article of W. Baehrens in *Hermes*, LXI (1926), pp. 382 sqq.; cf. below, note 18.

¹⁰ Cf. pp. 121–122.

¹¹ *Si proprium hoc fuerit*, line 31, *hoc* being evidently his skill or luck in hunting. For exactly this use of *proprius*, cf. Horace, *sat.* II, 6, 4 sq.: nil amplius oro,/ Maia nate, nisi ut propria haec mihi munera faxis. He hopes, that is, that what the god of luck has given him may not prove to be the fruits of a mere passing whim on good luck's part, to go suddenly and leave him as poor as ever. The name is scanned Mĭcon, which seems to indicate that the *i* of μικρός was occasionally short as early as Vergil.

¹² Lines 41 sqq. That this is Galatea's answer to Corydon has been seen by a number of scholars, as Cartault, Henze, W. Baehrens, and Mesk (see *Philologus*, LXXXIII, p. 454); but, needless to say, not by Conington. Her line, ite domum pasti, si quis pudor, ite iuuenci, is borrowed by Milton for the refrain of his *epitaphium Damonis*, ite domum impasti, domino iam non uacat, agni.

¹³ A lovely adaptation of a pretty passage of the ps.-Theokr., VIII, 78 ἁδὺ δὲ τῷ θέρεος παρ' ὕδωρ ῥέον αἰθριοκοιτεῖν. Vergil has added the detail of the moss about the fountains which supply the "running water" and, instead of simply mentioning the pleasure of sleeping in such a delightful place in hot weather, has made the grass softer than the sleep it induces (cf. Theokr., V, 51).

¹⁴ See p. 146.

¹⁵ Cf. Cartault, *op. cit.*, p. 197.

¹⁶ Meliboeus says (69) *haec memini*, which may mean perhaps that he has remembered all that happened, or more likely that there was more but he cannot recall it.

¹⁷ *Ex illo Corydon Corydon est tempore nobis*, 70. It is exactly the Vergilian figure which has so puzzled commentators on *Aen.*, VI, 882–883, heu miserande puer, si qua fata aspera rumpas,/tu Marcellus eris; cf. Rose in *Class. Rev.*, XLV (1931), pp. 51 sq., which misses part of Vergil's point.

NOTES TO CHAPTER VII

[18] In *Hermes*, LXI (1926), pp. 362 sqq. This is not quite adequate, but at least better than the despairing declaration of J. Mesk, *Philologus*, LXXXIII (1927-28), pp. 453-458, that there is no reason, ethical or artistic, for the decision, which comes merely because it had to; as if Vergil, always the freest of imitators, could not have left this contest undecided as he does that in *Ecl.* III.

[19] Certamen erat, Corydon cum Thyrside, magnum, 16.

[20] In *Class. Rev.*, XLVII (1933), pp. 216–219. The following details of Thyrsis' faults are taken with slight modification from this article.

[21] Ps.-Theokr., IX, 21.

[22] Cf. above, chap. v, note 1.

[23] *Ecl.*, VIII, 5–13, cf. p. 82.

[24] *Ibid.*, 16, incumbens... tereti... oliuae. Most commentators have seen that, as the irregular trunk of an olive-tree could not be called *teres*, this must be a staff of olive-wood.

[25] *Ibid.*, 2-4.

[26] *Ecl.*, V, 11, cf. p. 119.

[27] Catullus, 85, 1.

[28] This observation is made by G. Rohde, *De Vergili eclogarum forma et indole* (Berlin, 1925), p. 28.

[29] It was early morning with the dew still on the grass when Damon began (15) his song.

[30] Lines 29 sq., where the pronouns are sarcastically emphatic, *tibi* ducitur uxor ... *tibi* deserit Hesperus Oetam. Cf. A. Klotz in *Neue Jahrb. f. das klass. Alt.*, XLV/XLVI (1920), p. 153, "Es ist so unglaublich, dass man Mopsus selber daran erinnern muss."

[31] Theokr., II, 82, χὡς ἴδον, ὡς ἐμάνην, ὥς μοι περὶ θυμὸς ἰάφθη.

[32] Cf. p. 9.

[33] Theokr., III, 15 sqq., νῦν ἔγνων τὸν Ἔρωτα· βαρὺς θεός· ἦρα λεαίνας | μαστὸν ἐθήλαζεν, δρυμῷ τέ νιν ἔτρεφε μάτηρ, | ὅς με κατασμύχων καὶ ἐς ὀστέον ἄχρις ἰάπτει.

[34] Theokr., VII, 77, in a quite different context: ἢ Ἄθω ἢ Ῥοδόπαν ἢ Καύκασον ἐσχατόωντα.

[35] See chap. vi, n. 20.

[36] *Ecl.*, IV, 3, 11; see chap. viii.

[37] Cf. p. 94.

[38] *Ecl.*, VIII, 53–59; Theokr., I, 132-136. The words *omnia uel medium fiat mare* are a kind of touchstone of commentators. At the corresponding place in the Greek the expression is πάντα δ' ἔναλλα γένοιτο, and the stupider sort of reader and annotator, such as Cauer, Conington, and, very surprisingly, Elmsley, who must that day have been much below his usual form, cry with one voice that Vergil has taken ἔναλλα for ἐνάλια. The more acute, as Cartault, *op. cit.*, p. 311, note 1, P. Wilkinson in *Class. Rev.*, L (1936), pp. 120 sq., E. Dutoit, *L'adynaton* (Paris, Les Belles Lettres, 1936), p. 74, see that he has done nothing of the kind. He has changed all else, why insert a mistranslation of this one phrase? But it may be that the one Greek word suggested the other to him by resemblance of sound, and so gave him a lead to what change he should make.

[39] *Ecl.*, VIII, 60–62; Theokr., III, 25–27 (for the Leukadian rock, to which Theokritos is obviously alluding, and its curious ritual, which was certainly one of purification by air, see S. Eitrem in Λαογραφία 1922, pp. 127 sqq.); ps.-Theokr., XXIII, 21.

[40] Theokritos never published a collection of his poems, and the numbers in our editions have no ancient authority; but they are well known and convenient, and the attempt of Wilamowitz-Moellendorff, in his text, to restore the order of the ancient collected editions has since been shown mistaken, though ingenious, by the discovery of papyri of Theokritos.

[41] Line 97 specifies the palaistra of Timagetos, implying that there was at least one other.

[42] Line 68.

[43] She says (85 sqq.) that she became violently ill, could not leave her bed for ten days, and all her hair fell out. Even allowing for Alexandrian conventions in describing the physical effects of sudden and violent passion, this is exaggerated, for a little later she is manifestly attractive and capable of responding strongly to Delphis' caresses, 140 sqq. This is of course intentional; the speaker is a desperate and very lovesick girl.

[44] For the *iynx*, see A. S. F. Gow in *Jour. Hell. Stud.*, LIV (1934), pp. 1 sqq.

[45] Line 30 sq.

[46] *Ibid.*, 110.

[47] *Ibid.*, 38 sqq.

[48] Here (48) it is distinctly called a plant; the name is also used (as by Vergil, *Georg.*, III, 282) of an alleged secretion of mares in heat, used in black magic, and again of the supposed tubercle on the front of a new-born foal (cf. *Aen.*, IV, 515 sq., where see Pease's note).

[49] See *ibid.*, 159 sqq.; she utters a last and not very convincing threat to poison Delphis with drugs she has got from an "Assyrian stranger" (cf. the Pontic herbs in Vergil's imitation, line 95), and ends on a note of calm.

[50] *Aen.*, IV, 504 sqq.

[51] The water must be fetched "out," *Ecl.*, VIII, 65, from the store-jar or wherever it is kept, and there is a threshold, 93, 108. As she calls Daphnis her *coniunx* (67), they clearly are living together; it is not stated by Vergil and it would be quite profitless to enquire whether she is his *uxor, concubina,* or *contubernalis*.

[52] Cf. Pliny, *N. H.*, XII, 61 sq.

[53] The words are (67) coniugis ut magicis sanos auertere sacris/experiar sensus. Servius notes: aut a sanitate, aut "auertere" ait pro "aduertere," ut sit mutata praepositio, to which Daniel's Servius adds, aut certe in me conuertere. It is no doubt possible to make the words mean "turn his sober senses" (into madness), but I prefer to think *sanos* quasi-predicative, "turn his mind and make it sane."

[54] See Z. N. Hurston, *Mules and Men* (Philadelphia, Lippincott, 1935), pp. 251 sqq.; the authoress has the double qualification of being a well-trained anthropologist and an initiate of Hoodoo (or Voodoo).

[55] She says (80 sq.): limus ut hic durescit et haec ut cera liquescit [the jingle suggests old popular Italian verse]/uno eodemque igni, sic nostro Daphnis amore. It is a good example of that figure of "imperfect proportion" or "rhetorical enthy-

meme" to which I have drawn attention, *Harv. Stud.*, XLVII (1936), pp. 5 sqq. The reader is to supply something like *et ego odio illius*.

⁵⁶ Lucretius, II, 355 sqq.

⁵⁷ I take *bucula* (87) as a pitying diminutive, not as signifying a young cow or heifer, and reject the interpretation of the passage as describing the beast in search of her mate.

⁵⁸ We know from Macrob., *Sat.*, VI, 2, 20, that this line is from Varius.

⁵⁹ Cf. above, note 49.

⁶⁰ On *Ecl.*, VIII, 97; Filargirius is not sure whether it was his subtlety in magic or the changeableness of his nature which produced the phenomenon, that is, whether he was a natural werwolf or an artificial one. Cf. R. P. Eckels, *Greek Wolf-Lore* (diss., Philadelphia, 1937), pp. 32 sqq.

⁶¹ Petron., *Sat.*, 62.

⁶² Serv. on *Ecl.*, VIII, 99; he gives the wording as *neue alienam segetem pellexeris*, but the actual law would of course use the "future" imperative, not the perf. subj.

⁶³ Lines 101 sq.; for good interpretation, followed in the text, see A. Klotz in *Neue Jahrb.*, XLV/XLVI (1920), p. 156.

⁶⁴ Aesch., *Choeph.*, 98 sq.

⁶⁵ *Ecl.*, VIII, 103.

Excursus: The Chronology of the Eclogues

It will have been noticed that the foregoing chapters make no systematic attempt to draw up a list of the ten Bucolics in order of composition, nor to assign dates to most of them. The chief reason for this is that I consider the task both unimportant and impossible, save for such matters as have already been dealt with, i.e., that Nos. II and III precede V, V precedes IX, which in its turn is probably earlier than I, IV is earlier than VIII and in all probability than X, VI previous to the final loss of Vergil's estate, and VII more likely early than late. But whether, for example, VIII or X was composed first and whether VII or VI is the earlier seems to me not worth the trouble of finding out. This opinion has been arrived at after examining some of the modern attempts to reach a chronology of the poems. Of these, one of the fundamental works is that Ewald Krause, *Quibus temporibus quoque ordine Vergilius Eclogas scripserit* (diss., Berlin, 1884), on which Cartault largely draws. He starts from well-established facts, the statement of Asconius Pedianus (in "Probus," p. 323, 13 Hagen) that he "wrote" (*scripsit*) the Bucolics when twenty-eight years old, and that of Donatus (*Vita*, l. 89 Brummer; cf. Servius, Vol. I, p. 2, 8 sq., Thilo-Hagen) that the work took him three years. He was twenty-eight years old in 712/42, and therefore the two statements put together mean that he first tried his hand at pastoral poetry in that or the next year, i.e., before he was twenty-nine, and had the *Eclogues* finished and ready for the public (as opposed to circulation as single pieces among the author's own acquaintance) sometime in 715/39 or 716/38, which agrees very well with such indications of absolute chronology as can be gleaned from the text of the poems, e.g., from IV, 11 and VIII, 6 sqq. Unfortunately a not inconsiderable part of

Krause's further argument depends on the false identification of Vergil with Tityrus and Corydon. The latest attempt, and one of the most ingenious, which I have seen is that of C. F. Kumaniecki, in *Eos*, XXIX (1926), pp. 69–79. His criterion is the passages in which Vergil imitates or half-quotes himself, and is obviously weakened by its subjectivity, for it is seldom that any two critics will agree, in default of external evidence, which of two passages is the earlier; one certainly false result, in my opinion, is the conclusion at which he arrives that V is later than IX. But his article is of worth, not only for its subtle literary criticism, but also for the comparative table with which it ends, showing the results arrived at by several other moderns who have made researches in the same thankless field.

Notes to Chapter VIII: A Child Is Born

[1] Asconius (below, note 110) discussed it with Asinius Gallus.

[2] See p. 174.

[3] That the constellation Virgo is the same as Dike is an idea as old at least as Aratos, *Phaen.*, 100 sqq., and familiar enough to Latin poets, e.g., Ovid, *Metam.*, I, 149 sq., et Virgo caede madentes/ultima caelestum terras Astraea reliquit. Vergil means that Justice shall no longer be a far-off thing, visible to men only as a constellation, but shall return once more and converse familiarly with a now righteous earth.

[4] Teque adeo decus hoc aeui, te consule, inibit/Pollio, et incipient magni procedere menses./te duce, si qua manent sceleris uestigia prisci,/irrita perpetua soluent formidine terras, 11-14. Obviously it is possible to punctuate heavily either before or after *te duce*, but it makes little difference whether we say "when you are consul and leader, the Great Year shall begin again and the fear caused by old-time guilt shall pass away," or "when you are consul, the Great Year recommences, when you are leader, the fear, etc." The words *consule* and *duce* seem in either case to refer to one and the same thing, namely the respectable and still fairly powerful magistracy Pollio held in 710/40, though no doubt there is a side glance at his prominent position in public life, which his own vanity much exaggerated.

[5] Pacatumque reget patriis uirtutibus orbem, 17. There seems to be no deciding whether *patriis uirtutibus* should be taken closely with *pacatum* or *reget*, or ἀπὸ κοινοῦ with both.

[6] This quaint detail (lines 42-45: nec uarios discet mentiri lana colores,/ipse sed in pratis aries iam suaue rubenti/murice, iam croceo mutabit uellera luto,/ sponte sua sandyx pascentis uestiet agnos) throws a curious light on Vergil's reading, his methods of imitation, and the possibility that *Catal.* 5 is by him, if the emendation *Tarquitique* there is right (see chap. iv, note 38). Macrobius, *Sat.*, III, 7, 1-2, tells us that in a work of Tarquitius which is taken straight from an Etruscan treatise on portents and their interpretation (liber Tarquiti transscriptus ex ostentario Tusco) it is said that: purpuero aureoue colore ouis ariesue si aspergetur, princeps ordinis et generis summa cum felicitate largitatem auget, genus progeniem propagat in claritate laetioremque efficiet. The clumsy Latin distinctly suggests that the writer is translating pretty literally. If Vergil had this passage in mind, as seems likely (Servius auctus on 43 gives the gist of the same information, but without mentioning Tarquitius), it is clear that he changed the application of the wonder from a portent of good times coming to a detail of the good time which shall have come when the Golden Age returns.

[7] Talia saecula, suis dixerunt, currite, fusis/concordes stabili fatorum numine Parcae, 46-47. For the echo of Catullus, see p. 201; that *Parcae* and *fata* mean respectively Μοῖραι and εἱμαρμένη is rightly held by Leo and R. Helm, cf. the latter in *Hermes*, 1937, p. 87. The old mythological spinners (for, whatever their real nature, the Parcae were such to Vergil) are the agents of the impersonal and more philosophically conceived force of necessity or causality.

[253]

⁸ Incipe, parue puer, risu cognoscere matrem . . . incipe, parue puer; qui non risere parenti/nec deus hunc mensa dea nec dignata cubili est, 60, 62-63. The reading *qui non risere parenti*, having the support of Quintilian (see crit. edd.) and of the sense, is to be preferred to the *cui . . . parentes* of the MSS. The shift of number, *qui risere . . . hunc*, though not so common in Latin as in Greek, is perfectly legitimate in a generic statement of this sort, see Ethel M. Steuart in *Class. Rev.*, XL (1926), p. 156, and add to her examples, as an instance of such a use in the most dignified poetry, Lucretius, V, 857-859. The compromise reading, *qui non risere parentes*, could mean nothing in classical Latin but "those who have not made fun of their father and mother" (cf. *Aen.*, V, 181 sq.), which is manifest nonsense here. The point is that babies less than forty days old were supposed by the ancients never to smile (Censorinus, 11, 7), as in fact they cannot consciously do, though some slight distortion of the face quite early in life may suggest a smile. But a wonder-child may do so, as he may do any other precocious thing. Neither the infant Herakles (Theokr., XXIV, 31) nor the infant Vergil (Donatus, *Vita*, 2, 13 Brummer) cried; but the only known infant to smile (or laugh, *risisse*) on the day of his birth was Zoroaster, Pliny, *N. H.*, VII, 72, unless we count Nonnos' Beroe, *Dionys.*, XLI, 212, who is not much in point even if she were not so late, seeing that she is the child of Aphrodite and in this respect takes after her mother. See, for some imperfect parallels, D. R. Stuart, in *C. P.*, XVI (1921), pp. 212 sqq.

To shift these lines from the place where they stand to between 25 and 26 (R. Kukula, *Römische Säkularpoesie*, Teubner, 1911, p. 46) is to rob the poem of its perfect close. He does, however, see the point of them; only a wonder-child will grow to be the companion of gods and husband of a goddess. To collect, as, e.g., W. Warde Fowler does (*Class. Rev.*, 1919, p. 67), ethnological material on the supposed significance of a (normal) child's first smile is beside the point, nor has the smile of the infant Kypselos in Herodotos (adduced by J. H. Thiel, *Mnemos.*, LVIII, pp. 112 sqq., and a score of others) anything to do with the matter. He was destined to a great future, but was otherwise normal enough, and the point of Herodotos' story (V, 92 γ) is that the would-be murderers were too kind-hearted to kill a baby who was smiling at them. See further, D. R. Stuart, *loc. cit.*, pp. 209 sqq.

⁹ It is an astonishing fact that in the year 1933 (see *Rev. Et. Anc.*, XXXIII, pp. 33-40) Ph. Fabia found it necessary to explain, and support from Comedy, this elementary point. Those whom he enlightened included so excellent a scholar as P. Lejay. If a woman conceives, say, in January and her child is born full-time in October, we say, in all modern languages, that she has carried the infant nine months; the Romans regularly counted inclusively, reckoning both January and October, and called the same period ten months. Greek uses δεκαμηνιαῖον and ἐννεαμηνιαῖον (βρέφος) indifferently, see Hephaistion in *C. C. A. G.*, VIII, 1, p. 141, 17 sqq.; 145, 8. Vergil's words, therefore (61), matri longa decem tulerunt fastidia menses, mean no more and no less than that the mother has endured all the discomforts of a full-time pregnancy. H. Jeanmaire, *Le messianisme de Virgile* (Paris, Vrin, 1930), p. 8, translates the whole passage sympathetically and admi-

rably: "Allons, petit enfant, souriez à votre mère! Elle a bien souffert, votre maman! allons, petit enfant; les enfants qui ne font pas risette a leur mère n'auront part ni à la table des dieux ni au lit des déesses." He also interprets the perf. *tulerunt* rightly; Vergil writes these lines "anticipant sur un avenir très prochain."

¹⁰ Especially Menander Rhetor (Spengel, *Rhetores Graeci*, III, pp. 368 sqq., particularly 377 sqq.) and the opening chapters of the *ars rhetorica* falsely attributed to Dionysios of Halikarnassos and included in Reiske's and Usener-Radermacher's edd. See on this subject Kukula, *op. cit.*, p. 93; Fr. Marx in *Neue Jahrb.*, I (1898), pp. 105 sqq.; E. Pfeiffer, *Virgils Bukolika*, pp. 68 sqq. R. T. Kerlin, *A. J. Ph.*, XXIX (1908), has pointed out and elaborately detailed certain resemblances between this Eclogue and Theokr. XVII ('Ἐγκώμιον Πτολεμαίου). Both are encomia, both have something to say of the birth of a child (Theokr., 60 sqq., but the resemblance is very distant), both foretell a Golden Age (this is hardly correct, for Theokr. merely speaks of great prosperity under Ptolemy, 75), and there are some verbal echoes in Vergil of this and other Theokritean works (there are a few, but on the whole this is by far the least Theokritean piece of the whole collection). All these writers tend to exaggerate, but are right in looking for some kind of formal model. I hold that Vergil may have taken hints from such poems as that of Theokritos and from whatever older teachings lie behind the precepts of Menandros and ps.-Dionysios.

¹¹ Menand., pp. 412 sq., Spengel, cf. ps.-Dion., 3.

¹² Dittenberger, *O. G. I.*, 458.

¹³ Dittenberger, *Syll.*, 3d ed., 760 (Ephesos, 706/48).

¹⁴ Cf. Menander, p. 377, 31 sqq. Spengel; the technical term was (λόγος) ἐπιβατήριος, but similar formulae could be used for somewhat different occasions, *ibid.*, 385, 1 sqq., where the author shows how to apply them to a (λόγος) πάτριος, i.e., a speech in which the orator praises his own city.

¹⁵ Dittenberger, *Syll.*, 3d ed., 797.

¹⁶ Suet., *Calig.*, 22, 1: hactenus quasi de principe, reliqua ut de monstro narranda sunt.

¹⁷ So ps.-Dionysios, 2, 5: οἷον ὅτι Μενέλεως ἀθάνατος ἐγένετο διὰ τὸν γάμον τῆς Ἑλένης καὶ ὁ Πηλεὺς διὰ τὸν τῆς Θέτιδος, κτέ. (Vol. II, p. 264, 10, Usener-Radermacher.)

¹⁸ Cf. p. 201.

¹⁹ Cf. Rose, *Handb. Gk. Myth.*, p. 138.

²⁰ See Tacitus, *ann.*, VI, 12: post exustum sociali bello Capitolium (a mistake or loose statement, for the Social War proper was over some years earlier; in *hist.*, III, 72, he rightly says it was the Civil War, i.e., that between Marius and Sulla, in 671/83) quaesitis Samo Ilio Erythris, per Africam etiam et Siciliam et Italicas colonias carminibus Sibullae. To suppose, as H. Wagenvoort does (*Vergils vierte Ekloge und das Sidus Iulium*, in *Mededeelingen der Konkinklijke Akademie van Wetenschappen*, Afdeeling Letterkunde, Deel 67, Serie A, Amsterdam, 1929, p. 36), that "Africa" could include Alexandria and an oracle of Jewish colouring might have been picked up there, does violence to ancient geography and little credit to the critical abilities of the Quindecimuiri.

[21] See Wissowa, *Rel. u. Kult. d. Römer*, 2d ed., pp. 534 sqq.

[22] When Augustus became pontifex maximus, says Suet., *Aug.*, 31, 1, quicquid fatidicorum librorum Graeci Latinique generis nullis uel parum idoneis auctoribus uulgo ferebatur, supra duo milia contracta undique cremauit ac solos retinuit Sibyllinos, hos quoque dilectu habito. I.e., he confiscated some 2000-odd volumes of prophecies and burned them all except some which he decided, on examination, were genuinely Sibylline. There were therefore some Sibylline oracles in private or at all events non-official keeping. The surviving books, says Suetonius, he stored in the base of the great Palatine statue of Apollo; they thus presumably became part of the state collection. Sibylline oracles had been in circulation from at least the days of Aristophanes, see *Knights*, 61, *Peace*, 1095, 1116, to say nothing of earlier mentions.

[23] For the Sibylline Oracles now existing, see Christ-Schmid, *Gesch. d. griech. Lit.*, 5th ed., II, pp. 463 sqq. They are largely of Jewish origin, although containing some genuine, i.e., pagan, passages, for instance IV, 97 sq., which is to be found in Strabo. They vary in date between Antiochos Epiphanes and the first century A.D., with the exception of some palpably late passages, running down to M. Aurelius Antoninus (beginning of Bk. V), and the editorial work of the final compiler, who lived in the fifth or sixth century A.D. The whole has been Christianised, but not very heavily. As an example of clearly Alexandrian origin may be taken Bk. XI, which has much to say of Egypt and is especially interested in the time of Kleopatra VII.

[24] *Ecl.*, IV, 4.

[25] It is discussed in practically all the works quoted in the following notes.

[26] See Excursus. A good survey of relevant non-astrological doctrines is contained in F. Pfister's art. *Weltalter* in Roscher's *Lexikon*.

[27] *Ecl.*, IV, 10, tuus iam regnat Apollo; 8 sq., ferrea primum/desinet et toto surget gens aurea mundo. That Vergil, or any Augustan poet, does identify the sun and Apollo ought not to be assumed without proof, see J. E. Fontenrose in *Proc. A. P. A.*, LXIX (1938), pp. xxxvi sq., LXX (1939), pp. 439 sqq.; cf. *Am. Jour. Phil.*, LXI (1940), pp. 429 sqq.

[28] The best-known arrangements of the planets, in descending order of their supposed distances from the earth, imagined to be the centre of the solar system, is that implied in the names of our weekdays, viz., Saturn, Jupiter, Mars, sun, Venus, Mercury, moon. Cf., for other arrangements, A. Bouché-Leclercq, *L'astrologie grecque* (Paris, Leroux, 1897), pp. 63 sqq., 93 sqq. The week starts with the sun, regent of 12 midnight–1 A.M. Sunday, then of 7–8 A.M., and so on; Venus is regent of 1–2 A.M., Sunday, then of 8–9 A.M., etc., while Mercury becomes regent at 2 A.M., the moon at 3 A.M., thus being regent again at midnight on Sunday–Monday, Saturn at 4 A.M., and so forth. The sun is regularly in the middle, i.e., some planets are supposedly farther away from the earth than he is, others nearer; Saturn, being farthest out, could never come immediately before or after the sun in any enumeration which an astronomer or astrologer of Vergil's day would have accepted, or any handbook of the subject then have given. See, for more particulars, F. H. Colson, *The Week* (Cambridge, Univ. Press, 1926).

NOTES TO CHAPTER VIII

[29] C., II, 17, 17 sqq., he thinks he and Maecenas must have been born under the same sign (as if that were all that mattered; the degree of the sign, the position of the planets, and other factors must be taken into account in erecting the scheme of a nativity), but does not know which it is, although he could have found out by remembering the date of his birth and consulting an almanac. That Vergil knows that Saturn is a cold planet (*Georg.*, I, 336) and connects the tropical sign Cancer with the earthly "tropics" (*Ecl.*, X, 68) is insignificant; everyone knows that much.

[30] The *locus classicus* is Censorinus, *de die natali*, 17, 2 sqq.; for other authorities, see Pfister, *op. cit.*, 417; Wissowa, *op. cit.*, pp. 430 sqq.

[31] The first certain mention of this is Horace, *carm. saec.*, 21, see Pfister, *ibid.*

[32] See Rose, *Handb. Lat. Lit.*, pp. 229 sqq., and authorities there.

[33] Daniel's Servius on *Ecl.*, IV, 10: Nigidius de diis li b. iv, quidam deos et eorum genera temporibus et aetatibus (dispescunt), inter quos et Orpheus, primum regnum Saturni, deinde Iouis, tum Neptuni, inde Plutonis; nonnulli etiam, ut magi, aiunt Apollinis fore regnum, in quo uidendum est ne ardorem, siue illa ecpyrosis appellanda est, dicant. By *genera* he means world-ages. Cf. J. Bidez and Fr. Cumont, *Les mages hellénisés* (Paris, Les Belles Lettres, 1938), II, p. 361, n. 2.

[34] *Ecl.*, IV, 53–55: o mihi tam longae maneat pars ultima uitae,/ spiritus et quantum sat erit tua dicere facta. To hope that in some 30–40 years (the child, yet unborn, will be a full-grown man before the Golden Age comes, 37) a man now thirty will still be alive and capable of writing a poetic masterpiece is reasonable enough; but if Apollo is to govern an age, even no longer than the shorter Roman-Etruscan *saeculum*, Vergil is committed to the absurd hyperbole of hoping to live to be about 130 and still retain some measure of vigour, a silliness of which he would never be guilty.

[35] Notably E. Norden, *Die Geburt des Kindes* (Teubner, 1924), p. 15, who cuts the knot by simply declaring that Servius must be wrong on this point and Apollo is lord of the first age, not the last. Among other critics, Wagenvoort, *op. cit.*, p. 2, who for the most part agrees with Norden, draws attention to this, as had been already done by J. Jüthner in *Anz. d. Akad. d. Wissenschaften*, Vienna, LXII (1925), pp. 165 sqq., which Wagenvoort did not know of when writing his article.

[36] So, in effect, Wagenvoort, *op. cit.*, p. 7.

[37] P. 331, 9 sqq., Hagen.

[38] Hesiod, *W. D.*, 636. That his name was Dios is a misinterpretation of *ibid.*, 299, Πέρση, δῖον γένος.

[39] P. 73, 20 sqq., Hagen.

[40] P. 776 Hagen, note on *Ecl.*, IV, 4. That the note as Hagen publishes it is made up of several more or less correct copyings of the same scholion is obvious.

[41] Herrmann, *Masques et visages*, p. 77.

[42] *Aen.*, VI, 398, cf. Servius there.

[43] Hesiod, *W. D.*, 176 sqq., cf. the whole passage from 104.

[44] *Ibid.*, 174 sq.

[45] Norden, *op. cit.*, pp. 25 sqq.

[46] By Macrobius, *Sat.*, I, 18, 10, and Epiphanios, *Panarion*, LI, 22, 8 sqq.

NOTES TO CHAPTER VIII

[47] J. Carcopino, *Virgile et le mystère de la IV*ᵉ *Eclogue* (Paris, L'Artisan du Livre, 1930), pp. 111 sqq.

[48] *Op. cit.*, pp. 6 sq.

[49] In *C. Q.*, XXXI (1937), p. 41.

[50] Appian, *bell. ciu.*, IV, 7 Mendelssohn-Viereck: τοὺς δὲ (the triumvirs in 711/43) ἀποφῆναι μὲν αὐτίκα τῆς πόλεως ἄρχοντας ἐς τὰ ἐτήσια ἐπὶ τὴν πενταετίαν.

[51] That it is especially an Eastern doctrine is insisted on at some length by W. A. Heidel in *A.J. Ph.*, XLV (1924), pp. 205–237, who adduces a large number of illustrations. Cf. W. Weber, *Der Prophet u. sein Gott* (Beihefte zum Alten Orient, 3), Leipzig, Hinrichs, 1925, pp. 100 sqq.; K. Kerényi in *Klio*, 1936, pp. 1–35.

[52] *Op. cit.* (see note 35), p. 171.

[53] Thucydides, II, 8, 2: καὶ πολλὰ μὲν λόγια ἐλέγοντο, πολλὰ δὲ χρησμολόγοι ᾖδον ἔν τε τοῖς μέλλουσι πολεμήσειν καὶ ἐν ταῖς ἄλλαις πόλεσιν. Those who remember the popularity of Mme. de Thèbes in the Great War, or who notice the prominence of astrology and other forms of divination in connection with the present conflict, will feel no surprise. Human nature does not change perceptibly in so short a time as two or two and a half millennia.

[54] Tarn in *J. R. S.*, XXII (1932), pp. 135 sqq.

[55] See p. 206.

[56] *Orac. Sibyll.*, III, 356 sqq.; in *ibid.*, 51 sqq., the triumvirate is to be followed by the destruction of the world by fire from heaven. Tarn suggests that these represent respectively a Greek and a Jewish view; in both Kleopatra was expected to triumph, but the former looked for a Golden Age, the latter for the end of the world (and therefore the triumph of Yahweh) to follow; *op. cit.*, pp. 141 sqq.

[57] A glance at the list of parallel passages in Rzach's ed. of the *Orac. Sib.* (Prague, Vienna, and Leipzig, 1891) will show that although Homer is by far the commonest source, reminiscences of Hesiod are frequent.

[58] Juv., XIII, 28 sqq., nona aetas agitur peioraque saecula ferri/temporibus [the Iron Age, then, is over], quorum sceleri non inuenit ipsa/nomen et a nullo posuit natura metallo. I do not know why Housman (cr. note, *ibid.*) doubts the soundness of the reading. That it is not merely an exaggeration of Hesiod by Juvenal himself is shown by the specific *nona*, where surely a rhetorician would have contented himself with going the older poet one better and saying *sexta*.

[59] There are a few, but not many instances of the number ten's having some significance in Sibylline chronology, as III, 108–109 (cf. XII, 14–15), VIII, 199, XII, 42, 102. Cf. Wagenvoort, *op. cit.*, p. 4 and note 1, who cites the opinion of Kampers (*Werdegang der abendländischen Kaisermystik*, p. 93) that nine is the really important number.

[60] *Orac. Sib.*, VIII, 361 sqq., cf. the oracle in Herodotos, I, 47, 4.

[61] *Politicus*, 268 d sqq. I have discussed this matter in *C. Q.*, XVIII (1924), pp. 113–118, and further consideration of the subject has strengthened my conviction that my theory is entirely right and of some importance for the interpretation of this poem.

[62] *Ecl.*, IV, 21 sq.; ipsae lacte domum referent distenta capellae/ubera, nec magnos metuent armenta leones. In *Georg.*, III, 316, he says that goats (presum-

NOTES TO CHAPTER VIII 259

ably in Italy) normally come home of their own accord; it is therefore not a miracle nor a characteristic of the Golden Age that they do so here. The meaning is that goats (and the larger cattle) shall behave in the quietest and least troublesome way, like very tame Italian beasts in normal times, because the herds (and flocks), all the world over, even in countries like Africa, shall no longer be molested by wild creatures, which though they may still exist shall be weak and harmless (the position of *magnos* makes it emphatic, and the meaning is, not that there shall be no more lions, but that they shall not be large and terrifying). Hor., *Epod.*, 16, 33, which in wording is either imitated from this or is its original, is quite different in sense: credula nec rauos timeant armenta leones is a picture of a wonder-land where all manner of beasts live peaceably together, the cattle placidly trusting the lions to do them no harm and being justified in their trust.

[63] *Ecl.*, IV, 26 sqq.

[64] *Ibid.*, 32 sq. Contrast Pindar's picture of the life of the blessed, *Ol.*, 2, 63 sq., οὐ χθόνα ταράσσοντες ἐν χερὸς ἀκμᾷ | οὐδὲ πόντιον ὕδωρ | κενεὰν παρὰ δίαιταν. This does not describe the existence of the finally justified (*ibid.*, 68 sqq.), but that of men who are being rewarded for a life of righteousness during their latest sojourn on earth.

[65] Hesiod, *W. D.*, 156 sqq.

[66] Vergil would perhaps have said "for our sins," to judge from the allusions he makes to *scelus nostrum* (*Ecl.*, IV, 13), *prisca fraus* (31). This would appear to be Orphic, or Orphic-Pythagorean, more probably the latter, about which he would know something from Nigidius Figulus (cf. Carcopino, *op. cit.*, pp. 30 sqq.), since the former does not seem to have been much in evidence at Rome, save for literary acquaintance with its writings (see A. Boulanger in *Rev. Et. Lat.*, XV, 1937, pp. 121–135). S. Reinach in *Cultes, mythes et religions*, II, pp. 66–84, would explain nearly everything in the poem by Orphism, even supposing that child to be the Orphic Zagreus. This is an example of the exaggerated importance which at that date was attached to Orphic doctrine and influence. When he elsewhere (*op. cit.*, III, p. 349) says that original sin (or, more correctly, legends and beliefs like that which in Christianity led to the formation of such a doctrine) is in Greece *essentiellement populaire*, he is probably right, but when he adds *et orphique* he does not allow for its existence elsewhere.

[67] Plato, *op. cit.*, 269 d, e.

[68] *Ibid.*, 268 d.

[69] *Ibid.*, 271 e sq.

[70] *Ibid.*, 271 d.

[71] *Ibid.*, 272 b–d.

[72] I take the opportunity to mention that I refuse to enter into the discussion, which appears to me utterly futile and incapable of final solution, as to which of these two poems is the older.

[73] To cite only one of the best, it is the opinion of Cartault, *Etude*, p. 213.

[74] See above, notes 45, 47.

[75] Above, pp. 83 sqq.

[76] Dio Cassius, XLVIII, 32, 1–2.

⁷⁷ See *ibid.*, 20, 1-2, cf. Carcopino, *op. cit.*, pp. 111 sqq.

⁷⁸ Reinach, *op. cit.*, II, p. 73.

⁷⁹ That this is the real meaning of *saeculum condere* there is no doubt, cf. *lustrum condere*. Vergil, however, *Aen.*, VI, 792, chooses to make it there mean "found," "establish" (aurea condet/saecula qui rursus), a legitimate use of the verb and quite Vergilian in its departure from the usual meaning in this context.

⁸⁰ For authorities, see Wissowa, *op. cit.*, p. 430.

⁸¹ See *ibid.*; Pfister, *op. cit.*, 417 sqq.; C. Pascal, *Commentationes Vergilianae* [Mediolani-Panormi, MDCCCC], pp. 97 sqq.

⁸² Suet., *Claud.*, 21, 2: fecit [Claudius] et saeculares [supply *ludos* from the preceding sentence] quasi anticipatos ab Augusto nec legitimo tempori reseruatos, quamuis ipse in historiis suis prodat intermissos eos Augustum multo post diligentissime annorum ratione subducta in ordinem redegisse. Obviously the passage from Claudius' historical work was written before his accession loosened his tongue, and was the politic, official account expected of a little regarded member of the Imperial house.

⁸³ See above, note 31.

⁸⁴ If we count exclusively, 715/39 is the 110th year after 605/149, but inclusively (as, e.g., the third day before the Ides of May is May 5, not 4), it is 714/40.

⁸⁵ W. Weber, *Der Prophet und sein Gott*, p. 75, upholds a curious form of what is essentially the same doctrine. If Caesar had not been assassinated and had carried out his plan of a Parthian campaign, he might have been expected back in Rome about the end of 713/41, and so could have held his *ludi triumphales*, which on the calculation given in the text could have been also *saeculares*, the following year. See the following pages of his monograph for some ingenious but extremely doubtful further conjectures and combinations.

⁸⁶ *Op. cit.*, pp. 2 sqq.

⁸⁷ For examples, see Weber, *op. cit.*, pp. 61 sqq.

⁸⁸ Wagenvoort, *op. cit.*, pp. 12 sqq.

⁸⁹ Above, p. 90.

⁹⁰ Pliny, *N. H.*, II, 94, citing Augustus' memoirs: ipsis ludorum meorum diebus sidus crinitum per septem dies in regione caeli sub septentrionibus est conspectum. id oriebatur circa undecimam horam clarumque et omnibus terris conspicuum fuit. eo sidere significari uulgus credidit Caesaris animam inter deorum immortalium numina receptam, quo nomine id insigne simulacro capitis eius quod mox in foro consecrauimus adiectum est. haec ille in publicum, interiore gaudio sibi illum [sc., cometam] natum seque in illo nasci interpretatus est. et, si uerum fatemur, salutare id terris fuit. Suet., *Iulius*, 88 and Cassius Dio, XLV, 7, 1 go back one way or another to Augustus, as do the notes of Servius on *Ecl.*, IX, 46, most of the information given by Baebius Macer in Daniel's Servius, *ibid.*, and Serv. on *Aen.*, VIII, 681.

⁹¹ Wagenvoort, *op. cit.*, p. 29.

⁹² *Ibid.*, pp. 29 sqq. For the Hebrew expression, see Daniel, 7:25, 12:7; Rev., 11:2, 13:5 paraphrases it by "forty-two months," and models upon it the three

NOTES TO CHAPTER VIII

days and a half for which, in 11:9-11, the bodies of the two witnesses lie unburied, after they have prophesied for 1260 days, *ibid.*, 3, i.e., 3½ years of 360 days each; cf. 12:6.

⁹³ Horace, *sat.*, I, 5, 100.

⁹⁴ See p. 189.

⁹⁵ *Ecl.*, IV, 4 sqq.: ultima Cumaei uenit iam carminis aetas;/magnus ab integro saeclorum nascitur ordo./iam redit et Virgo, redeunt Saturnia regna;/iam noua progenies caelo demittitur alto./tu modo nascenti puero, quo ferrea primum/ desinet ac toto surget gens aurea mundo,/casta faue Lucina; tuus iam regnat Apollo.

⁹⁶ I must here draw attention to another point of elementary Latinity, for it has been misinterpreted a score of times. *Nascenti* means "during parturition," "while he is being born," and does not say, what no participle can say in either of the classical languages, when that event is taking place, but only that it and Lucina's favour are contemporaneous.

⁹⁷ St. Augustine, *ep. in Rom. incohata expositio*, 3 (Migne, *P. L.*, Vol. XXXV, 2089).

⁹⁸ See H. W. Garrod in *C. R.*, XIX (1905), p. 37; J. B. Mayor in *Virgil's Messianic Eclogue* (London, Murray, 1907), pp. 87 sqq.

⁹⁹ Mayor, *op. cit.*; T. F. Royds, *Virgil and Isaiah* (Oxford, Blackwell, 1918).

¹⁰⁰ It says much for Mayor's learning and honesty that one of the most convenient lists is given by him, *op. cit.*, pp. 123 sqq. See the commentators on the fourth Eclogue for more details.

¹⁰¹ That there is an as yet undetermined amount of Oriental influence in much Greek poetry of early date is likely if not certain. See, for a somewhat exaggerated claim of this kind regarding Hesiod, F. Dornseiff in *L'antiquité classique*, VI (1937), pp. 231-258.

¹⁰² See Norden, *op. cit.*, p. 38.

¹⁰³ A. Erman, *Literatur der Aegypter* (Leipzig, Hinrichs, 1923), pp. 152 sqq., gives one of the best-known examples, the prophecy of Nefer-Rehu. The date seems to be the reign of Amenemhet I (1995-1965), whose coming is clearly foretold. King Snefru asks to see a wise man, and when in answer Nefer-Rehu, a learned priest (*cher-heb*) of Bast, is produced, bids him speak of the future. Nefer-Rehu foretells a time of utter ruin and disaster of all sorts, to be ended by the coming, from the south, of "Ameni" (a sort of pet name for Amenemhet), the son of a Nubian woman, who shall put all right again.

¹⁰⁴ See any account of Zoroastrianism, e.g., N. Turchi, *Manuale di storia delle religioni* (Torino-Milano-Roma, Bocca, 1922), p. 367; texts (Yasht XIX, 88 sqq.) in A. Bertholet, *Religionsgeschichtliches Lesebuch* (Tübingen, Mohr, 1908), p. 355.

¹⁰⁵ See F. Pfister, art. EPIPHANIE, in *Realenc.*, Suppl. IV, 307 sqq.

¹⁰⁶ See Erman, *op. cit.*, p. 336, where the king of the Chatti says to Ramses II, "du bist der Sohn des Re, der aus seinen Gliedern hervorgegangen ist." Cf., for the popularity of the divine child, particularly Harpokrates (Har-pe-chrat, Horus the Child), Norden, *op. cit.*, pp. 73 sqq., which also deals with the begetting of Egyptian kings by a god upon a human woman, the queen mother.

[107] *Orac. Sibyll.*, III, 652 sqq.

[108] See A. Alföldi in *Hermes*, LXV (1930), pp. 369-384, and plate.

[109] Schol. Bern., pp. 775-777 Hagen. As usual, the text as Hagen publishes it is a medley of several copies of the same note.

[110] Serv. Dan. on *Ecl.*, IV, 11.

[111] Antony, see below, note 140; Octavian and Scribonia, e.g., Warde Fowler, *Messianic Eclogue*, p. 84, and two or three others whom he quotes there. It might almost be called the orthodox view, although, as is shown below, it is absolutely impossible.

[112] Sir Wm. Ramsay, cited *ibid.*, p. 55, after Heyne-Wagner.

[113] Reinach, *op. cit.*, III, pp. 73 sqq. (Zagreus); Th. Pluss, cited by Cartault, *Etude*, p. 234 (son of Liber and Libera). See *ibid.*, pp. 228 sqq., for a list of the identifications proposed up to 1897.

[114] Norden, *op. cit.*, pp. 44 sqq.

[115] I do not waste time considering purely freakish suggestions, as that the child was Octavian himself.

[116] For a sympathetic sketch of it, see Conway in *Messianic Eclogue*, pp. 22 sqq.

[117] See R. Syme in *C. Q.*, XXXI (1937), pp. 39-48, from whose article the following arguments are chiefly drawn.

[118] On Vergil, see above, notes 109, 110; Horace, Porphyrio on C., II, 1, 15: *cui laurus aeternos honores*, ideo hoc dicitur quia Pollio Salonis urbe ex Dalmatis capta triumphauit. Cf. ps.-Acro, *ibid.*: laurus hic pro uictoria posuit, Salonas enim Pollio Dalmatarum ceperat ciuitatem, unde et filium suum, eo quod natus ibi erat, Saloninum appellauit.

[119] Daniel's Servius on *Ecl.*, IV, 1: Asinius Pollio, ductor Germanici exercitus, cum post captam Salonam, Dalmatiae ciuitatem, primo meruisset lauream, post etiam consulatum adeptus fuisset, eodem anno suscepit filium, quem a capta ciuitate Saloninum uocauit, cui nunc Vergilius genethliacon dicit. quem constat natum risisse statim, quod parentibus omen est infelicitatis, nam ipsum puerum inter ipsa primordia perisse manifestum est.

[120] See the two notes last preceding.

[121] The day of his death was the *dies lustricus*, see Plutarch, *quaest. Rom.*, 102, with my comment, *Roman Questions of Plutarch* (Oxford, Clar. Press, 1924), p. 210.

[122] Tacitus, *ann.*, III, 75.

[123] For the facts about C. Asinius C. f. Gallus, to give him his full name, see the *Realenc.*, *s.u.* (I, 1585 sqq.). He was born about 713/41 (1585, 12) and died A.D. 33 (1586, 55).

[124] See the dictionaries under *paco*. In Caesar, the word is used repeatedly in the sense of "conquer," "reduce to submission," see Merguet, *Lexikon zu den Schriften Cäsars* (Jena, Fischer, 1886), *s.u.*, and so, e.g., in Ovid, *Metam.*, VII, 405, of Theseus conquering the brigands, etc., of the Isthmus; Verg., *Aen.*, VI, 803, of Herakles overcoming the boar of Erymanthos; hence figuratively of cultivating land, as Horace, *epp.*, I, 2, 45, and in ethics of overcoming the passions, etc., hence *pacata mente*, Lucr., V, 1203. Thus Ovid, *Fast.*, I, 3, can use

pacato uultu to mean a countenance expressing calm of mind resulting from having conquered anger (at the poet's offences). Livy (XXIV, 20, 10; XL, 57, 4; 58, 1) rather oddly uses *pacatum agmen* of an army on the march which does not ravage the country, i.e., is "subdued" by discipline.

[125] *Aen.*, VII, 45 sq.

[126] E.g., Warde Fowler in *Mess. Ecl.*, p. 82, note 1: "conceive a poem addressed on the birth of his son to a President of the United States without any allusion to his fatherhood!"

[127] For some of them, see Cartault, *Etude*, p. 231, note 2, citing P. A. H. Wimmers for refutation of their theory. Add L. Herrmann, *Masques et visages*, p. 92; cf. below.

[128] See *Prosop. Imp. Rom.*, art. OCTAVIA.

[129] Herrmann, *op. cit.*, pp. 98 sq., argues for 714/40 as Marcellus' birth year, but his conclusions are not generally accepted.

[130] It is maintained by D. A. Slater in *C. R.*, XXVI (1912), pp. 114-119; cf. Herrmann, *loc. cit.*, and in *Musée Belge*, XXXIV (1930), pp. 83-87.; Marion Smith in *C. J.*, XXVI (1930), pp. 141-143.

[131] Catullus, LXIV, 384 sqq.

[132] *Ibid.*, 397 sq.

[133] *Ecl.*, IV, 13 sqq.

[134] *Ibid.*, 6, cf. note 3.

[135] Cat., LXIV, 338 sqq.

[136] *Ecl.*, IV, 36.

[137] Cat., LXIV, 323-381.

[138] It seems at least as likely as the extremely ingenious idea of J. Carcopino, *op. cit.*, p. 57, note 1, that the total number of Vergil's lines, being seven times nine, has a Pythagorean significance, a grand climacteric of verses. But it is very difficult to judge to what extent plays of this sort with numbers would be liked or understood. Vergil's friends were not mystery-mongers, and though he may well have read Nigidius Figulus, he did not write to please him or his following.

[139] Herrmann, *op. cit.*, pp. 58 sqq.

[140] In *Le messianisme de Virgile* (Paris, Vrin, 1930).

[141] This is made clear by *Ecl.*, IV, 49, cara deum suboles, magnum Iouis incrementum, a verse almost the same as *Ciris*, 398, where it is used of the Dioskuroi. It is true that *incrementum* has a variety of meanings, "process of growth," "concrete thing which increases the size or value of something," "seed, germ," "child, offspring," see Tenney Frank in *C.P.*, XI (1916), pp. 334-336, but, as he rightly holds, only the last of these is possible here, not only for the reasons he gives, but also because of the common Vergilian habit of making the two halves of a line say the same thing in different ways; now *deum suboles* can mean nothing but "offspring of the gods," hence any such meaning as "germ of a [future] Iuppiter" (so Munro, see Conington *ad loc.*) is put quite out of court. The child is divine, and so a descendant of Iuppiter, whether directly begotten of him or not, for Iuppiter is the all-father.

[142] Jeanmaire, *op. cit.*, p. 29, who points out the Dionysiac nature of the plants

which earth produces as the child's playthings (19 sqq.; note especially the ivy) and of the things which shall be abundant in the world over which he is to rule, wine (29), milk (21–22), honey (30), cf. Eur., *Bacch.*, 142 sqq. I do not find his arguments very cogent.

[143] *Ibid.*, p. 30.

[144] *Ibid.*, p. 45; see Plutarch, *Antonius*, 26.

[145] *Ibid.*, pp. 50 sq. Cf. my article, "The Departure of Dionysos," in the Liverpool *Annals of Archaeology and Anthropology*, XI (1924), pp. 253 sqq.

[146] Jeanmaire, *op. cit.*, pp. 54 sq.

[147] *Ibid.*

[148] *Ibid.*, pp. 180–182 for his chronological scheme.

[149] *Ibid.*, p. 28.

[150] *Ibid.*, citing Fr. Boll., *Aus der Offenbarung Johannis* (Teubner, 1914), p. 111.

[151] *Ibid.*, p. 112, cf. Cicero, *de rep.*, VI, 12.

[152] *Ibid.*; some significant dates are, fall of Troy, according to the then received chronology, 1184 B.C.; censorship of Cato the Elder, 184; burning of the Capitol, 84.

[153] See above, note 54 for reference.

[154] Tarn, *op. cit.*, p. 155.

[155] *Ibid.*, p. 158.

[156] *Ibid.*, p. 159.

[157] Horace, *sat.*, I, 5, 32 sq. For the date, which cannot be 714/40, as wrongly stated in my *Handb. Lat. Lit.*, p. 269, see the introduction to the poem in P. Lejay's edition (Vol. II of Plessis-Lejay, *Œuvres d'Horace*, Paris, 1911).

[158] Macrob., *Sat.*, I, 18, 10.

[159] Norden, *op. cit.*, p. 44 sqq., *q.u.* for further refs.

[160] For Ianus-Aion, see Wissowa, *op. cit.*, p. 108 and note 2; for the lack of a Greek parallel to Ianus, Ovid, *Fast.*, I, 89 sq.

[161] Horace, *carm.*, II, 5, 13 sqq.: currit enim ferox/aetas et illi [Lalagae] quos tibi dempserit/adponet annos.

[162] No ancient records the exact time of Julia's birth; but it is easy to calculate approximately, for: (1) It was in 715/39, and the same day as Scribonia's divorce, Cassius Dio, XLVIII, 34, 3. (2) The marriage of Octavian and Livia followed with indecent haste, see Suet., *Aug.*, 62, 2: cum hac [Scribonia] quoque diuortium fecit ... ac statim Liuiam Drusillam matrimonio Tiberi Neronis et quidem praegnantem abduxit. Let *statim* be thought rhetorical and a delay of some few days or weeks supposed, the two events are still close together. (3) When Livia married, her son Tiberius was three years old, Velleius Paterculus, II, 94, 1: Ti. Claudius Nero, quo trimo ... Liuia ... Caesari nupserat. His birth was on November 16, 712/42, Suet., *Tib.*, 5: natus est Romae in Palatino XVI kal. Dec., M. Aemilio Lepido iterum L. Munatio Planco coss. Hence the marriage was not earlier than November 16, 715/39 nor later than the same date in 716/38. Hence, at the very earliest, Julia was born about October, 715/39, and may have been later, though not after December 31 of that year.

[163] It seems to me off the point (but cf. Norden, *op. cit.*, pp. 73 sqq.) to adduce the begetting of Egyptian royalties by Re or another god. Nothing in Vergil indicates that the child is to have a real and a putative father, the former a god; his father is to be a human being, whose *facta* are recorded in books which the child will one day read, lines 26 sq.

[164] See *Georg.*, I, 498 sqq.

[165] *Aen.*, VI, 792 sq.

INDEX

INDEX

ABELLA, 63
Achilles, 98, 164, 170, 200 sqq.
Actium, 18, 167
Adam, 187
Addison, 98
Admetos, 38, 177
Adonis, 13, 131, 137
Aegle, 95
Aegon, 72
Aeneas, 98 sq., 203
Aeschylus, 160
Africa, 123, 126 sq., 133, 171
Agamemnon, 98
Agrippa, M. Vipsanius, 19
Ahriman, 181, 195
Ahura Mazda, 181
Aiolic dialect, 14
Aiolid, 176
Aion, 178, 195, 208, 210
Aitolia, 34
Aktaion, 34
Alcon, Alkon, 119 sq.
Alexander, 70, 133
Alexander Helios, 205 sq.
Alexandria, Alexandrian literature, cult, etc., 4, 6, 11, 16, 23, 38, 66, 73, 95 sq., 99, 119, 127, 139, 172, 180, 192, 195, 206, 208 sq.
Alexis, 26 sqq., 69 sq., 72, 127, 144
Alkaios, 14
Allegory, 22, 49, 117 sqq., 212
Alphesiboeus, 72, 147 sqq.
Alps, 105, 107; Brescian, 56, 62
Amaryllis, 33, 46, 70 sq., 150, 153, 156 sq., 160
Amata, 31
Amenemhet I, 178
Amenophis IV, 209
Amphrysos, 177
Amyntas, 41, 118
Andes, 52 sqq., 233
Anna Perenna, 210
Anne, Queen, 19

Anser, 71
Anthology, Greek, 10
Antiope, 34
Antonius, L., 79 sqq., 109 sq.
Antonius, M. (Mark Antony), 18, 55, 79 sqq., 108 sq., 187, 191, 196, 200 sqq.
Apelles, 192
Aphrodite, 13 sq., 103, 131, 135; -Isis, 205
Apollo, 38, 41, 48, 87, 95 sqq., 104, 113 sq., 118, 127, 136, 163, 166, 174 sq., 182, 186, 193, 205, 211 sq., 216; and the Sun, 172 sqq.
Apollonios of Rhodes, 98
Appian, 79
Aquarius, 217
Arakynthos, 34
Archilochos, 14
Arethusa, 12
Argo, Argonauts, 98, 164, 183
Arion, 152
Aristophanes, 65
Aristotle, 208
Arkadia, Arkadians, 65, 94, 105, 117, 142 sq., 149, 154
Armenia, 127
Artemidoros, 11, 16
Artemis, 137, 143, 163; -Hekate, 154
Asconius Pedianus, 196, 198
Asia, province of, 168 sq.
Asianic prose, 2
Asklepiades, 10
Askra, 65
Assos, 169
Astrology, 123, 131, 135, 173, 186, 214 sqq.
Atalanta, 96, 103
Athens, 120
Atticus, 72, 76
Augustine, St., 118, 194
Augustus, 21, 44, 70, 129 sq., 167 sq., 190 sq., 196, 212; *see also* Octavian
Avernus, 64

[269]

INDEX

BACONIAN CRYPTOGRAM, 117
Baehrens, W., 145
Bakchos, Bacchus, 127
Barbary States, 171
Bavius and Mevius, 40, 69 sqq., 125
Berne scholia, 176, 196
Bessuti, Mgr. A., 232 sq.
Bianor, 57
Bible, 215
Bion, 12 sqq., 131; *Lament for*, 12 sqq., 100, 131
Birt, Th., 77
Boiotia, Boiotian, 34, 143, 181
Boll, Fr., 217
Bologna, 78
Brasilas, 57
Braunholtz, Professor, 54
Bronze Age, 176, 184
Brundisium, 77, 81 sq., 179 sq., 187
Brussels, 71
Brutus, M., 79, 108, 124, 126
Burns, Robert, 14
Byzantines, 216

CAECILIVS EPIROTA, Q., 72
"Caelius," 69
Calpurnius Siculus, T., 22
Calvisano, 56 sq.
Calvus, C. Licinius, 72
Camaldoli, 64
Campania, 63
Canadian Expeditionary Force, 197
Capitol, 171, 190
Carcopino, J., 179
Carpenedolo, 56 sq.
Cartault, A., 97, 124, 134
Casalpoglio, 56
Cassius, C., 76, 79, 124, 126
Catullus, C. Valerius, 16 sqq., 25, 29, 72, 76, 99, 101, 122, 127, 170, 201 sqq.
Caucasus, 96
Cebes, 70
Chaonia, 89
Chiese, river, 56
Choirilos of Samos, 22

Christ, 193 sq., 196 sq.
Christianity, Christians, 117, 172, 178, 193 sq., 196, 215
Christmas, 178
Chromis, 94
Chronokratories, 173, 214 sqq.
Cicero, M. Tullius, 25, 72 sq., 118, 174
Cinna, Helvius, 69, 72, 121
Ciris, 101
Claudius, Emperor, 190
Clodia-Lesbia, 25
Clodius Pulcher, P., 68
Codrus, Kodrus, 69, 71, 119 sqq., 143
Conington, J., remarks in criticism of Ecl. II, 26
Conway, R. S., 54 sqq.
Cordus, Cremutius, 121 sq.
Cornificius, Q., 121 sq., 126 sqq., 138, 143
Corydon, 26 sqq., 43, 63, 69, 71, 115, 121, 126, 142 sqq.
Cremona, 55 sqq., 74, 81 sq., 87, 233
Crete, 120
Cumae, Kyme, 162, 171, 175 sq., 192, 194
Cumont, Fr., 214
Cynthia, 109
Cytheris, 70, 72, 108 sqq., 243 n. 44; *see also* Lycoris, Volumnia

DALMATIA, 151, 196
Damoetas, 38 sqq., 70, 72
Damon, 72, 147 sqq.
Dante, 53
Daphnis, 15, 63, 70 sq., 105, 110, 114, 117 sqq., 139 sqq., 152, 156 sqq.; and Chloe, *see* Longus
Delia, 42
Delphis, 154 sq.
Delphoi, 205
Demophon, 119
Demos, 65
Deukalion, 96, 103
Diana, 137
Dido, 99
Diniarchus, 25

INDEX

Diodoros, 2
Diomedes, 110
Dionysos, Dionysiac rites, 123, 132 sqq., 204 sq.
Dios, 176
Dodona, 89
Domitian, Emperor, 86
Domitius Calvinus, Cn., 179
Domitius Marsus, 72, 119, 125
Donatus, 77, 124, 198
Doric dialect, 1, 12, 14, 139
Dosiadas, 10
Drew, D. L., 130, 132

EARTH (goddess), 103, 133
Egnatius, 52, 100
Egypt, Egyptians, 194 sq., 209, 216; Graeco-, 205
Eileithyia, 163
Einsiedeln poet, 22
Elegiacs, 5, 16
Elizabethan drama, 167
Engelbrecht, August, 217
English, "standard," 14
Ennius, Q., 29
Epicurus, Epicureanism, 44, 67, 76, 92, 96, 132, 155
Epidius, 74 sq.
Epiphany, 178
Eros, 13 sq., 135, 150 sq.
Erythrai, 171
Etruscan dynasty, 171; world-ages, 173 sq.
Euphorion, 97, 99, 106, 122; -*is cantores*, 73, 97
Euripides, 137, 151, 166, 208
Eurotas, 95, 97

FACETVS, meaning of, 24 sq., 142, 158, 226
Fate, 135, 164
Fates, 201 sqq.
Faunus, 37
Firmicus Maternus, 216
FitzSimon, Vincent A., 117
Flaccus, alleged brother of Vergil, 124 sq.

Fonteius Capito, 207
Fulvia, 79, 108
Fundamentalism, 193

GAIVS (Caligula), 169, 212
Galate(i)a, 8 sq., 15, 34, 36, 38, 41 sq., 46, 70, 120, 144, 150
Gallus, C. Cornelius, 19, 55, 66, 69 sq., 73, 76, 78, 81, 88, 92 sqq., 117, 138, 206
Games, Great, 4 sq.
Gaul, Gauls, 38, 67, 107, 132; Cisalpine, 80, 125
Georgia, 197
Germany, 107; army of, 197
God, 185, 193, 215
Golden Age, 63, 96, 103, 130, 137, 161, 163, 165, 169 sq., 172 sqq., 193, 210 sqq.
Great Year, 172, 175, 195, 206
Greece, 95, 109 sq., 115
Greek, 31, 150; computation, 190, 254 n. 9
Grynion, 96 sq.

HAMMER, SEVERINUS, 102 sq.
Hannibal, 129
Hebrew mythology, 187
Hekate, 2; *see also* Artemis
Helen, 170
Helikon, 103
Helios, 103, 178, 180, 209
Hephaistion of Thebes, 216 sq.
Hera, 103
Herakleitos, 208
Herakles, 66, 136
Herculaneum, 76
Hermes, 136, 215
Heroic Age, 184, 201 sq.
Herrmann, L., 71 sq., 117, 119, 176
Hesiod, 11, 96, 104, 176 sqq., 215
Hieron II, 3 sq., 88
Hippolytos, 135
Hippomenes, 103
Hirtius, C., 76
Hollywood, 14

Homer, 12, 45, 97, 120
Hoodoo (voodoo), 157
Horace (Q. Horatius Flaccus), 20, 23 sqq., 39 sq., 72, 82, 124 sq., 173, 187, 192, 207; scholiasts on, 197
Hylas, 96, 103

IANVS, 210
Ilion, 171
Illyricum, 197
Inuus, 37
Iollas, 37, 72
Ionic dialect, 14
Iron Age, 176 sq., 184, 193, 210
Isaiah, 194
Isis, 205
Islands of the Blessed, 184
Italian colonies, 171
Italians, Italy, 14, 22, 40, 45, 50, 62 sqq., 73, 78 sqq., 109 sq., 115, 129, 132, 136, 142, 164, 173 sq., 180 sqq., 213
Iuppiter, 41, 174, 176
iynx, 154, 156

JASON, 151
Jealousy, 151
Jeanmaire, H., 204 sqq.
Jerome, St., 53, 198
Jews, 172, 180 sqq., 192, 194 sq.
Johnson, Samuel, 98
Julia, 196, 210, 212, 264 n. 162
Julius Caesar, 18, 21, 48, 67, 70, 76, 90, 124 sqq., 169, 174, 191, 195, 212; his calendar, 168
Justice, 163, 192, 202
Jüthner, J., 181
Juvenal, 34, 182

KALLIMACHOS, 4, 5, 122
Keightley, 26
Kern, O., 182
Kirke, 156
Kleopatra VII, 181, 204 sqq.; Selene, 205
Kos, 6, 10, 22, 32

Kronos, 96, 103, 163, 175, 177, 185, 187, 212
Kydnos, 204

LARIONE, river, 51
Latin attitude to Greek techniques, 22; language, etc., 17, 29, 150
Latinus, 98, 199
Lavinius, river, 78
Leo, F., 48, 65, 101 sq., 111
Leria, 70
Lesbos, 14
Leukas, 153
Liber Pater, 132, 136
Libethros, 143
Linos, 96 sq.
Livy, 21, 51
London, 95
Longus, 16
Louisiana, 156
Love, *see* Eros
Lucilius, 39
Lucina, 163, 193
Lucretius, 66, 96, 100, 131, 157
Lyciae sortes, 99
Lycidas, Lykidas, 10, 47 sqq., 90, 144, 151
Lycoris, 69 sq., 72, 105 sqq.; *see also* Cytheris, Volumnia

MACER, AEMILIUS, 119 sq., 122
Macrobius, 209
Maecenas, 20, 70 sqq., 77 sq., 82, 86, 93, 207
Magi, 174
Magic, 3, 154 sqq.
Magii, 50, 59; Magius, 56
Mainalos, 113, 149
Manius, 79
Mantua, Mantova, 18, 26 sq., 44 sqq., 70, 82, 86 sqq., 94, 104, 117, 122, 142
Marcella minor, 206
Marcelli, 200
Marcellus, 196, 200 sqq.
Martial, 62
Mede(i)a, 151 sq.
Mediterranean area, 155

INDEX

Meliboeus, 45 sqq., 92, 134, 142 sqq.
Menalcas, Menalkas, 33, 38 sqq., 47, 53, 69 sq., 72, 87, 89, 112 sq., 118 sqq., 139 sqq.
Menander, Menandros (comedian), 108; (rhetorician), 167 sqq.
Menelaos, 170
Messalla Corvinus, C. Valerius, 77
Messianic prophecies, 194
Metals, the planetary and the secular, 172 sq.
Micon, 72, 143
Midas, 64
Milan, 74
Milon, 140
Milton, John, 6, 12, 123
Mimes, 1
Mincio, Mincius, 51 sqq., 94, 142, 151
Mnasyllus, 94
Moeris, 47 sqq., 79, 90, 154 sq.
Moirai, 164
mollis, meaning of, 24, 43, 226
Monte Rosa, 7
Mopsus, 48, 72, 118 sqq., 148 sqq.
Moschos, 12
Muses, 11, 23, 75, 89, 96 sq., 102, 104, 115, 136, 143, 162
Music, shepherds', 6 sq.
Mussolini, 188

Nais, 140
Naples, 49, 60 sq., 74
Nardi, B., 51
Nemesianus, M. Aurelius Olympius, 22
Nemi, 137
Neptune, 174, 176
Nero, 212; age of, 16
New York, 95
Nigidius Figulus, 174 sq.
Norden, Ed., 178 sqq., 208 sq.
Nymphs, 10, 113; of Libethros (Muses), 143
Nysa, 148 sqq.

Ocnus, 57
Octavia, 187, 196, 200 sqq.

Octavian, 18 sqq., 44, 46 sq., 55 sq., 65 sqq., 69, 74, 78 sqq., 117, 125 sq., 128 sq., 179, 183, 187 sq., 191, 203, 205 sqq.; *see also* Augustus
Octavius Musa, 55, 77, 86 sq.
Odysseus, 120
Oidipus, 30
Old Testament, 193 sqq.
Olpeus, 152
Orphism, Orpheus, 148, 152, 174, 176, 182, 196, 259 n. 66
Osiris, 205
Osone, river, 51
Ovid, 14, 73, 122, 130 sq.

Pacatvs, meaning of, 199
Paetus, L. Papirius, 76
Palaemon, 39 sqq.
Pan, 13, 37, 113 sq., 165
Pansa, C. Vibius, 76
Paris (city), 95; (son of Priam), 38
Paros, 14
Parthenios, 72
Parthia, 205, 212
Participles, 261 n. 96
Pasiphae, 96, 103
"Pathetic fallacy," inverted, 33
Paullus, Fabius Maximus, 168
Peleus, 170, 203; and Thetis, *see* Catullus
Peloponnesos, 120; Peloponnesian War, 181
Penelope, 110
Permessos, 96, 138, 241 n. 23
Persius, 39
Perusia, 80 sqq., 205
Petronius Arbiter, 159
Phaethon, 96, 102 sq.
Pharaoh, 194
Philippi, 46, 55, 78
Philitas, 10
Phillimore, J. S., 73, 119
Philodemos of Gadara, 72, 76
Philomela, 97, 102 sq.
Phoibos, 180
Phronesium, 25

274 INDEX

Phyllis, 42, 119 sq., 144
Pietole, 53 sqq., 69
Pindar, 5
Piso, L. Calpurnius, 76
Planets, 173, 214 sqq., 256 n. 28; see also Astrology, Chronokratories, Metals
Plato, 183 sqq., 212
Plautus, 25, 166
Pliny the Elder, 132, 191
Pliny the Younger, 83
Pluto, 174
Po, Padus, 51, 100
Poetry, relations to prose, 30, 166; bucolic, rules of, 120, 151
Pollio, C. Asinius, 19, 40, 69 sqq., 78, 80 sqq., 120, 151, 162 sqq.
Polyphemos, 8, 120, 144, 146, 150, 152
Pompeius Magnus, Cn. (Pompey the Great), 133
Pompeius, Sex., 188
Poseidon, 103, 176
Poseidonios, 216
Posilipo, 64
Priapos, 143, 146
Priscus, Iavolenus, 83
Probus, 52 sqq., 77, 175 sq.
Proitos, 96, 103
Prometheus, 96, 103
Propertius, 83, 88, 100, 109
proprius, meaning of, 248 n. 11
Proteus, 140
Ptolemy II, 4, 88
Punic lions, 127; War, First, 191
Puteoli, 64
Pyrrha, 96, 103
Pythagoreanism, neo-, 174

Qvindecimviri, 171, 190
Quintilian, 86

"R. W. R.," 117
Ramsay, Sir William, 54, 58
Rand, E. K., 58
Re, 195
Reinach, S., 189, 192

Revival of Letters, 193
Rhetoric, 166 sqq.
Rhine, 105
Romans, Rome, 4, 46, 49, 60, 65, 70, 74, 95, 169, 171, 180 sq., 187, 192, 196 sq., 199: brides, 159; coins, 195; computation, 190, 254 n. 9; prejudice against actors, 118
Rumour, 133

Sabbadini, 52
Sabinus, Sex., 75
Sabinus, the "muleteer," 75, 77
saeculum, 130, 162, 173 sq., 186, 189 sqq.; *saeculares ludi*, 190
Salonae, 196 sq.
Saloninus, 196 sqq.
Saoshyant, 195
Sallust, 118
Samos, 171
Sandbach, F. H., 145 sq.
Saturn, 65, 173 sqq., 193
Sayers, Dorothy, 139
Schiller, 111
Scott, Sir Walter, 62
Scribonia, 196, 210
Seilenos, Silenus, 64, 71 sq., 88, 94 sqq.
Seneca the Younger, 111
Septuagint, 194
Servius, 11, 48, 55, 57, 65, 67, 70 sq., 97 sqq., 105, 108 sqq., 117, 119 sq., 124, 134, 160 sq., 172 sq., 182; Daniel's, 55, 68, 97, 121, 159 sq., 174, 196 sq.
Shakespere, 8, 45
Sherman, 197
Sibyls, 162, 171 sqq.
Sicily, 2, 4, 22, 26, 33 sqq., 109, 120, 135, 140, 142, 162, 171
Sikelidas, 10; *see also* Asklepiades
Silo, 124 sq.
Silvanus, 113
Silver Age, 176, 184
Simaitha, 33, 153
Simichidas, 10, 32; *see also* Theokritos
Siron, 44, 59, 64, 71 sq., 75 sq., 87, 100

Skutsch, Fr., 97 sqq.
Skutsch, Otto, viii n. 1
Skylla, 97, 101, 102 sq.
Slater, D. A., 203 sq., 206
Sophron, 1 sqq., 221 sq.
Sosibios, 5
Statius, 30
Stesichoros, 135
Stimichon, 71
Stoicism, Stoics, 92, 155, 174 sq., 177, 216
Suetonius, 132, 169
Sulla, 11
Sun, 172 sq.; *see also* Apollo, Helios
Syme, R., 179
Syracusans, Syracuse, 1 sqq., 12, 25, 65

TACITVS, 118, 171
Tarentum, 88
Tarn, W. W., 181, 206, 208
Taylor, Phoebe Atwood, 139
Tennyson, 6
Terence, 39, 108
Tereus, 97, 102 sq.
Terpandros, 4
Thebes, war of, 184
Theokritos, 3 sqq., 22, 32 sq., 35, 47 sqq., 57, 64, 83, 88 sqq., 105 sq., 110, 114, 116, 130 sq., 134 sqq., 144, 148 sqq.; pseudo-, 139 sqq., 148, 152
Theon, 11
Theseus, 137
Thessaly, 177
Thestylis, 32, 154 sq.
Thetis, 170, 203
Thyrsis, 71, 121, 142 sqq.
Tiberius, Emperor, 122, 198, 212
Tibullus, 14, 113
Tityrus, 45 sqq., 70 sqq., 92, 139, 152
Tommy Atkins, Roman, 85
Tragedy, proper subject of, 43
Trojan War, Troy, 183 sq., 200, 206
Twelve Tables, 160
Tucca, 77

VALCKENAER, 141
Valgius Rufus, 72, 121
Varius Rufus, L., 69 sq., 72, 77, 120
Varro, M. Terentius, 62, 160, 171, 174
Varus, Alfenus, 48, 55, 67, 69 sqq., 72 sq., 76, 78, 81, 86 sqq., 94, 102 sqq., 116, 125
Varus, Quintilius, 70, 72, 124 sq.
Varus, tragic poet, 70
Venice, 52
Venus, 49, 130 sq., 157, 203
Vergil (P. Vergilius Maro), the poet, *passim*; date, 18; diction, etc., 12, 28 sqq., 145; friends, 69 sqq.; home, 45 sqq.; imitation, methods of, 111: of Catullus, 76, 201; of Theokritos, 9, 22, 26, 47, 112, 134, 149 sqq.; called Menalcas, 47, 69, 87; models, 166 sqq.; philosophy, 44; sense of humor or proportion, 43; studies, 74 sqq.; tastes, 18
Vergil, *works of*: *Aeneid*, 97 sqq., 130, 166, 183, 187; Appendix Vergiliana mostly not his, 237 n. 44; *Catalepton*, how far genuine, 237 n. 45; discussed, 44, 59, 75 sqq., 84, 104; No. 5, exegesis, 235 n. 38; *Culex* not by, 75
Vergil, *Eclogues* of, allegory in, *see* Allegory; dates of, 151, 251; numbering, 54; riddles in, 226; seven "bucolic," 138, 244 n. 51; title of, 21
Vergil, *Eclogues*, individual, discussed: I, chap. iii; II, III, chap. ii; IV, chap. viii; V, chap. vi; VI, chap. v; VII, VIII, chap. vii; IX, chap. iii; X, chap. v
Vergil, *Eclogues*, passages in expounded: Ecl. I, 27 sqq., 228 n. 2; III, 55–57, 226 sq., 109–110, 225 n. 31; IV, 11–14, 253 n. 4, 21 sq., 258 n. 62, 42–45, 253 n. 6, 49, 263 n. 141, 60 sqq., 254 nn. 8, 9; VI, 33, 240 n. 6; VII, 70, 248 n. 7; VIII, 53–59, 249 n. 38, 80 sq., 250 n. 55; IX, 16, 232 n. 84; X, 2–3, 242 n. 30, 44, 243 n. 36

Vergil, *Georgics*, 77, 83
Vergil the elder, father of the poet, 18, 27, 53
Vergilia, 56
Vergilii, 50, 59, 124
Vergilius, P., 53
Verona scholiast, 121
Vienna, 217
Virbius, 137
Volumnia, 70, 72, 108; *see also* Cytheris, Lycoris
Volumnius Eutrapelus, P., 72, 108
Vulcanius, Vulcatius, 174

WAGENVOORT, H., 190 sqq.
Weiss, J., 217
Welsh magic, 157
Werwolf, 159
William Tell, 120

YAHWEH, 182, 195
Yorkshire, 159

ZAGREUS, 196
Zeus, 10, 34, 96, 103, 141, 163 sq., 177, 184
Zoroastrianism, 181, 195

www.ingramcontent.com/pod-product-compliance
Lightning Source LLC
Chambersburg PA
CBHW021656230426
43668CB00008B/642